INVENTING INTERNATIONAL SOCIETY

ST ANTONY'S SERIES
General Editors: Alex Pravda (1993–97), Eugene Rogan (1997–), both
Fellows of St Antony's College, Oxford

Recent titles include:

Mark Brzezinski
THE STRUGGLE FOR CONSTITUTIONALISM IN POLAND

Peter Carey (*editor*)
BURMA

Stephanie Po-yin Chung
CHINESE BUSINESS GROUPS IN HONG KONG AND POLITICAL
CHANGE IN SOUTH CHINA, 1900–25

Ralf Dahrendorf
AFTER 1989

Alex Danchev
ON SPECIALNESS

Roland Dannreuther
THE SOVIET UNION AND THE PLO

Noreena Hertz
RUSSIAN BUSINESS RELATIONSHIPS IN THE WAKE OF REFORM

Iftikhar H. Malik
STATE AND CIVIL SOCIETY IN PAKISTAN

Steven McGuire
AIRBUS INDUSTRIE

Yossi Shain and Aharon Klieman (*editors*)
DEMOCRACY

William J. Tompson
KHRUSHCHEV

Marguerite Wells
JAPANESE HUMOUR

Yongjin Zhang and Rouben Azizian (*editors*)
ETHNIC CHALLENGES BEYOND BORDERS

St Antony's Series
Series Standing Order ISBN 0–333–71109–2
(*outside North America only*)

You can receive future titles in this series as they are published by placing a standing order.
Please contact your bookseller or, in case of difficulty, write to us at the address below with
your name and address, the title of the series and the ISBN quoted above.

Customer Services Department, Macmillan Distribution Ltd
Houndmills, Basingstoke, Hampshire RG21 6XS, England

Inventing International Society

A History of the English School

Tim Dunne
Lecturer in International Politics
Department of International Politics
University of Wales
Aberystwyth

 in association with
ST ANTONY'S COLLEGE, OXFORD

First published in Great Britain 1998 by
MACMILLAN PRESS LTD
Houndmills, Basingstoke, Hampshire RG21 6XS and London
Companies and representatives throughout the world

A catalogue record for this book is available from the British Library.

ISBN 0-333-64345-3 hardcover
ISBN 0-333-73787-3 paperback
ISBN13 9780-333-64345-7 hardcover
ISBN13 9780-333-73787-3 paperback

First published in the United States of America 1998 by
ST. MARTIN'S PRESS, INC.,
Scholarly and Reference Division,
175 Fifth Avenue, New York, N.Y. 10010

ISBN 0-312-21545-2

Library of Congress Cataloging-in-Publication Data
Dunne, Timothy, 1965–
Inventing international society : a history of the English school
/ Timothy Dunne.
p.   cm. — (St. Antony's series)
Includes bibliographical references and index.
ISBN 0-312-21545-2 (cloth)
1. International relations—Philosophy—History.   2. International
relations—Study and teaching—Great Britain—History.   I. Title.
II. Series.
JZ1242.D86   1998
327.1'01—dc21   98–17291
                                                          CIP

This book is printed on paper suitable for recycling and made from fully managed and
sustained forest sources.

Transferred to digital printing 2002
Printed and bound in Great Britain by
CPI Antony Rowe, Chippenham and Eastbourne

For Alan and Elizabeth Dunne

Contents

Acknowledgements

In the course of writing this book, I have had a considerable amount of support from family, friends, and academic colleagues. The first and most lasting intellectual debt is to my mentor Steve Smith, who along with the late Martin Hollis, introduced me to the world of ideas at the University of East Anglia in the late 1980s. After completing my undergraduate degree, it was Steve who encouraged me to take up a postgraduate place at Oxford. Throughout the four years as an ESRC funded M.Phil and a D.Phil student, I benefited greatly from Andrew Hurrell's guidance and his excellent judgement. The decision by the British International Studies Assocation to award my D.Phil thesis 'International Relations Theory in Britain: The Invention of an International Society Tradition' the prize in 1994 in part reflects the first-class supervision Andrew provided.

These were intellectually stimulating years. Many of my close friends, such as Geoffrey Wiseman, Marrianne Hansen, Jennifer Welsh, Shu Sun, Ngaire Woods and Iver B. Neumann had been taught by John Vincent, acquiring his sense of fun as well as critical engagement. Although I never met John, I feel he would have appreciated the intellectual journey I embarked upon, particularly in so far as it builds a bridge between two of his foremost influences, E.H. Carr and Hedley Bull. It was John who used to refer to my college, St Antony's, as a 'mini-United Nations', a term no doubt used to capture the hierarchy of the institution as well as its multiculturalism. In the course of the daily round of college life, I developed long-term friendships with people who indirectly contributed to my education in Oxford, in particular David Nickles, Mats Berdal, Richard Hanson, Shelly Leanne and Ana Covarrubias. One such bond was severed tragically when Holly Wyatt-Walter died in 1996. Other members of the Inter-national Relations community in Oxford provided encouragement and personal support; here I have in mind Geoffrey Martin Ceadel Best, Rosemary Foot, Alex Pravda (the then St Antony's Series General editor), Adam Roberts, Avi Shlaim and Andrew Walter.

One week after submitting the D.Phil thesis, I moved to Aberystwyth to take up a lectureship in international politics. I realised at the time that I was coming to a Department with a famous past; four years on, I have a strong conviction that our Department has an even better future. The principal reason for the energy and creativity in the Department is, of course, the leadership of Steve Smith. Ten years after first hearing him lecture, he continues to inspire as a teacher, writer and friend. Standing alongside Steve on the bridge of the ship called *Interpol* has been Ken Booth. I feel privileged to have had the opportunity to listen to Ken's critical voice draw from his stock of sound-bites, and since the early part of 1997, to work with him and our 'big ed' Michael Cox on the *Review of International Studies*.

Like all good teams, the Department of International Politics is about more than the reputations of its star. At the other end of the corridor from the professorial suites there is a wealth of knowledge about the subject and a strong measure of good humour to be found in the busy offices of colleagues and research students. One friend and colleague in particular, Nick Wheeler, has had a profound impact on my thinking on the subject. I have been a constant borrower from his thinking on a whole range of ideas, from human rights to normative International Relations theory in general. His intellectual generosity has extended as far as reading the entire manuscript (some chapters more than once); in a phrase which he will instantly recognise, his 'influence' can be found 'on every page of it'. In addition, Nick encouraged me to draw directly from previously published co-authored material in Chapter 7. The interpretation of Hedley Bull presented here is very much the result of a shared interest in and commitment to one of the great scholars of modern International Relations.

Outside of Aberystwyth, I have received support for this project from a variety of sources. Within academic International Relations, I would like to acknowledge the advice of Michael Donelan, James Mayall, Cornelia Navari, Stephanie Lawson, Richard Little, Robert Jackson, Nicholas Rengger, James Richardson, Hidemi Suganami, and Peter Wilson. I have been inspired by the words – written and spoken – of four other scholars in the field who have in different ways brought critical insights to bear on the English School; here I have in mind Chris Brown, Andrew Hurrell (who has provided critical feedback on Chapters 1, 7 and 8), Roger Epp (who read draft chapters and helped me in particular with the Christian realism of Wight and Butterfield) and Andrew Linklater (apart from providing helpful comments on earlier drafts of Chapters 1 and 2, he has more than anyone inspired mine and Nick's attempt to bridge the English School with critical international theory).

Given that the book draws from a range of unpublished papers and correspondence, I would like to thank the following individuals and institutions for their help: Mary Bull for allowing me to quote from the Hedley

Bull papers; the University of Cambridge Library for access to Herbert Butterfield's papers, and Peter Butterfield for his permission to copy them; the University of Wales, Aberystwyth, for access to their archives in regard to E.H. Carr's years as the Woodrow Wilson Professor; Kenneth W. Thompson for granting permission to quote from his correspondence with Butterfield in regard to the origins of the British Committee; the Royal Institute of International Affairs library for access to their collection of British Committee papers; Adam Watson for permission to quote from his correspondence with Wight and Bull regarding the leadership of the group after Butterfield had passed on the responsibility; and Gabriele Wight for allowing me to draw upon Martin Wight's correspondence. These rather formal acknowledgements disguise how indebted I am to those closest to the main characters in the book for their anecdotes and advice. Here I have in mind lengthy conversations with Carsten Holbraad, Brian Porter, Adam Watson, and especially Mary Bull, Angela Vincent and Gabriele Wight.

In the final few months, the burden of completing the manuscript has been eased by the technical expertise of Elaine Lowe, and by Rob Dixon, who helped to compile the bibliography and index. It only remains for me to acknowledge my immediate and extended family for the support they have given in more ways than I could possibly mention. Thank you to Alan, Elizabeth, Andrea, George, Malcolm, Christiane, Eileen, and Caroline, thank you for being you and for being with me.

TIM DUNNE
Aberystwyth

Introduction

> There is more to international relations than the realist suggests but less
> than the cosmopolitan desires.[1]
>
> Andrew Linklater

E.H. Carr's explanation for the failure of 'utopianism' in his magnificent
work *The Twenty Years' Crisis* is often regarded as the first real analysis of
International Relations since its inception as a formal academic discipline.
After Carr, the history of academic International Relations 'crosses' the
Atlantic, as it were, to consider the wave of early post-war realist writings
by scholars such as Hans Morgenthau.[2] The subsequent privileging of
American thinkers in shaping the contours of the discipline has led to a distortion in the 'self-images' of the discipline, and a concomitant discounting
of the importance of International Relations in Britain.

One of the most significant moments in British International Relations
thinking occurred in the late 1950s when a group of scholars gathered to
form a Committee to investigate the fundamental questions of 'international theory'. The first formal meeting of the British Committee, in
January 1959, signifies the symbolic origins of the English School.
Although the ideas and arguments of key British Committee scholars have
been debated within the wider International Relations academy, this
evaluation has taken place in the absence of a contextual account of the
intellectual community which they themselves identified with. The principal aim of the book is to provide such an account, thereby adding a new
chapter to the incomplete historiography of International Relations.

A secondary aim, although potentially more significant from a normative point of view, is to reveal the radical potentiality of the Grotian or
Rationalist tradition. Beneath this task lay the belief that the leading
thinkers in the English School, contained in the volume, represent more
than just an important voice in the historiography of the discipline. Carr's
dialectical method, Wight's historical sociology of culture and identity,
Bull's reflections on alternative notions of community, and Vincent's
prescriptions for a radical redistribution of wealth from the 'haves' to the
'have-nots', all speak to a broadly defined critical agenda for International
Relations theory. In tune with the politics of the 1990s, thinkers like
Wight, Bull and Vincent show that there can be a radical centre to the
study of global politics.

The book is being published at a time when interest in the English School is growing. This is not to suggest that those identified with the School have been immune to criticism; to the contrary, in recent years there have been a number of polemical pieces suggesting that their contribution to International Relations was at best unfulfilled, and at worst, positively harmful. Chapter 1 puts this debate in the context of a broader discussion about the English School, its defining elements, and its 'members'; this includes those who refuse on principle to join any 'club' which will have them.

The interpretation of Carr presented in Chapter 2 of the book illustrates the interplay of the two key aims set out above. Consistent with the normative project, the interpretation of Carr draws on arguments made in recent years by Ken Booth and Andrew Linklater who have sought to rescue *The Twenty Years' Crisis* from the previously dominant realist reading. But unlike these attempts to release Carr from the grip of realism, the chapter will also show how his thinking contributed to the invention of an international society tradition from the late 1950s onwards. Carr is the appropriate point of departure for a study of the English School, for the following reasons. His *The Twenty Years' Crisis* had an immense impact on the development of international theory here in Britain. He was the first theorist to broaden the study of International Relations from its narrow focus on law and organisation which dominated the first wave of scholarly work on the subject. For Carr, realism was a weapon to be turned against those who espouse universalist principles, revealing the play of interests and exclusion behind the moral mask. But crucially, Carr was dissatisfied with 'pure' realism, both in *The Twenty Years' Crisis* and even more clearly in his other war-time writings. In its place, he posited a form of 'utopian realism' which placed economic and political reform at the centre of the domestic and international agenda for post-war reconstruction. By the end of his tenure as Woodrow Wilson Professor at Aberystwyth in 1947, Carr's intellectual interest shifted eastwards towards the Soviet Union thereby finally signally his exit from the International Relations academy. What is interesting here is the way in which Carr was later to express a degree of embarrassment, both about the works he wrote whilst at Aberystwyth and more broadly about the status at that time of the discipline itself. In his words, 'we tried to conjure into existence an international society', but 'no international society exists'.[3] With this admission, Carr is associating his contribution to International Relations with the central concern of later English School thinkers, namely, the invention of international society.

Chapters 3 and 4 will show how the early work of Martin Wight and Herbert Butterfield also participated in propagating certain ritualistic claims associated with realism. Throughout the 1940s, Martin Wight was the most articulate critic of the 'shallow' and 'discredited' progressivism which had been built into the landscape of the early twentieth century. Despite the paucity of his published output, Wight exerted a powerful influence on the British Committee, particularly in the early years. Yet it was his lectures on 'international theory', given at the London School of Economics from the early 1950s, which are the primary reason for his reputation as the high priest of the English School. In these lectures, Wight went beyond a one-dimensional realism, recognising that 'reality' was captured by a three-way conversation between the 'three Rs' of realism, rationalism and revolutionism. Subsequent English School scholars have carried on this conversation over the last four decades.

Herbert Butterfield is a central character in the English School 'story' principally for two reasons. His arguments against progressivism in history demonstrate how widespread the tenets of realism were embedded in the intellectual climate of the age. He shared with E.H. Carr and Martin Wight not only a rejection of progressivism but the identification of the collapse of international order within a broader crisis of secular civilisation. After 1950, Butterfield was increasingly drawn to the study of the causes of international conflict and the means by which conflict could be regulated. By the end of the decade, he had come to believe that there was a need for an institutional enquiry into the fundamental principles and problems of international relations. It was this context of decaying realism that led Butterfield to inaugurate the British Committee on the Theory of International Politics following the lead given by Kenneth Thompson (of the Rockefeller Foundation) who was the anchorman of the parallel American Committee.

Chapter 5 begins by retracing the origins of the Committee, which remain something of a mystery in the history of academic International Relations. In brief, Butterfield chose Martin Wight as his co-organiser since he recognised the convergence of their intellectual positions and regarded him as a specialist in International Relations. Around this core gathered Desmond Williams (diplomatic history), Michael Howard (military historian), Donald Mackinnon (theology), Hedley Bull (international relations), Geoffrey Hudson (international relations), Adam Watson (Foreign Office), and William Armstrong (Treasury). The book will distinguish two successive phases in the history of the British Committee. It was in the formative years (1959–1962) that the collection of essays published as *Diplomatic Investigations* were written and discussed by the Committee. The preface to the volume provides significant evidence for the invention of a conception of international society which was interposed between a

Hobbesian state of nature (anarchy) and a Kantian zone of peace (community). As the editors of *Diplomatic Investigations* put it, their 'frame of reference' had been 'international society' itself.[4]

Chapter 6 examines the second phase of the British Committee's work, which traces their growing interest in methodology and a comparative sociology of historical states systems. From 1964 onwards, the members of the Committee were increasingly conscious of the differences between their approach to international theory in contrast to the developments in American International Relations. The Committee's desire to understand the nature and limits of modern international society led them to examine historical states-systems and the degree to which their survival was dependent upon cultural unity. On one level their endeavour was unsuccessful as it was intended to lead to a second collaborative publication. However, it will be argued that the significance of this period must be judged according to the foundations which these papers laid for future publications on states-systems by Martin Wight and Adam Watson.[5] In the mid to late 1970s, the Committee had evolved into a more purposeful structure under the guidance of Adam Watson and Hedley Bull. The publication of the edited volume *The Expansion of International Society* in 1984 marked the culmination of the British Committee's work.[6]

The final two chapters examine in more depth the theories of international society put forward by Hedley Bull and R.J. Vincent. Although Bull's early British Committee papers reveal a deep hostility towards a Grotian or 'solidarist' conception of international society, in Chapter 7 we see how his later thinking reveals a growing recognition of the inability of 'pluralism' to provide for anything other than a 'thin' conception of international ethics. Picking up where Bull left off, Vincent examined the tension between pluralism and solidarism as it was played out in the theories and practices of human rights in international society. The discussion in Chapter 8 shows how Vincent tried to build a bridge between pluralism and solidarism; despite a sensitivity to cultural diversity, he believed that certain rights were universal in scope and preceded political and cultural differences. What is interesting about Vincent is the way in which he believed that states have the capacity to be a civilising force and that by acting as agents of cosmopolitanism, states would be strengthened rather than undermined.

The Conclusion considers the contribution of the English School to International Relations. At this point the book moves from an internal history to a theoretical evaluation. On the positive side, from its symbolic 'birth' at the first meeting of the British Committee in January 1958, the English School has consistently opposed the sterility of a realist-cum-positivist approach to the discipline. Its recognition that all theory is normative theory, that forms of human association are changing, and that order without justice is ultimately unstable, are themes which contemporary critical international society theorists have taken up. The 'dark' side of the English School legacy questions how far our sense of moral awareness can be extended before the norms of international society are stretched to breaking-point. This all too often leads to prescriptive solutions which are 'second best', thereby narrowing the moral horizon which Carr believed modernity had opened up.

NOTES

1. Andrew Linklater, 'Rationalism', in Scott Burchill and Andrew Linklater *et al.*, *Theories of International Relations* (London: Macmillan, 1996), 95.
2. The following argument of Fred Halliday's is an exemplar in this respect: 'With the crises of the 1930s, '"idealism" gave way to "realism", initially in the work of E.H. Carr ... and later in the work of a range of US-based writers, including Hans Morgenthau, Henry Kissinger and Kenneth Waltz.' See Fred Halliday, 'The Pertinence of International Relations', *Political Studies*, 38 (1990), 506.
3. Letter from E.H. Carr to Stanley Hoffmann (30 September 1977). Quoted in R.W. Davies, 'Edward Hallett Carr 1892–1982', *Proceedings of the British Academy*, LXIX (1983), 486.
4. Butterfield and Wight bracketed international society with 'the diplomatic community' and 'the states-system'. Herbert Butterfield and Martin Wight (eds), *Diplomatic Investigations: Essays on the Theory of International Politics* (London: Allen and Unwin, 1966), 12. For an introduction to the context of the British Committee, see Adam Watson's preface to James Der Derian (ed.), *International Theory: Critical Investigations* (London: Macmillan, 1995), ix–xvii.
5. Martin Wight, *Systems of States* (Leicester: Leicester University Press, 1977). Adam Watson, *Evolution of International Society* (London: Routledge, 1992).
6. Hedley Bull and Adam Watson (eds), *The Expansion of International Society* (Oxford: Clarendon, 1984).

1 The English School

The evolution of the discipline of International Relations has been conditioned by a number of factors, principal among them are debates which are internal to the academic community, ignited by the publication of a key book or article which sets the agenda for the next stage in the discipline's history. Another source of influence on the internal development of a discipline is derived from encounters with other academic communities such as political theory, sociology, law and history. At a deeper structural level, the ideas which dominate a particular field of enquiry are shaped by wider social forces embodied in, for example, scientific or ideological revolutions.

In the historiography of International Relations the last two factors have tended to dominate the received understanding of the identity of the discipline. The stories we have told ourselves about ourselves have either been 'read off' as a response to changes in world politics *or* tied to new ideas and methodologies adopted by other disciplines. On this reading, idealism was wiped out by an admixture of the collapse in the interwar order *and* a shift away from liberal progressivist assumptions across the human sciences; traditional realism was in turn wiped out by science; pluralism and structuralism were thrown up by the new international political economy of the 1970s; and the realism exhumed by Waltz reflected the return of neo-conservative ideological hegemony. These conventional accounts of the history of the field tend to assume that 'events within world politics have had a determinative and causal effect upon the development of the discipline'.[1] A more sophisticated approach to the history of the discipline would be attentive to the context within which the internal debates were carried forward, retracing the footsteps of academics who self-consciously and institutionally understood themselves as carrying on a distinctive conversation about International Relations. One of the principal objectives of the book is to provide an account of the internal history of the English School, thereby contributing to the new or revisionist historiography of the discipline.[2]

To anticipate the guiding argument of the book, the English School is an important voice in academic International Relations which has either not been heard or has been misrepresented as a derivative of realism. An example of the former is the so-called 'inter-paradigm debate' between realism, pluralism and structuralism which was prevalent in the 1970s and 1980s (particularly in text book surveys of the field).[3] From the borderlines of the discipline, postmoderns have (with one exception) tended to bury the School under the rubble of realism, seeing thinkers like Carr, Wight and Bull as examples of a discredited positivism.[4] This line of argument portrays the history of the discipline as a kind of epic struggle between an undifferentiated positivism characteristic of the 'backward discipline' and the differentiated post-positivist voices of feminism, critical theory and post-structuralism.

The new constellation in International Relations, particularly in the US, is structured around the polar distinction between 'rationalism' and 'reflectivism'.[5] Rationalism was being used in its epistemological sense, as a view of the world which existed independently of our thinking about it and which was amenable to scientific investigation. The fact that an earlier (and very different) kind of 'rationalism' had been pioneered by Martin Wight in the 1950s was not acknowledged by Robert Keohane, the principal exponent of this new constellation. This point is not meant to imply evidence of unscholarly practice, rather, it illustrates the way in which key English School scholars have been no more than a marginal presence in the dominant self-images of the discipline.

The project of bringing the English School back in to contemporary debates in the discipline draws on a different approach to historiography. It rejects contextualism, either of the kind found in International Relations or the history of ideas.[6] The problem with contextualism is that it imputes causality to the world, relegating theory to an effect of changes 'out there' (an often repeated example in the literature is of idealism being defeated by the outbreak of World War 2). In addition, this book is not a plea to add the English School to the inter-paradigm debate as though this will achieve a more authentic understanding of the discipline's past.[7] As Schmidt puts the point eloquently, 'the issue is not one of the authenticity versus inauthenticity of a particular historical account but rather of focusing on recapitulating the main contours and content of a circumscribed realm of discursive activity conventionally designated as international relations.'[8] In order to recover the contribution of the English School to International Relations it is necessary to reconstruct the conversation which took place between members of the School. The subject matter is therefore the published works, book reviews, conference papers, and most important of all in the context of this particular study, the manuscripts and transcripts from the British Committee on the Theory of International Politics meetings.

A second and more ambitious objective for *Inventing International Society*, is to provide an evaluation of the English School's contribution to the discipline, particularly in the context of the new wave of normative theory which has swept across the field in the last two decades. There is a sense in which the emphasis in the first six chapters is on the reconstruction of the beginning of the English School conversation through to the point in the mid-1980s when the formal organised setting for the School was jettisoned. The final two chapters and the Conclusion will privilege the normative dimension of the project, in order to consider the legacy of the English School and the possibilities that exist within it to shape new thinking on the theory and practice of International Relations. The immediate aim of this chapter is to focus in more depth on the way in which the English School has been interpreted in the orthodox history of the discipline. This leads into an extended discussion of the boundaries of the English School, and the vexed question about insiders and outsiders.

Opening the Closure of the English School

When the English School has been present in the discursive history of International Relations, it has regularly been subjected to a double-closure. In the first instance, the closure has resulted from the opprobrium the label has generated and the concomitant unwillingness among English School scholars to respond effectively to this problem. Second, and more importantly, the English School has suffered from its dismissal as just another form of realism. Yet the School developed precisely as a 'move' away from pure realism, as the concluding part of this section will demonstrate.[9] (Crucially, this does not mean that the English School rejects all aspects of realism, rather, it is to argue that the School is not identical with it.)

Labels and Closures
The 'new great debate' in the late 1960s between the 'classical approach' and 'behaviouralism' first put on the agenda the idea that the contending approaches in academic International Relations could be explained in part by national or cultural factors.[10] This identification of discipline and country returned in the 1980s debate on the 'English School'.[11] Ironically the label 'English School' was first used in a polemical article by Roy E. Jones who rather perversely argued for the closure of the school which he had helped to create. In the intervening period, there has been a marked lack of consensus concerning a range of issues about the 'School' from the formal to the substantive. A central point of contention concerns the act of naming, in other words, is the 'English School' an accurate label? Or is the connection between nation and scholarly community itself an act of closure which sets limits on how far the ideas associated with the School

can resonate? More importantly, does the 'English School' represent a distinctive approach to International Relations, one with a coherent research agenda which has made an important contribution to the field?

The most frequently cited objection to the epithet English School is that a number of its most important 'pupils' were not English. Some accounts of the history of the School include Charles Manning, who was a South African, in their number (an argument which is rejected below); and *all* hitherto references to the School have included the Australian Hedley Bull. For this reason, a number of writers have preferred to denote the Wight-Bull-Vincent lineage as 'the classical approach' or the 'international society tradition'.[12] These labels have the advantage of revealing something compelling about the ideas in question (in the same way that realism or liberalism do) rather than simply grouping their representatives according to the nationality of the majority.[13]

Another revisionist attempt to establish a more accurate empirical criterion for the School is to use the label British rather than English. This move in many respects constitutes a regression since it effectively projects aspects of traditional English culture onto regions and nations in the rest of the United Kingdom who define themselves, linguistically or otherwise, in opposition to those values. Here, in particular, I have in mind the Oxbridge values embodied in the *mentalité* of the British Committee in the late 1950s. There is a sense in which the proceedings of the Committee reveals a very English preference for the conduct of academic inquiry *qua* polite conversation. Therefore, the term British School does not overcome the problem of linking a body of thought to a particular territory, and brings with it additional cultural difficulties as well as not receiving widespread recognition in the discipline.

Although certain élite English values undoubtedly penetrated the origins of the 'English School', it could be argued that, almost four decades after the founding of the School in 1958, the idea of Englishness has changed significantly. Today there is a complete lack of consensus among cultural historians as to what constitutes 'Englishness', with no unique ethnic or cultural factors which separate English identity from other nations or states. Just as English culture has become heterogeneous, so has the cultural identity of the English School. In this sense, the gates of the School have been opened to anyone who is broadly aligned with its central assumptions and seeks to carry on its debates.

Realism in Drag?

The second closure is more serious since it is attacking the theoretical arguments sustained by the School rather than the nomenclature. Critics of the English School argue that it is just a tamer version of realism. This argument is not entirely hollow, since the English School overlaps with core claims associated with realism, in particularly recognising the limits of achieving co-operation under anarchy. But points of contact between the two bodies of thought does not signify their convergence. In short, the English School shares certain arguments with realism, but crucially, it is not reducible to it.

This attempt to dress up the English School in realist clothes can be uncovered in the writings of realists and certain radical thinkers. Robert Gilpin, for example, has tried to align key members of the English School, such as Hedley Bull, to the 'classical' wing of realism.[14] Others infer from the School's defence of order, the priority they place on the balance of power, and the scattered passages on the security dilemma as evidence of their realism.[15] Certain writers on the radical wing of the discipline treat the English School as a Trojan horse for realism, a way of smuggling in power politics in a language of community.[16] There are two key counter-arguments that can be made in defence of the English School as a distinctive and coherent position. In the first instance, members of the English School believed themselves to be participating in a post-realist dialogue. The second counter does not rely on the accuracy or otherwise of the self-definitions of members of the English School. Instead, it places clear blue water between the School and realism by revealing their conformity to an approach which is incompatible with mainstream realist theories. In short, this book seeks to challenge the prevailing view that the English school is nothing other than 'a group of realists on this side of the Atlantic'.[17] These arguments will be explored in greater detail below.

Three Preliminary Articles of the English School

To return to an earlier theme, one of the problems with the English School label is the implicit suggestion that all International Relations thinking in Britain conforms to its 'canon'. This is clearly not the case. A number of significant theorists in the British International Relations academy have rejected one or more of the propositions outlined below. Instead, what follows is an attempt to articulate the 'family resemblances' shared by members of the English School; aspects of their thinking which are interwoven and distinct. I have referred to these family resemblances as 'preliminary articles', a starting point for thinking about a genealogy of the English School rather than presenting the boundaries as fixed and immutable. Like all families, these resemblances have been and will continue to be contested.

(i) Self-Identification with a Particular Tradition of Enquiry

A necessary condition for being a member of the English School is an awareness of a body of literature, a set of central questions and a common agenda. This approximates to what Alasdair McIntyre has called a 'tradition of enquiry', which he defined as: 'more than a coherent movement of thought: it is such a movement in the course of which those engaging in that movement become aware of it and of its direction and in self-aware fashion to engage in its debates and carry its enquiries forward.'[18]

Although to an extent the early work of Carr, Butterfield and Wight drew from a similar stock of realist ideas, there is a lack of conscious direction on the part of these thinkers: they did not, in the 1940s, identify themselves as participating in a particular tradition of enquiry. The element of conscious agency becomes apparent only with the beginning of the British Committee on the Theory of International Politics. During the first three years of the Committee, their papers began to evince a 'community of assumptions' about theory, leading to a heightened sense of awareness about the distinctiveness of the group. By this stage, the embryonic English School had constructed its own canon of classical texts and a body of diplomatic papers which together constituted its political vocabulary and constrained its moral imagination.

This sense of collective identity was fuelled in the mid-1960s with the recognition that a divide was opening up on either side of the Atlantic. From then on, the Committee papers and the minutes of their discussions demonstrate a convergence around a research agenda which sought to enquire into the historical sociology of states systems. The conscious development of a research programme is perhaps even more marked in the last two decades of the Committee's deliberations, from the first paper on states systems by Herbert Butterfield, to the publication of the papers from the final stage of the Committee's proceedings around the theme of European international society and its expansion into a global international society.

There are two other important 'indicators' which highlight the existence of a community of scholars inhabiting a particular 'School'. First, there are the personal ties, particularly in evidence in the pedagogical bond which unites successive generations of English School scholars. The obvious example here is the relationship between Martin Wight and Hedley Bull. Wight was Bull's intellectual mentor, providing him with a training in International Relations theory which he had not received as an undergraduate in Sydney nor as a postgraduate at Oxford. In his memorial lecture for Martin Wight, Bull describes how he had been a 'constant borrower' from Wight's lectures on 'international theory'.[19] R.J. Vincent openly admitted to borrowing from Bull; he was, after all, his Ph.D. student at the Australia National University in the early 1970s. Even after Bull's death, Vincent noted the influence Bull exerted on 'every page' of his book, *Human Rights and International Relations*. The lineage between Herbert Butterfield and Adam Watson conforms to a similar pattern. Butterfield taught Watson, brought him in to the British Committee and exerted 'the most long-standing influence' on him.[20]

A second indicator of the existence of an English School can be discerned from the self-identification with the School by the members themselves. In the case of Hedley Bull, in a talk to the Grimshaw Club at the London School of Economics, boldly titled 'The Appalling State of International Relations Studies at the London School of Economics and Elsewhere', he noted how 'someone at BISA said there was no British school. Nonsense'.[21] Similarly, R.J. Vincent openly categorised his own thinking as belonging to the English School.[22] Identification by 'insiders' is matched by a recognition among some sympathetic 'outsiders' of the existence of the School, evident, for instance, in Stanley Hoffmann's introduction to the second edition of *The Anarchical Society*.[23] Less sympathetic outsiders were hostile to the English School because of its rejection of the scientific revolution sweeping through politics departments in American Ivy League Universities.

(ii) An Interpretive Approach
The second theme which underpins the English School of International Relations concerns a broadly interpretive approach to the subject. From the outset, scholars identified with the English School were sceptical of the possibility of a scientific study of International Relations. Even Carr, who opens *The Twenty Years Crisis* with the sentence 'the science of international politics is in its infancy', and proceeds to identify realism with science,[24] recognises the interdependence between subject (scholar) and object (world). In Carr's words, 'the facts about capitalism are not, like the facts about cancer, independent of the attitude of people towards it.'[25] Carr resolves his desire to make International Relations more scientific whilst recognising the limits of this possibility with a Weberian compromise; in other words, although politics cannot be removed from the realm of values and judgement, it can nevertheless be pursued according to certain objective criteria.

Although Bull's article 'International Theory: The Case for a Classical Approach'[26] is often seen as the paradigmatic English School response to the scientific revolution, it was Martin Wight who pioneered an interpretive approach a decade earlier. In order to go beyond realism, Martin

Wight looked back to the classical ideas from European international society relating to the management of International Relations, in particular the writings on international law, diplomacy and the balance of power. It was this stock of knowledge which the English School sought to interrogate, a corpus untouched by the early debate between realism and idealism. These classical writings on law and morality were identified first by Martin Wight and then by Hedley Bull as constituting a 'Grotian' or rationalist tradition.[27] The attraction to rationalism in the English School is explained because it provides the most compelling answer to the central question for English School international theory, namely, 'what is international society?' Here we see how the methodology of the English School becomes intertwined with their ontological defence of international society.

Whilst the English School focuses on the nature and possibilities for international society, it remains acutely aware that the practices of the society of states are threatened by the ever present realities of the 'state of war' and global transnational relations. Thus, the ideas of realism and revolutionism are not merely the outer boundaries of a rationalist *via media*. The rationalist desire for international order is constantly undermined by the realist pursuit of self-interest and the revolutionist quest for transnational justice. Although these positions are intellectually distinct, and internally coherent, they are not mutually exclusive in practice. In Wight's own words, they 'are streams, with eddies and cross-currents, sometimes interlacing and never long confined to their own river bed'.[28]

The approach to international theory adopted by Martin Wight should be seen as a *conversation* between these three positions, one whose original function was pedagogical. Subsequent English School scholars have reinvigorated the 'three Rs' either by examining the ideas of philosophers who had not previously been considered in detail,[29] or by refining the categories themselves in the light of recent scholarly critiques of tradition-building, as Bull had begun to do with the Grotian tradition at the time of his death (a project diligently sustained by Ben Kingsbury and Adam Roberts).[30] Recently, attention has been given to patterns of international thought which are not adequately captured by these positions, in particular the additional category of 'fideism' which ironically, given Wight's religious beliefs, is not accommodated convincingly in his three traditions.[31] This attempt by the School to both broaden and deepen our knowledge of pre-twentieth century international thought is evidence of a living tradition of enquiry carrying forward the 'classical theory' adumbrated by Wight and Bull.

There are a number of aspects of the English School's interpretive approach which remain conceptually underdeveloped. At this juncture, I will briefly open up possible lines of critique which will be addressed in more length elsewhere in the text. One line of attack concerns the status of key concepts like 'international order'. At times it is presented as a cause of certain kinds of state practice and on other occasions, an effect. Similarly, their approach to international history is open to a number of objections. Apart from the substantive question about whether or not the particular thinkers are suitable representatives of their 'tradition', the relationship between the traditions and 'the world' remains unclear. Is reality created by the particular tradition? Is there anything out there other than the language and discursive practices of lawyers, diplomats and state leaders? If rationalism is constituted by these practices, how can rationalism ever be wrong?[32] The broader danger is one in which epistemology is reduced to a form of classification; something is real only in so far as it can be classified. A final 'meta' problem with the interpretive approach of the English School concerns their ambivalence on the structure-agent questions. Aside from the fact that they never really address the question whether it is meaningful to talk about states as agents, the dynamics of the structuration between states and international society remains unclear.

Three decades after the so-called 'second great debate' between the American 'scientists' and the English School 'traditionalists', it is apparent that more was at stake than simply 'how-to' questions about methodology. For the English School, the most important questions in international relations were not amenable to empirical verification (as the would-be scientists demanded). The state, international society, diplomatic community and so on, were all knowable even if they were not observable. Here we see how a debate which was ostensibly focused on methodology, brought to the surface far deeper cleavages about the scope and purpose of theory (discussed below).

(iii) International Theory as Normative Theory

Martin Wight can justly be regarded as the father of the English School not only for pioneering an interpretive approach to the history of international relations, but also for placing ethics at the centre of theoretical enquiry. Each of Wight's traditions represents a distinctive moral position: rationalism and its desire to blend prudence and moral obligation; realism and non-perfectionist ethics; revolutionism and the quest for universal justice. Moreover, Wight's later British Committee work sought to interrogate the ethics of rationalism, the belief that the society of states may not be perfect but is not the worst of all possible worlds. If there is an international society, 'there is an order of some kind to be maintained, or even developed.'[33] This clarion call for a normative enquiry into the bases of international society was taken up by Hedley Bull, and laid bare in *The Anarchical Society*.

The English School's exploration into the nature of international society is widely recognised as its most important contribution to International Relations. It has also been referred to in the debate on the English School as the 'distinguishing power' of the School.[34] But what does the term *society* mean in the context of relations between states? Clearly it is a *different* kind of society, one with fewer members than civil societies, where the gap between the strongest and the weakest is far greater, and where there are no legitimate institutions which can enforce the will of the collectivity. Despite the differences between domestic and international society, there are also clear overlaps. Both societies can be defined, in a Rawlsian sense, as co-operative arrangements for securing the mutual advantage of the members. Both have highly developed systems of rules which start out from the premise of formal equality (at least in democratic societies). In the case of international society, equality is stipulated by sovereignty, a right which implies obligations to (at a minimum) refrain from interference in the affairs of other states and to respect their territorial integrity.

Bound up with the ontology of international society is the idea that states are not, as has often been assumed, strangers to the moral world. Two related arguments contribute to this normative predisposition. The first concerns the recognition that diplomats and state leaders have agency. The society of states has been constructed by 'the handiwork of real people' and is reproduced by their 'ongoing activity'.[35] Recognising that it is state leaders who have spun the web of international society leads necessarily (as noted above) to an interpretive mode of enquiry which seeks to uncover the principles guiding their conduct and the meanings they give to their actions. To judge their actions, Wight argued, 'means judging the validity of their ethical principles.'

The spectrum of choices facing the agents (i.e. state leaders) in formulating their foreign policies is constrained by layers of legal principles and 'settled norms' which form the structure of international society. A central tenet of the English School is the belief that the agents are socialised by the structure. This comes through strongly in Hedley Bull's often-quoted definition of international society:

> A society of states (or international society) exists when a group of states, conscious of certain common interests and common values, form a society in the sense that they conceive themselves to be bound by a common set of rules in their relations with one another, and share in the working of common institutions.[36]

Although this passage presents a powerful case for the existence of international society as a social and political fact, it obscures to a degree two different normative accounts of the nature of the common values to which states adhere. Here we see an important division within the English School between a 'pluralist' account which embodies a 'thin' morality, and a 'solidarist' position representing a 'thick' morality.[37]

The thin morality of the society of states holds that states can agree to a framework of international order which permits them to co-operate for their mutual advantage. International society is not, according to this reading, a mid-point along the path to a universal community of humankind. Rather, it is a more or less optimal solution to the problem of how to accommodate a plurality of cultural values within a well-ordered international system.[38] Since states are the legitimate containers for cultural difference, the task for international society is to formulate norms and procedures which 'separate and cushion'[39] the units in the states system. This leaves the English School open to the criticism that it is too complacent, neglecting the empirical evidence that far too many states behave inwardly like 'gangsters' rather than 'guardians' of the well-being of their citizens.[40]

Recognising that the ethical defence of pluralism begins to break down if it enables repressive governments to hide behind the norm of sovereignty, the solidarist wing of the English School see the society of states as having the potential to enforce universalist ethics such as respect for human rights. The extent to which the collectivity of states has the moral resources within it to enforce new standards of international legitimacy built upon world-order values, is a theme which critical international society theorists have taken up in recent years. Central to this project is the on-going dialogue between staple English School texts and the growing body of social and political theory which has facilitated a greater understanding of the relationship between citizen and community, justice within and between states, and the historical and social construction of collective identity.

The distance between these two accounts of the normative bases of international society can easily be exaggerated, indeed, there is a point at which the distinction between procedural and substantive ethics breaks down. Pluralism and solidarism do, however, provide useful background theories for understanding how the society of states should respond to some of the key normative questions addressed by the English School, for example, on the causes and conduct of war, the justification or otherwise of intervention, the distribution of global resources, and the content of human rights.[41]

Insiders, Outsiders and Dissidents

Although the 'preliminary articles' cited above do not signify definitive boundaries of the English School, they nevertheless provide strong clues as to the identity of the 'core' members. For instance, members of the original British Committee defined themselves as part of a collective enquiry into international theory, despite the fact that many of them came from different disciplinary backgrounds; the key point is that all the members of the British Committee *believed* themselves to be participating in a dialogue about foundational theoretical questions. The emphasis in the paragraphs below is not so much on the central figures in the School, for the reason that they receive considerable attention elsewhere in this book. What is important at this stage is to justify why certain thinkers have been left out of the internal discursive history of the English School, and why some are best thought of as living on the borderlines.

Given that this book traces the origins of the English School back to the British Committee, it follows that those scholars who were not invited to participate in this forum should be seen as 'outsiders'. In this respect, my argument challenges two of the central assumptions of the English School debate hitherto: that the London School of Economics is the 'institutional home' of the School, and that Charles Manning was the progenitor.[42] Although many of the most important English School scholars have worked at the London School of Economics, it is also true to say that the Australia National University, Oxford, and Keele can also claim to have nurtured English School thinking at different times. Peterhouse, Cambridge, has the strongest case to represent the institutional setting of the English School, given that it was the site for most of the British Committee meetings from 1958 to 1968. The affinity between the English School and the British Committee effectively displaces Charles Manning from being a member of the School, as he was never invited to participate in the Committee's proceedings.[43] There were undoubtedly personal reasons for this, as the correspondence on the Committee recorded in Chapter 5 testifies. Whilst Manning's characterisation of a society of states[44] was to an extent influential on Hedley Bull, his impact on international theory was barely recognised by Wight. Perhaps this was because of their diverging methodologies, Manning's being a unique blend of phenomenology and jurisprudence which was at odds with the philosophy of history adumbrated by Wight.

The question of E.H. Carr's relationship to the English School is an altogether more complex one. In terms of the first 'article' of the English School – the conscious act of identification with a particularly community of scholars – he is certainly an outsider. He does, however, approximate to the second and third of the preliminary articles, thereby rendering his status an ambivalent one. As Chapter 2 argues, the tension between Carr's two 'planes' of 'realism' in 'utopianism' mirrors the ambivalence in Wight as to whether they are coexisting elements of 'reality' or whether history unfolds through the interplay and final resolution of the dialectic (in the case of Carr) and trialectic (in the case of Wight).[45] There is a less ambiguous answer to whether Carr conforms to the third preliminary article. His work is clearly normative, inspired by the desire for greater equality and social justice between individuals and people. The crucial normative disjuncture between Carr and later English School writers centres on their different conceptions of agency. On both normative and instrumental grounds, Carr believed that the state was increasingly unable to deliver economic and welfare goals, and an international society of *states* was therefore stillborn as an agent for progressive change.

Perhaps the best way to describe Carr's role is that of a dissident in the School, a voice which can always be heard but is never in complete harmony with the conversation conducted by the leading players. If Carr is the dissident voice, *The Twenty Years' Crisis* is the dissident work of the English School, because it articulates 'difference, not identity: the questioning and transgression of limits, not the assertion of boundaries or frameworks; a readiness to question how meaning and order are imposed, not the search for a source of meaning and order already in place.'[46] It is Carr who continually reminds later members of the School that 'meaning and order' are not neutral but 'imposed', and that we need to be constantly vigilant to ensure that states do not abuse their power. Later English School thinkers never fully escaped from Carr's critical question, international order *for whom*? Carr undoubtedly believed that the society of states benefited the 'haves' rather than the 'have-not' powers.

Another key figure who was active in the field at the time of the birth of the School was F.H. Hinsley. One of the reasons for his exclusion from the proceeding was that he appears not to have been held in high regard by Martin Wight, at least not if one was to take his review of Hinsley's *Power and the Pursuit of Peace* as a guide.[47] There is further anecdotal evidence recorded in Chapter 5 which suggests that Hinsley was regarded by other members of the School as being too much of a realist, thereby excluding him on the basis of the third as well as the first preliminary articles.

By the mid-1970s, the work of the Committee began to impact upon a second generation of English School scholars, all loosely conforming to the three preliminary articles cited above. In particular, the working group at the LSE associated with Michael Donelan and James Mayall can be regarded as self-consciously building on the work of the British Committee, drawing upon classical theories in their methodology and addressing important normative questions.[48] As an American scholar put it, 'the Donelan-Mayall group' works in a 'Wightean mode'.[49] Another parallel international theory discussion group was organised at the University of Leicester, around figures like Peter Savigear, Murray Forsyth and Maurice Keens-Soper. This group was modelled on the British Committee, seeking the advice of Butterfield on the appropriate goals and procedures.

Two decades after Kenneth Thompson and Herbert Butterfield raised the question of the inauguration of a British Committee other academics working in Britain were becoming public in their criticism of the 'classical approach'. In 1976 Stephen George published an attack on the English School for their hostility to predictive theory, preferring a synthesis between the British and American approaches.[50] But it was Roy Jones's polemical destruction of the English School which brought the identity and the arguments of the School into the centre stage of the British International Relations academy. However, of the six 'seminal thinkers' Jones lists in the first paragraph, only three (Wight, Bull and Donelan)[51] approximate to the preliminary articles outlined above.[52] Manning is singled out for particular abuse, for 'darting about in lofty philosophical-anthropological-jurisprudential regions best known to himself' – ironically for almost exactly the same reasons why Manning was excluded by Butterfield, Wight and Bull from the British Committee. Aside from the question whether Jones was aiming at the right target, it is evident that epistemology was over-determining his critique. As an empiricist, he regards holistic ideas like 'international society' as nonsense on stilts. Characterising international society in a not dissimilar way to the portrayal of civil society by a recent Prime Minister, Jones argued that 'a society is what individual men and women inhabit'. Further, he castigated Wight's approach as historicist, thus echoing the now discredited critique of Marx by Popper twenty-five years earlier.

Roy Jones's attack on the School prompted, during the 1980s, a number of replies. The first considered commentary came from Hidemi Suganami. He argued that there was a distinctive approach to International Relations theory in Britain, evident in the work of Manning, Bull, Northedge and James. Suganami identified five factors which unite the School: their commitment to value free enquiry; rejection of behaviourism; use of sociological method and institutional analysis; a belief in the autonomy of academic International Relations; finally, a rejection of utopianism.

Although these factors are definitely in evidence to varying degrees in the work of many English School writers, it would be hard to argue that these distinguish the School from a good deal of traditionalist-cum-realist writings. A further weakness with the Suganami criteria is that it appears to lack the element of self-conscious identification on the part of the members with the School and its research agenda.

Sheila Grader and Peter Wilson agreed that the defining feature of the School was its commitment to international society, but disagreed on the coherence or otherwise of the concept. As Grader put it, 'the question really is – are they talking about the same thing?'[53] She concludes that the representation of international society in the work of Manning, Bull and Northedge is inconsistent. The fact that she is surely right on this point does not demonstrate the bankruptcy of the English School, rather, it suggests that Grader has made the mistake of comparing the treatment of international society across the work of three distantly related academics. The reason for their disagreement is the explanation why Manning and Northedge are not members of the School.

In the 1990s, the commentaries on the English School have broken the habit of identifying the School with former professors at the London School of Economics irrespective of the content of their arguments. There is now an emerging consensus that the legitimate founders of the School are Martin Wight, Herbert Butterfield, Hedley Bull and Adam Watson.[54] Carr is making a comeback, Northedge has virtually disappeared and Manning is on the way out.[55] More importantly, as an epistemic community, the membership of the English School in the 1990s has increased considerably, drawing in theorists like Andrew Linklater who broadly conform to the three preliminary articles although with greater critical self-awareness of the limitations of the School. But perhaps the most significant development of all is that it has become genuinely transnational. The English School is no longer an island. Some of its most ardent supporters are resident in North America (particularly in Canada), Norway, Germany, Italy, and Australia.[56]

Conclusion

Until recently, the English School as an organised and self-aware community of scholars has been left out of conventional accounts of the history of International Relations. This can be explained in part because International Relations is an American social science; writers like Wight and Bull were neither of these. Indeed, they were articulating an interpretive approach at a time when the promise of positivism was attracting a new generation of research students, junior faculty and funding for policy relevant research. Although the 'fad' of behaviouralism waned in the 1970s, the acceptance of 'naturalism' (the idea of a unified scientific method) remained largely unchallenged. Liberals like Keohane and neorealists like Waltz both ascribe to forms of scientific enquiry which believes that theory is an instrument for explaining the world, not for changing it. More than any other factor, the English School's recognition that theories can never be value-neutral, explains why the School did not make much of an impact in the American International Relations community in the 1960s and 1970s. Only a few years before Waltz published *Theory of International Politics*, a text which sought to build a genuinely scientific theory of world politics, Bull argued that 'in my view no strictly scientific theory can come to grips with the central issues of the subject.'[57]

A useful insight into the relative neglect of the English School by leading American thinkers came to light in a recent interview with Kenneth Waltz. 'While you are broadly speaking in a Realist school', Fred Halliday put it to Waltz', 'what's called the English School seems to play very little role, both in the sense of citation and engagement with Carr, Wight, Bull and others.' Waltz replied by noting the respect with which he held Martin Wight and Hedley Bull (perhaps thinking mistakenly that this is what his interviewers wanted to hear) before adding 'but they did theory in a sense not recognized as theory by philosophers of science.'[58]

The motivation for writing *Inventing International Society* is, however, less to do with adding to the chorus of voices calling for the International Relations community to take the English School seriously than the wider issue of understanding the role of the School in the discursive history of the discipline. To this end, the main body of this chapter has focused on the three key distinguishing factors: the realisation that theory-building must take place in a formal institutional setting, drawing from a shared body of knowledge and ideas; the invention of an interpretive approach to the history of ideas about International Relations; and the recognition that the society of states embodies rules and norms which must be the subject of academic scrutiny and critical judgement. The claim which is being made is that these three factors broadly define the limits of the English School, and by implication, the question of who is 'in' and who is 'out' can be evaluated (or contested) in the light of their affinity with these principles. The more normative concern about the rules and practices of the society of states itself, has not received much attention thus far. Later in the book, I will consider the argument that the School has been too preoccupied with developing an account of the 'handiwork' of state leaders rather than putting the victims of repressive states at the centre of their theoretical investigations.

NOTES

1. Brian C. Schmidt, 'The Historiography of Academic International Relations', *Review of International Studies* 20 (1994), 350. Schmidt mounts a powerful critique of conventional accounts of the discipline's history, that the development of International Relations has evolved through idealist-realist-behaviouralist phases, often characterised in terms of a succession of 'great debates'. For a sample of this kind of history see Ray Maghroori 'Introduction: Major Debates in International Relations' in Ray Maghroori and Bennett Ramberg (eds), *Globalism versus Realism: International Relations' Third Debate* (Boulder, Colorado: Westview, 1982).
2. In addition to Schmidt's revisionist historiography of the discipline, expounded in more length in his *The Political Discourse of Anarchy* (New York: SUNY, 1998), see also Jens Bartelson, 'Short Circuits: Society and Tradition in International Relations Theory', *Review of International Studies* 22 (1996), 239–360, and Richard Price, 'Interpretation and disciplinary orthodoxy in international relations', *Review of International Studies* 20 (1994), 201–204.
3. See Michael Banks, 'The Inter-Paradigm Debate' in Margot Light and A.J.R. Groom (eds), *International Relations: A Handbook of Current Theory* (London: Pinter, 1984), 7–26. For an interesting attempt to re-visit the debate in the light of the post-positivist turn, see Ole Waever, 'The Rise and Fall of the Inter-Paradigm Debate', in Steve Smith, Ken Booth and Marysia Zalewski (eds), *International Theory: Positivism and Beyond* (Cambridge: Cambridge University Press, 1996), 149–185.
4. An example of a post-positivist reading of the historiography of International Relations as a Cold War discipline, see Jim George *Discourses of Global Politics: A Critical (Re) Introduction to International Relations* (Colorado: Lynne Reinner, 1994), especially 69–89. The exception, among postmodern accounts, is James Der Derian 'Introducing Philosophical Traditions in International Relations', *Millennium* 17 (1988), 189–193.
5. Robert Keohane, 'International Institutions: Two Approaches', in his *International Institutions and State Power*, 158–182.
6. See the essay by Quentin Skinner, 'Meaning and Understanding in the History of Ideas' in James Tully (ed.), *Meaning and Context: Quentin Skinner and his Critics* (Princeton, 1988).
7. Barry Buzan has hinted that the English School might be a 'possible fourth' paradigm. Buzan, 'The Timeless Wisdom', in Smith, Booth, Zalewski, *International Theory*, 55.
8. Schmidt, 'The Historiography', 364.
9. The development of the English School out of realism is recognised in Robert Jackson 'Is there a Classical International Theory?' in Smith, Booth and Zalewski (eds), *International Relations Theory Today* (Cambridge: Cambridge University Press, 1996), 203–17.
10. Steve Smith (ed.), *International Relations: British and American Perspectives* (Oxford: Blackwell, 1985).
11. See especially R.E. Jones 'The English School of International Relations: A Case for Closure', *Review of International Studies* 7 (1981), 1–13. Hidemi Suganami, 'The Structure of Institutionalism: An Anatomy of British

Mainstream International Relations', *International Relations* 17 (1983), 2363–81. Sheila Grader 'The English School of international relations: evidence and evaluation', *Review of International Studies* 14 (1988), 29–44. Peter Wilson 'The English school of International Relations: A reply to Sheila Grader' *Review of International Studies* 15 (1989), 49–58. See also Christopher Hill 'The study of International Relations in the United Kingdom' in Hugh C. Dyer and Leon Mangasarian (eds), *The Study of International Relations: The State of the Art* (London: Macmillan, 1989); and Gene M. Lyons, 'The study of International Relations in Great Britain: Further Considerations', *World Politics*, 38 (1986), 626–45. The most recent debate about the English School has taken place in a Nordic journal; see Ole Waever 'International Society: Theoretical Promises Unfulfilled?', *Cooperation and Conflict* 27 (1992), 97–128 and the reply by Timothy Dunne, 'International Society: Theoretical Promises Fulfilled?', *Cooperation and Conflict* 30 (1995): 125–54.

12.   The first use of the term was by Christopher Hill, 'R.J. Vincent (1943–90)', *Political Studies*, 39 (1991), 158–160:159. There were also references to an international society tradition in the special issue of *Millennium: Journal of International Studies*, Special Issue, 'Beyond International Society', 21 (1992).

13.   I have previously argued that since the English School converges around the notion of international society, then it is preferable to reconstruct the English School along the lines of an international society tradition thereby avoiding the problems associated with 'nationalising' a particular stream of thinking. In the course of re-writing the original thesis, I have shifted my position on this issue principally for two reasons. From a pragmatic point of view, alternative labels have there own drawbacks, and more importantly, it is the label English School which has gained common currency. In addition, the normative problem with the association of 'nation' and 'approach' is less problematic once the identity of Englishness is recognised to be both contested and in part constructed by its relations with South African citizens, Australians, Indians, and North Americans.

14.   Robert Gilpin, 'The Global Political System', in J.D.B. Miller and R.J. Vincent (eds), *Order and Violence: Hedley Bull and International Relations* (Oxford: Clarendon, 1990), 112–139.

15.   Holsti subsumes the Grotian tradition into a 'classical' realist position, see K.J. Holsti, *The Dividing Discipline: Hegemony and Diversity in International Theory* (London: Unwin Hyman, 1995), 33. Other examples of reading English School thinkers as realists include: Francis A. Beer and Robert Hariman (eds), *Post-Realism: The Rhetorical Turn in International Relations* (East Lansing: Michigan State University Press, 1996), 5; George, *Discourses*, Ch. 3. For an innovative reading of Bull as a realist, see Martin Griffiths, *Realism, Idealism and International Politics: A Reinterpretation* (London: Routledge, 1992), especially Ch. 7 and Ch. 8.

16.   Fred Halliday, 'International Society as Homogeneity: Burke, Marx and Fukuyama', *Millennium*, 21 (1992), 435–61. Other radical voices are far more sensitive to the differences between the English School's rationalism and realism. For example, Andrew Linklater notes that '[w]hereas realism and neo-realism more specifically than often refer to an international system

in quasi-mechanistic terms, rationalism highlights the cultural dimensions of world politics, and specifically the national and international ideas and beliefs which weave societies together in a greater society of states. This focus upon the "normative" and "institutional" dimensions which give international politics its separate "logic" distinguishes rationalism from other perspectives'. Andrew Linklater, 'Rationalism' in Scott Burchill, Andrew Linklater et al, *Theories of International Relations* (London: Macmillan, 1996), 99–100.

17 Fred Halliday, 'The Pertinence of International Relations', *Political Studies* 38 (1990), 506.

18. MacIntyre, quoted in Hedley Bull, Benedict Kingsbury and Adam Roberts (eds), *Hugo Grotius and International Relations* (Oxford: Clarendon, 1990), 54.

19. A related point concerns the remarkable amount of time and energy Bull lent to the project of disseminating Wight's ideas more widely than he had succeeded himself during his lifetime. For a flavour of their pedagogical relationship, see Hedley Bull, 'Martin Wight and the Theory of International Relations', in Martin Wight, *International Theory: The Three Traditions* (Leicester: Leicester University Press, 1991), ix–xxiii.

20. Adam Watson, *The Evolution of International Society: A Comparative Historical Analysis* (London: Routledge, 1992), 5.

21. Hedley Bull, 'The Appalling State of *International Relations* Studies at the LSE and Elsewhere', notes from an unpublished talk give to the London School of Economics 17.1.1980.

22. R.J. Vincent, 'Change in International Relations', *Review of International Studies*, 9 (1983), 69.

23. In his 'Foreward: Revisiting "The Anarchical Society"', Hoffmann notes that the first edition of *The Anarchical Society* did not receive the attention it deserved because 'its "Britishness" did not fit with the prevailing American approaches'. See Hoffmann in Bull, *The Anarchical Society: A Study of Order in World Politics* (London: Macmillan, 2 ed., 1996), vii. Terry Nardin has written the most extensive text on international society in American International Relations, although he admits that 'Britain provides an exception to the assertion that the expression "international society" has fallen out of favour'. Terry Nardin, *Law, Morality and the Relations of States* (Princeton, Princeton University Press, 1983), footnote 4, 27–28.

24. In his chilling words, realism 'places its emphasis upon the acceptance of facts and on the analysis of their causes and consequences'. E.H. Carr, *The Twenty Years' Crisis 1919–1939: An Introduction to the Study of International Relations* (London: Macmillan, 1 ed., 1939), 14.

25. Carr, *The Twenty Years' Crisis*, 7.

26. Hedley Bull, 'International Theory: The Case for a Classical Approach', in Klaus Knorr and James N. Rosenau (eds), *Contenting Approaches to International Politics* (Princeton: Princeton University Press, 1969), 21–38.

27. Wight, *International Theory*, 14–15. Hedley Bull *The Anarchical Society: A Study of Order in World Politics* (London: Macmillan, 1977), Ch. 2.

28. Wight, *The Three Traditions*, 260. Once the cross-over between the 'three Rs' is recognised, the whole system of classification begins to break-down. Arguably this was less problematic for Wight than for Bull. In his memorial

lecture for Wight, Bull suggested that the debate Martin Wight conducted, using great thinkers as his instruments, 'ceases to be one that has actually taken place, and becomes one that he has invented'. Bull, in Wight, *The Three Traditions,* xviii

29.   For example, R.J. Vincent, 'Edmund Burke and the Theory of International Relations', *Review of International Studies*, 10 (1984), 205–218. Another example of 'classical thinkers' being added to the categories include Andrew Hurrell, 'Kant and the Kantian Paradigm in International Relations', *Review of International Studies*, 16 (3): 183–205. Perhaps the single most important collection of essays to 'read' classical thinkers through the 'three Rs' is by Ian Clark and Iver B. Neumann (eds), *Classical Theories of International Relations* (London: Macmillan, 1996). The idea behind the volume was inspired by Vincent's teaching and writing.

30.   H. Bull, B. Kingsbury and A. Roberts (eds), *Hugo Grotius and International Relations,* (Oxford: Clarendon Press, 1990).

31.   M. Donelan, *Elements of International Political Theory* (Oxford: Clarendon Press, 1990).

32.   Colin Wight draws out the implications of this position nicely. 'The world, reality, the cosmos itself just is as *we* say it is. Humanity becomes firmly secured in its rightful place, as meaning-bestowing, reality-creating manifestations of Geist/God.' Colin Wight, 'Incommensurability and Cross-Paradigm Communication in International Relations Theory: What's the Frequency Kenneth?', *Millennium* 25.2 (1996), 291–319 (303).

33.   Wight, 'Western Values', 103.

34.   Pete Wilson, 'The English school of International Relations: A reply to Sheila Grader'. *Review of International Studies* 15 (1): 49–58.

35.   Robert Jackson, 'The Political Theory of International Society' in Ken Booth and Steve Smith (eds), *International Relations Theory Today* (Cambridge: Polity, 1995), 113.

36.   Bull, *The Anarchical Society*, 13.

37.   The terms 'pluralism' and 'solidarism', in connection with international society, were first used by Hedley Bull in his 1962 British Committee paper 'The Grotian Conception of International Society', published in Herbert Butterfield and Martin Wight eds, *Diplomatic Investigations* (London: Allen and Unwin, 1966), 51–73.

38.   This argument is well made by Robert Jackson, who suggests that international society 'presupposes the intrinsic value of all states and accommodates their inward diversity', Robert Jackson, 'Martin Wight, International Theory and the Good Life', *Millennium* 19 (1990), 267. For other compelling articulations of the pluralist system of ethics which underpins the English School interpretation of international society, see Nardin, *Law, Morality* and Chris Brown 'International Theory and International Society: The Viability of the Middle Way', *Review of International Studies* 21 (1995), 183–96.

39.   R.J. Vincent, *Human Rights and International Relations* (Cambridge: Cambridge University Press, 1986), 123.

40.   This, of course, is only part of the 'guardian-gangster' dichotomy lucidly explored by Wheeler. See Nicholas J. Wheeler, 'Guardian Angel or Global Gangster: A Review of the Ethical Claims of International Society', *Political Studies* 44 (1996), 123–135.

41. These questions, addressed by the English School, are included in Mervyn Frost's list of 13 'central questions for normative theory'. See Mervyn Frost, *Ethics in International Relations*, (Cambridge: Cambridge University Press, 2nd edition, 1996), 76–77.

42. Roy Jones noted how 'the English School claims and acclaims' Manning as its 'principal source of inspiration'. Jones, 'The English School', 3. Recently, Martha Finnemore described Manning and Wight as the founders of the English School. Rather than use this label, Finnemore argued: 'A more appropriate term might be "the LSE School" because the London School of Economics has been the institution at which most of these scholars came together.' Martha Finnemore, *National Interests in International Society* (Cornell; Cornell University Press, 1996), 17, note 28.

43. An additional reason for Manning's exclusion from the Committee may have had something to do with his openly pro-Apartheid politics. In addition, Manning gave 'evidence' to the International Court of Justice on this question, published in 'Collective Selfhoods: An Element in the South West Africa case being the Testimony of an Academic South African' (London: The South Africa Society, 1965). Manning was at the time the chair of the South Africa Society. Two aspects of Manning's testimony are worthy of note. The first is his definition of the discipline. In response to the opening question, 'what did your teaching of international relations involve?', Manning replied: 'From the outset I saw my subject not so much as a branch of history or of conventional political science but rather as a species of political sociology, focused as it was on human history in its widest dimension, its world-wide dimension. I saw it in principle and in fact as a kind of sociology of the social universe, a cosmology of the social universe perhaps.' This is not a definition of the field which Bull or any other member of the English School would subscribe to without qualification. Under intensive cross-examination from Ernest A. Gross, member of the New York Bar, Counsel for the Governments of Liberia, who asked Manning what he thought of 'the international human rights norm of non-descrimination', Manning noted his 'distaste for any doctrinaire or ideological approach to a problem which seemed to me to be one of social gardening …' (meaning social engineering). Manning, 'Collective Selfhoods', 19. I am grateful to Chris Brown for drawing my attention to Manning's defence of apartheid.

44. There is no doubt that Manning's work was pioneering to the extent that he understood the rule-governed identity of international society, and the fact that it is reproduced by the actions of 'those quasi-persons, the sovereign states'. See Charles Manning, *The Nature of International Society* (London: Macmillan, 2nd ed., 1975), xxiii.

45. The term 'trialectic' is used by Kingsbury in conjunction with the three tradions. See Benedict Kingsbury, 'Grotius, Law, and Moral Scepticism: Theory and Practice in the Thought of Hedley Bull', in Ian Clark and Iver B. Neuman (eds) *Classical Theories of International Relations* (London: Macmillan, 1996), 59.

46. Richard Ashley and R.B.J. Walker, 'Speaking the Language of Exile: Dissident Thought in International Studies', *International Studies Quarterly* 34 (1990), 265. This representation of Carr as a dissident,

mirrors his relationship to British culture more broadly. As Tamara
Deutscher said of him, 'Carr was *in* the British tradition and yet was not
quite *of* it'. Tamara Deutscher, 'E.H. Carr – A Personal Memoir', *New
Left Review*, 137 (1983), 79.

47. Martin Wight, 'Does Peace Take Care of Itself', *Views* 2 (1963), 93–95.
Wight described the book as 'an idiosyncratic essay based on patchy scholarship', 94.

48. Michael Donelan's group began meeting in 1974. Publications from this
group include: Michael Donelan (ed.), *The Reason of States* (London: Allen
and Unwin, 1978); James Mayall (ed.), *The Community of States* (London:
Allen and Unwin, 1982); Cornelia Navari (ed.), *The Condition of States*
(Buckingham: Open University Press, 1991).

49. Gene Lyons, 'The Study of I.R. in Great Britain', *World Politics* 28 (1986),
625–645: 633.

50. Stephen George, 'The Reconciliation of the "Classical" and "Scientific"
Approaches to International Relations', *Millennium* 5 (1976), 28–40.

51. Although, as we will see in Chapter 7, Bull and Donelan had antithetical
understandings of the bases of itnernational society, Donelan believing in
primordial community of humankind and Bull viewing it as constructed
through the practices of states.

52. Jones also includes F.S. Northedge, who was not a theorist, and Robert
Purnell who did not agree with the substance of the English School apart
from the title of his one major work *International Society*.

53. Grader, 'The English School', 38.

54. Little, 'Neorealism and the English School', 32.

55. Robert Jackson adds Carr to the list of founding English School members.
Jackson, 'Is there a classical international theory', 213. Buzan includes Carr,
but also Manning (despite admitting that Manning was 'too convuluted' to
attract 'much of a following'). Barry Buzan, 'From International System to
International Society: Structural Realism and Regime Theory meet the
English School', *International Organization* 47 (1993), 327–52.

56. The English School in the 1990s could be said to include, among others, the
following theorists: David Armstrong Geoffrey Best, Barry Buzan, Martin
Ceadel, Ian Clark, Michael Donelan, Jack Donnelly, Roger Epp, Murray
Forsyth, Gerrit Gong, Andrew Hurrell, Christopher Hill, Robert Jackson,
Alan James, Benedict Kingsbury, Tony Knudsen, Andrew Linklater, Paul
Keal, Richard Little, Samuel M. Makinda, James Mayall, Cornelia Navari,
Brian Porter, Iver B. Neumann, James L. Richardson, Adam Roberts,
Hidemi Suganami, Adam Watson, Jennifer M. Welsh, Nicholas J. Wheeler,
Peter Wilson.

57. Hedley Bull, 'New Directions in International Relations Theory',
International Studies 14 (1975), 279.

58. Fred Halliday and Justin Rosenberg, transcripts of an 'Interview with Ken
Waltz' (LSE, 7 May 1993), 4–5.

2 E.H. Carr

E.H. Carr would have been more comfortable with the self-description 'intellectual activist' rather than 'international theorist'. His interest in international relations was motivated by his desire to influence policy, whether it related to the response of the West to the Soviet Union or the economic imperative of reconstructing postwar British economy and society. This concern to shape the course of history in the early 1940s led to something of a collision between his two worlds of academe and policy-making when it came to the attention of the Woodrow Wilson board that their Professor was more engaged in the politics of *The Times* than the Department of International Politics at Aberystwyth. Compared to the controversies within the English speaking academic world that his writings on International Relations and Soviet history were to generate, this fall-out at Aberystwyth was no more than a little local difficulty.

In the discipline of International Relations, Carr's reputation stands or falls largely according to competing interpretations of *The Twenty Years' Crisis*. During the years of the 'first great debate', Carr found himself in the unfortunate position of being caught in the cross-fire between different sides, neither wanting to claim him (or his work) for their own. Predictably, liberal idealists in the late 1930s and 1940s saw Carr as something of a menace.[1] But what is surprising is that the godfather of American realism, Hans J. Morgenthau, uttered the highest opprobrium.[2] In contrast to his reputation in the early post-war period, Carr's stock has risen dramatically in recent years. In an influential piece written in the mid-1980s, Robert Gilpin identified Carr as one of the all-time 'three great realist writers'.[3] At the radical end of the discipline, participants in the post-realist debate such as Ken Booth, Robert Cox and Andrew Linklater, all appropriate from Carr key building blocks for the construction of a new stage in international relations theory.[4] Postmodernists have not dwelt long on *The Twenty Years' Crisis*, which is surprising given Carr's twin attractions to power and pragmatism.[5] None of this is to suggest that Carr's work does not continue to provoke criticism from all political sides, as important recent critiques testify.[6]

E.H. Carr's involvement with academic International Relations ended after the war. His voyage into the history of the Soviet Union enabled him to revisit his love of Russian literature and politics. Through this monumental study, Carr was able to engage deeply in academic inquiry, as well as influencing Western opinion on the Soviet Union. Just as he sought, in *The Twenty Years' Crisis*, to 'counteract the glaring defects' of state leaders in the 1930s, his representation of the Soviet Union similarly aimed to balance the 'propaganda' about the regime which was disseminated by the West during the Cold War. Here Carr was entering deeply troubled political waters, provoking vituperative attacks from the 'right' shortly after his death, and relative alienation from all but the Marxist left during his life.

The focus for this chapter is not to enter the fray about whether or not Carr's *History* was flawed, or whether Carr's works in International Relations are contradictory.[7] It will, however, draw on the inter-related spheres of Carr's biography, ideology and his place in the academy, in order to address the following three themes. First, the question what did Carr mean by 'realism' and 'utopianism'? It will be argued that the realism of *The Twenty Years' Crisis* is not a theoretical construct but a critical weapon that Carr turned against 'utopianism'. Crucially, he was dissatisfied with a non-utopian realism,[8] privileging in the final analysis a complex relationship between the two constructs. This tension has been lost in the orthodox interpretation of the work as a founding text in the realist canon. The point here is not to deny that there are realist arguments in *The Twenty Years' Crisis*, but rather, the aim is to reveal the ambiguities inherent in the unstable relationship between 'realism' and 'utopianism'.

The second theme to be addressed concerns the extent to which Carr was a moral relativist. How did Carr seek to ground his ideas about a new global order after World War II: in reason, or in power (as his critics suggest)? Here the focus will shift to Carr's idea, outlined in *What Is History?*, of achieving progress through 'the widening horizon'. Finally, the chapter will examine where Carr stands in relation to the English School. Clearly Bull believed he stood on the 'outside', after all, it was Bull who argued that one of the consequences of Carr's relativism was that he 'jettisons the idea of international society itself'.[9] What is intriguing is that Carr's own reflections on his role in the establishment of International Relations, suggest the opposite, namely that Carr believed he *had* participated in an attempt to *invent* an international society.

Carr and IR: 'Political Thought is itself a Form of Political Action'[10]

Carr's education in international politics flourished whilst he was a diplomat in Riga, from 1925 to 1929, where his interest in Russian culture and history first took hold. Being rather a loner, he opted out of the opera circuit beloved of charmed diplomatic circles, preferring to read nineteenth century Russian literature.[11] There was also a political dimension to these works. Carr saw in these writers a powerful critique of bourgeois capitalist society. In addition to his work as a diplomat and biographer, Carr developed a third vocation, that of a commentator and essayist. In some respects, it is in this last capacity that Carr was at his most brilliant, combining an agile discursive style with an impressive breadth of historical learning.[12]

Between 1930 and 1933 Carr acted as a Foreign Office adviser on League of Nations Affairs. In a critical review of *The Twenty Years' Crisis* Sir Alfred Zimmern admitted that Carr had 'sat in the Foreign Office with an observing eye'.[13] A good example of his dual role of diplomat and commentator is recounted in *The Twenty Years' Crisis* where Carr notes how he was profoundly influenced by a statement made by the Yugoslav foreign minister who criticised the 'things-will-right-themselves' school of economists, who failed to see that free markets operated 'at the expense of the weakest.'[14] This critique of the liberal doctrine of the 'harmony of interests' became the starting point for Carr's construction of 'political realism'. More broadly, it signified Carr's increasing disenchantment with liberalism's twin foundations of capitalism and democracy. This opened the door to what Carr saw as the main attraction of Marxism, its ability to 'debunk' the moralistic claims of liberal democracy.

Upon Carr's acceptance of the Professorship at Aberystwyth in 1936 he soon undermined the idea of liberal internationalism associated with the former American President in whose name the chair was created.[15] For David Davies, the realism that Carr brought to the position was the final nail in his idealist coffin. He bitterly regretted the way in which the department 'has worked consistently against the programme I have spent most of my time and money advocating; namely, the development of the League with a real international authority.'[16] Endowing chairs, Davies was forced to conclude, 'is a very dangerous experiment.'[17]

When viewing Carr's tenure as Wilson Professor, we should not be too swayed by Davies' fanaticism for the League and his concomitant rejection of reasoned criticism of idealism. As the historian of the University College of Wales put it colourfully, 'hell hath no fury like an idealist disillusioned'.[18] In many ways, Carr's years at Aberystwyth were remarkably productive. Within three years he had published three major works in addition to his war-time service at the Ministry of Information as director of foreign publicity.[19] After a dispute with the new Minister, Sir John Reith, Carr increasingly devoted himself to writing editorials for *The Times* although continuing to publish books and pamphlets, mainly on the challenges of constructing the coming peace.[20] Carr's involvement with

The Times caused some conflict with his responsibilities at the University College Wales.[21] Carr resigned from the Chair at Aberystwyth in 1946[22] and began his fourteen-volume work on *A History of Soviet Russia*,[23] described by Brian Porter as 'one of the supreme achievements of modern British scholarship'.[24] Before considering the controversy surrounding the interpretation of Carr's *A History*, it is worth noting that after his 'resignation' from the Wilson Professorship, Carr was passed up for a number of academic positions for which he was well qualified.[25] The most obvious explanation for his exile from the academy is that Carr's sympathy for the Soviet experiment had become a professional liability with the onset of the Cold War. As Haslam put it, 'Britain, too, had its equivalent of McCarthyism.'[26]

Why did Carr become a disenchanted liberal? In his short autobiographical notes, Carr recalled how at the peace conference 'my Liberal principles were still intact.'[27] By the early 1930s, his views were thoroughly pro-Soviet. Carr was not alone in holding these views in élite circles. He was part of a generation of disenchanted liberals, who saw capitalism failing, democracy faltering and were exceedingly sceptical of the capacity for the West to deliver the progress the nineteenth century had once promised. However, it is arguable that Carr moved further from a position as a liberal dissenter, accepting key tenets of Marxism. In the preface to *Britain: a Study of Foreign Policy From the Versailles Treaty to the Outbreak of War* Carr noted that 'there are now few thinking men who will dismiss with confidence the Marxian assumption that capitalism, developed to its highest point, inevitably encompasses its own destruction.'[28] International Relations scholars are fond of pointing out that Soviet foreign policy makers rapidly shed their revolutionary clothes and become diplomats.[29] In the case of E.H. Carr, the diplomat became a revolutionary.

Theories as Weapons: Realism in The Twenty Years' Crisis
The Twenty Years' Crisis was published at the end of 1939, just after Britain officially declared war on Nazi Germany. To date the book has run to two editions and has been reprinted several times. It is interesting to note that by the end of the war Carr dismissed the work as 'a study of the period' which 'must be treated on its merits as such.'[30] Judging by the importance of the work in the historiography of academic International Relations, it is fair to say that Carr's assessment of the book is not shared widely within the discipline. Not only is it one of the first books students read, it is a book which more mature scholars often return to. More graphically, it might be one of the few books in the field 'which leaves us nowhere to hide.'[31] It is the only book written by a British International

Relations theorist to have been adopted as a key realist text in the American academy. Stanley Hoffmann called it 'the first "scientific" treatment of modern world politics'.[32] More recently, Michael Joseph Smith argued that 'from its first appearance *The Twenty Years' Crisis* was treated as a challenge to the predominant intellectual approach to international relations, and it is still read today as a classic statement of realism.'[33] Not only has the text travelled well in the English speaking International Relations world, its significance has been reified by the elevation of the work as the winner of the so-called first 'great debate' between realism and idealism.[34]

The analysis of *The Twenty Years' Crisis* offered below endorses Ken Booth's view that it is a 'brilliant' but 'flawed' work which has been 'misunderstood' by those who view it through a realist's lens. The 'brilliance' lies in its use of realist theory as a weapon to undermine specious claims to universal truth and morality. 'Flawed' because the arguments on which he bases his critique does not stand up to close scrutiny (discussed below). Carr's use and abuse of history is not the reason why most writers have criticised *The Twenty Years' Crisis*, citing instead Carr's subordination of morality to power, and utopianism to realism. It is in this sense that the work has been 'misunderstood', since it fails to recognise the genuine (if ambiguous) goal of utopianism, and moreover, wrongly construes the charge of 'relativism' so frequently laid at Carr's door. Where the analysis departs from that offered by Booth is in the rejection of his charge that *The Twenty Years' Crisis* has been an 'unhelpful influence on the development of the subject.'[35] Arguably, it contains within it the possibility of an immanent critique of a number of core claims made by contemporary defenders of the international society project. In particular, as discussed in the last part of the chapter, Carr's application of the sociology of knowledge to diplomacy enables us to penetrate the consciousness of actors in order to reveal the material forces and social structures which are shaping their actions, and crucially, distorting their self-definitions and explanations for their own actions. Furthermore, Carr's critique of the inequality of power in the international system poses deeply problematic questions for later writers on international society, who supposed that power could be confronted by norms of sovereign equality and new principles of international legitimacy.

E.H. Carr's motives in writing the book were both realist and utopian. Looking to the future, *The Twenty Years' Crisis* was dedicated to 'the makers of the coming peace', who would one day face the responsibility of building a new post-war utopia. Looking in the opposite direction, the book was written, in Carr's words, with the 'deliberate aim' of countenancing the 'almost total neglect of the factor of power' which had beset Anglo-American thinking in the interwar period.[36] The label Carr allocated to these 'children of lightness' was, of course, 'utopians'. But *who* were the 'utopians', *how* were they responsible for the 'underlying' rather than 'immediate' cause of the breakdown in international order? What false diagnosis did they prescribe? And how could the malaise they identified be removed and the theory and practice of international politics be reinvented?

The first and most obvious point to make about Carr's treatment of the 'utopians' is the pejorative way in which he uses the term, particularly in the early stages of the text. To be a utopian is to be immature, infantile; to prefer wishing rather than thinking. In Orwellian language, utopians are the humans (two legs bad), realists the pigs (four legs good). His initial referent for utopianism is the discipline itself, which is evolving out of its 'primitive' phase – an evolutionary form that he attributes to all 'sciences'. One of the defining characteristics of this phase is the privileging of the 'end' over the 'means', a tendency embodied in Woodrow Wilson's famous quote about the League, 'if it won't work, it must be made to work.'[37] Notice here the shift in the referent for 'utopianism' from the discipline to particular state leaders. Utopians tend to privilege general principles, or 'absolute standards', rather than practical questions about how principles are to be applied in practice. From utopian state leaders, the referent then shifts to the terrain of the political 'left', who tend to advocate ideas in preference to problem-solving approaches. Moving from the political to the philosophical, we discover that utopianism is as old as the Enlightenment tradition; the epistemology of utopianism is 'rationalism', the belief that reason can deliver unvarnished truth.[38]

Carr's expansive remarks on utopianism, make way in Part Two of the text to a more analytical consideration of the ways in which utopian thinking contributed to 'the international crises'. Faith in human reason articulated in philosophical sketches by Bentham and Kant began in the early part of the twentieth century to shape world-views of state leaders and western publics, who increasingly came to hold the opinion that reason could ground democracy, and democracy conquer anarchy. The referent for utopianism has now become 'democratic rationalism'.[39] Projected onto the international realm, rationalism was codified in the League of Nations covenants, with its universal standards for maintaining peace through collective security. Because these standards were self-evident, and applicable across time and space, any deviation from what is rational is designated as pathological. Hence, as Carr points out, the characteristic of utopian thinkers from 1931 onwards to describe the actions of revisionist states (and the lack of response to them) in *ad hominem* adjectives like 'wicked', 'egotistic', 'cowardly'.

What is evident from the detour into utopianism is the generality (and inconsistency) with which Carr assigns the category to a multitude of referents, from individual thinkers and particular texts, to different disciplines and finally to domestic and international political orders (blurring its ontological status as 'principle' or 'action' in the process).[40] The next move in *The Twenty Years' Crisis* is to show *how* a theory of utopianism has *caused* the breakdown in the interwar order. Here we come across the central explanatory theme which is said to unite all strands of utopianism across different disciplines, namely, the belief in a 'harmony of interests'. In philosophy, utilitarianism holds out the promise that self-interest promotes the general good; neo-classical economics brings together the interests of the individual with the efficient functioning of the market; and finally, liberal internationalism argues that there are no essential conflicts of interest between nation-states. The slow recognition from the turn of the century onwards, that interests collided in international relations (between great powers and small states for example) just as they conflict in the domestic labour market, is revealing the hollow nature of the hegemonic liberal conception of morality that has dominated political thought 'for a century and a half'.[41] This brings Carr to conclude: 'The inner meaning of the modern international crises is the collapse of the whole structure of utopianism based on the concept of the harmony of interests.'[42]

The analysis of the breakdown in the inter-war system presented in *The Twenty Years' Crisis* is open to a number of objections. Even if 'the harmony of interests' pervaded thinking in France, Britain and the League as a whole between 1919 and 1939 (itself a contestable claim), it was clearly not part of the vocabulary of post-revolutionary Russia and the other revisionist states in the 1920s like Italy and Japan, who rejected liberal economic and political principles long before the descent into war. Similarly, how does the natural liberal harmony explain the US's decision to remain outside of the League structure, an event which would appear to signal a clear disconnect between the national and international interest. A useful way to illustrate the weakness in the analysis provided in *The Twenty Years' Crisis* is counter-factually: even if state leaders in the 'satisfied' powers had recognised the reflection of their own national interests in the mirror of international principles, it is highly unlikely that this would have prevented the outbreak of general war. Nationalist forces and ideologies beyond the control of Western states were the primary cause of the Second World War, not illusions of perpetual peace harboured in liberal states.

Realism is the term Carr uses to describe the critique of utopianism. As will become clear below, it is of paramount importance to make a formal distinction between 'realism' as a theory of international politics, and Carr's version of realism as an epistemic 'tool' or 'weapon'. Using an analysis familiar to Marxists,[43] Carr refutes the harmony of interests doctrine, reducing it to 'the ideology of a dominant group concerned to maintain its predominance by asserting the identity of its interests with those of the community as a whole.'[44] For example, Britain's arguments in the nineteenth century for universal free trade reflected her particular advantages in securing such an outcome. Similarly, the Treaty of Versailles represented the interests of the satisfied victor powers, and not those of all humankind.[45] The utopian assumption that there is an international invisible hand which can masterfully co-ordinate a world common good out of the pursuit of a plurality of separate national interests is an illusion. Conflicts of interest are, Carr argued, '*real* and *inevitable*'.[46]

The purpose for realism is, therefore, to relativise all claims to a universal good in order to reveal the partial interests which underlie those claims. The 'absolute standard' which Carr was fighting was the law and the morality of the satisfied powers:

What matters is that these supposedly absolute and universal principles were not principles at all, but the *unconscious* reflexions of *national policy* based on a particular interpretation of national interest at a particular time.[47]

Applying this lesson to international relations, he concludes that there can be no international order outside the interests of the dominant powers. Clearly this was a devastating critique of the idealist movement to institutionalise a legal and moral order in the international realm. It is also a critical weapon that must eventually be turned against Carr's successors like Martin Wight, Hedley Bull and R.J. Vincent, who sought, however tentatively, to defend an international order in which all states had a stake.

As the following section will consider in greater detail, the relativism of realism is the issue which Carr's critics are united in condemning. For Carr it is precisely this relativism which represents the apotheosis of realist thought:

The weapon of the relativity of thought must be used to demolish the utopian concept of a fixed and absolute standard by which policies and actions can be judged.[48]

Where does Carr derive this formula of realism-as-relativism from? Probably the most important source for the argument in *The Twenty Years' Crisis* was the Hungarian sociologist, Karl Mannheim.[49] Carr acknowledges his debt to Mannheim in the 'preface' to the work, but the extent of his influence is more apparent in a later essay by Carr published in the *Times Literary Supplement* in 1953. Mannheim's principal academic innovation, Carr argues, was to systematise a body of ideas known as the 'sociology of knowledge'. The core claim here is the embedded nature of political thought in the social order, in other words, the sociology of knowledge is the appropriation of Marx's argument that ideas (superstructure) are a reflection of material circumstances (base), whilst denying a specifically economic character to the base. The intellectual impact of Mannheim's ideas on Carr is given prominence by Charles Jones. 'Mannheim deserves consideration by students of international relations', Jones argues, 'chiefly because he provided Carr with the dialectical structure of *The Twenty Years' Crisis* and a distinctively postpositivist social scientific methodology that would mark him off from the dominant positivism of the Anglo-Saxon world of his day.'[50]

Carr's exegesis on Mannheim is at the same time a vindication of his own method. As Carr said of Mannheim, 'he struggled hard against the imputation of "relativism"'. His one criticism of Mannheim suggests Carr's struggle against relativism was even greater. Carr resisted the idea, propounded by his mentor, that intellectuals could be quasi-autonomous. In a typically adroit comment, Carr wrote: 'The question is not where we are to find the standard-bearers, but where we are to find the standard.'[51]

Bringing Utopianism Back In

In his article '*The Twenty Years' Crisis* Thirty Years On', Hedley Bull argues that Carr's work is an exercise in critique which fails to construct from what has gone before. The same claim is made by less sympathetic critics. In Morgenthau's words, Carr surrenders 'to the immanence of power'.[52] Leonard Woolf dismisses Carr as a realist with no sense of morality reducing the complexity of the text to the crude formulae: 'Power is a reality; force is a reality; war is inevitable; peace is utopian.'[53] Whittle Johnson asks how Carr is able to prevent his argument being 'washed over the rapids into a normless relativism?'[54]

These convergent representations of *The Twenty Years' Crisis*, and Carr's work in general, commits three related errors (each of which is considered below): first, they do not adequately consider the specific recommendations made by Carr in order to facilitate peaceful change in international politics; second, the antinomial relationship between realism and utopianism is fundamentally misunderstood; third, they understate the extent to which Carr was aware of the need to provide moral foundations. By rethinking Carr's philosophy of history, it is evident that he provided (albeit cautiously) a grounding for reason in history (thereby overcoming relativism).

These commentaries on Carr's work uncritically accept a logocentric understanding of the relationship between realism and idealism; in other words, the power of realism displaces the wishful thinking of idealism. Carr never endorses this in an unqualified form. Even in the opening chapter of *The Twenty Years' Crisis* Carr admits that realism is a 'corrective' that must itself be counteracted by 'utopianism'. A revisionist understanding of the relationship between these 'two poles' highlights the movement of history and science through dialectical stages where the line between truth and falsehood is blurred rather than sharply defined opposites according to conventional logic. The case for a revisionist account is not helped by the fact that Carr 'slides' from a dialectical understanding to one in which realism and utopianism coexist in space rather than evolving through time.[55] The important point is not to try and unravel the precise relationship between 'realism' and 'utopianism', but to recognise the interpenetration of the two elements. This is precisely what was lost in the sound and fury of the so-called 'great debate'. T.L. Knutsen neatly articulates this argument:

> whereas Carr in the late 1930s had emphasized the dynamic interaction between utopianism and realism, scholars of the late 1940s often saw the two in static opposition. Post-war students, unaccustomed to Carr's dialectics, simply considered utopianism a naive alternative to realism; they treated it as a straw man which they could knock over in order to better portray the mature wisdom of the realist alternative.[56]

As a consequence of the colonisation of *The Twenty Years' Crisis* by the realists, little attention has been paid to the way in which Carr uses the term 'utopianism' in a constructive sense. After the realist weapon has penetrated the mask of national interests, Carr recognised the need to build a new utopia. What was *his* idea of a utopia? At this juncture it is useful to draw on the distinction between 'end-point utopias' and 'process utopias'.[57] Carr's target, as discussed earlier, was the theorists and practitioners who signed up to an 'end-point utopia', such as total disarmament or the renunciation of the use of forces, as though the conditions for its realisation were already in existence. But nowhere in *The Twenty Years'*

Crisis does Carr dismiss the reformist steps of process utopianism. Indeed, in a later work, Carr describes utopianism as moving towards a goal 'even if this goal is never fully attained or attainable.'[58]

The problem of how to 'effect necessary and desirable changes' without war[59] was a prevalent utopian theme in the 1930s.[60] For Carr, British appeasement of Germany embodied the two sufficient conditions for peaceful change, the element of power and the element of morality.[61] But Carr does not address how we are to judge the synthesis of these two planes. For example, how many borders should Hitler have been allowed to change before the element of force was required to counteract the ethical accommodation of Germany's revisionist demands? The strength of Carr's dialectic for change is that it allows for the interplay of *both* elements of morality and power. But the weakness in the argument, like the difficulty with the balance between the background theories of realism and utopianism, is that Carr does not explain *how* it is possible to have both elements. 'All one can do', as one critic put it, 'is see-saw between them.'[62]

Hedley Bull argued that Carr's defence of appeasement highlighted the moral bankruptcy of relativism, which 'denied all independent validity to moral argument.'[63] Yet this reading of his work does not take into account that Carr was clearly aware of the paucity of political programmes that were devoid of ethical content. As Carr argued in a contribution to a volume entitled *Foundations for World Order*, although morality cannot be separated from the influence of power 'we must believe – in an absolute good that it is independent of power.'[64] Not entirely confident that morality could provide any firm 'foundations', he nevertheless provided important prescriptions for international reform, including, an end to discrimination between 'individuals on grounds of race, colour or national allegiance', striving to find 'commonly accepted ground on which to meet and discuss differences' between states, and the provision of basic needs for all of humanity.[65]

These sketches of utopian thought in Carr's work serve to undermine the simplistic dismissal of Carr as a slave to power politics. They do not, however, amount to a theoretical escape from the relativism he encounters as a result of signing up to the sociology of knowledge. In *What Is History?* we find Carr's attempted escape route, although it would be premature to argue that this traces the path leading to utopia on the outside, rather than merely another point inside the walls of the realist prison. When dealing with the vexed question about grounding moral judgements, Carr once again reiterates that there are no ahistorical standards by which actions can be judged. But in the final lecture in the George

Macauley Trevelyan series, Carr opens up an ethical space which he refers to as 'the widening horizon'. In this space, Carr recalls romantically the age of the great nineteenth century liberal historian, Lord Acton. His age, argued Carr, 'possessed two things both of which are badly in need of today: a sense of change as a progressive factor in history, and belief in reason as our guide for the understanding of its complexities.'[66] Here we see how 'reason' and 'progress', the two utopian scourges that Carr sought to banish in the early chapters of *The Twenty Years' Crisis*, are returning to provide the foundations for a new and more inclusive social order.[67]

What has Carr got to do with It?

There are without doubt fundamental tensions between Carr's 'utopian realism' and the theories of international society propounded in elementary form in the British Committee, and more fully in the work of Bull and Vincent. These can usefully be divided into two sets of questions: the first will deal with Carr's interpretation of international society. Did Carr's realism exclude 'the good of international society as a whole' as Bull so forcefully argued,[68] or can we find within Carr's body of thinking on international politics a defence of the practices of the society of states? The second question concerns the personal dynamics between Carr and other scholars in the International Relations field working in Britain. This is important if we are going to try to locate Carr within the origin and evolution of the English School.

The idea of an international society was part of Carr's vocabulary, as it was for most writers on International Relations of the period. As we see from *The Twenty Years' Crisis*, it was precisely the realist denial of the existence of international society that called utopianism into existence:

> But pure realism can offer nothing but a naked struggle for power which makes any kind of international society impossible. Having demolished the current utopia with the weapons of realism, we still need to build a new utopia of our own, which will one day fall to the same weapons.[69]

Carr appears to use the term 'international society' in a distinctly constructivist manner. In the first instance, there is a notion of a socially constructed international society, for the reason that 'people talk, and within certain limits behave, as if there were a world community.[70] Patterns of societal behaviour are evident in the widespread recognition among state leaders and diplomats that states have obligations to one another.[71] Carr frequently cites examples of the way in which revisionist states justified their actions by reference to legal custom or general convention. Moreover, the tendency to personify states as legal persons, both in theory and practice, reinforces this idea of a community of states. The problem with international society, identified by Carr and recurrent in other English School writings, is that the degree of solidarity (Carr uses the term 'loyalty') is 'not *yet* powerful enough' to deflect states from the pursuit of 'vital national interests'.[72]

What, then, can be done to increase this latent loyalty (implied by the term 'yet')? Carr recommends a practice of 'give-and-take' which requires 'sacrifices' by the powerful states. 'If we could apply this analogy to international relations', he argues, 'conciliation would come to be regarded as a matter of course.'[73] This process should operate not only within the existing order, but in terms of challenges to the order itself. The problem here, as with Carr's defence of appeasement, is that he does not supply a moral criteria for judging the justice (or otherwise) of the challenge to the existing order. This is precisely the dilemma Bull faced in his later works on the 'revolt against the West'. Although Third World states had a strong case for distributive justice, the lack of consensus on this issue, which prevailed in the West, meant that 'give and take' had ultimately to be decided on grounds of preserving order.[74]

Whilst recognising the existence of a society of states, Carr does not seek to defend it as a legitimate architecture for world order. This point comes through strongly in a letter Carr wrote to Stanley Hoffmann in 1977, reflecting on the role he played in setting up the discipline:

Whatever my share in starting this business, I do not know that I am particularly proud of it. I suspect that *we tried to conjure into existence an international society* and a science of international relations. We failed. No international society exists, but an open club without substantive rules.[75]

The principle reason why the society of states is a myth, according to Carr, is the structural inequality built into the system. Any society which accepts as 'normal or permissible' discrimination between individuals, 'on grounds of race, colour or national allegiance', lacks the basic foundation for a moral order. Not only is there institutionalised inequality between peoples, but also between states. The present legal norms cannot effectively mitigate the massive inequality among states. For this reason, 'a world order constructed on such a basis contradicts the principle of true equality and lacks any solid moral foundation.'[76]

Therefore, despite interesting overlaps between Carr and later English School theorists about the nature of international society and its limits, the crucial factor that ultimately prevents Carr's assimilation into the School, is his recognition of the intrusion of power into all aspects of ethics and politics. Power for Carr, unlike Bull or Vincent, goes all the way down.[77] There can be no treaties signed, no concessions made, no aid given, no alliances forged, without 'the intrusion of power'. Crucially, power goes so far down that it penetrates the subconsciousness of state leaders, it looks over their shoulders, seeps into their dispatch boxes, and distorts their understanding of the underlying reality of international politics.

On purely theoretical grounds, Carr stands in relation to the English School in something of a semi-detached position. What brings him in to the School is the importance key thinkers like Bull and Vincent attached to his work, and perhaps more significantly, the shadow *The Twenty Years' Crisis* cast over these later English School writers. Following Carr, Vincent frequently wielded the weapon of the relativity of thought as a way of revealing the play of interests behind the mask of morality. It is also worthy of note that Vincent showed a greater subtlety in his reading of Carr than other English School writers, recognising the infusion of solidarist sentiments in Carr's work.[78] This latter point cannot be said of Bull; as we have seen above, in his 1969 review essay, he rather uncritically endorsed a one-dimensional realist reading of *The Twenty Years Crisis*. Moreover, despite berating Carr for failing to provide a defence of international society, Bull himself never supplies a foundationalist argument for evaluating the practices of states and the way in which they contribute to world order. Indeed, Carr's realist critique is mobilised by Bull to serve as a corrective to his growing sense of 'cosmopolitan moral awareness' (a point which will be picked up in Chapter 8).

Conclusion

E.H. Carr believed the realist-relativist critique to be the great strength of realism. For his critics, it was the Achilles heel of *The Twenty Years' Crisis* and Carr's work in general. There is near unanimity among them that Carr was a brilliant deconstructionist but a poor constructionist. In this respect, the critics tried to debunk the great debunker. But were they successful?

One response to Carr's critics is to contend that their argument against Carr relies on a misreading of his theory of realism as though it represented an unalloyed victory over utopianism. In place of this one-dimensional reading, the chapter considered alternative formulations of the relationship between the two planes of realism and utopianism. In the final analysis, Carr provides textual evidence to support three versions: realism and utopianism as a dualism (opposites), duality (interpenetrating) and dialectic (successive moments in the resolution of opposites). By locating the issue in the body of his thinking, particularly his philosophy of history, I would argue that the most compelling reading is that realism and utopianism form the two components of a remorseless dialectic. The key phrase is Carr's recognition that 'we still need to build a new utopia of our own, which will one day fall to the same weapons.'[79] Therefore, whilst *The Twenty Years' Crisis* was a powerful assault on the 'naiveté' of utopianism, it was also a warning against the 'sterility' of realist thought. For this reason, the description of Carr as a 'utopian realist' is a convincing one. The only problem with this label is it obscures the fact that utopianism remains an unstable category, one which is never adequately grounded despite Carr's hope that reason might open a 'wide horizon' for a social democratic politics to occupy. Given this instability, perhaps a more appropriate label would be 'postmodern realism'. This term picks up on the (admittedly fragmentary) pragmatist epistemology found in Carr's work[80] and moreover, the deeply held belief that ethics cannot escape the intrusion of power politics.

A second important reason for de-coupling Carr from orthodox realism concerns his departure from a strict state-centric position. Carr even went as far as to suggest that 'the national unit seems at best irrelevant to contemporary ideals of social justice and at worst recalcitrant to them.'[81] Carr viewed world history to be moving away from liberalism and the nation-state, hence his search for an alternative set of political principles. To overcome the crisis of liberal-capitalism, Carr charts the increasing importance of economic planning. Planning, collectivisation, spheres of influence, were all more important than the 'half-discarded truths' of liberalism with its notional sovereign equality, unrealisable collective security and unfair 'free' trade. In short, it was communism, and not liberalism, that personified the highest stage of reason in history. The problem with the belief that history is on your side is the easy temptation to regard *necessity* as a priority over *freedom*.[82] In retrospect, Carr is clearly guilty of overlooking the tragic human consequences of Soviet policies. This point was not lost on Martin Wight who reminded Carr of the dangers of historicism: '[t]he replacement of the old-fashioned and inefficient tyrannies in Eastern Europe by modern stream-lined efficient tyrannies does not confer meaning upon the historical process.'[83]

Whilst there are good reasons for doubting the hegemonic portrayal of Carr as a one-dimensional realist, a more important question for the purpose of this volume is how does Carr relate to the development of the English

School from the late 1950s onwards? Reading Carr's confession regarding his role in attempting to 'conjure into existence an international society', there is a danger of underestimating vital points of contact between Carr's arguments and those articulated by card carrying members of the English School in more recent times. One progressive consequence of Carr's work for the development of the English School concerns his role in broadening the discipline away from its legal institutionalist origins. International Relations in Britain after Carr could no longer be accused of being a surrogate of international law or international history. This did not mean that Carr's work signalled a shift away from normative thinking, only that there can be no meaningful analysis of law and ethics independent of the political order in which they are located. A second legacy of Carr, and one which Bull picked up and ran with in the mid-1960s, was the recognition that International Relations could not be assimilated to the methods of the physical sciences. In the social sciences, there can be no simple break between the subject and the object of investigation – as Carr put it, 'in the process of analysing the facts, Marx altered them.'[84] A further overlap with the 'classical approach' is evident in the way in which *The Twenty Years' Crisis* brings together history, philosophy and legal thinking (albeit in a critical way).

Ironically, perhaps Carr's single most important contribution to the development of the English School was to provoke writers like Martin Wight into in seeking a *via media* between realism and utopianism. Dissatisfied with Carr's thorough-going critique of the society of states as nothing other than a discursive act of legitimation on the part of the satisfied powers, Wight believed that the theory and practice of international relations demonstrated patterns of conflict and co-operation, barbarism and civilised intercourse (explored in depth in Chapter 3). Hence the attempt by Wight initially, and then the British Committee under his guidance, to resolve the dialectic between realism and utopianism, to find a synthesis which recognises that power and self interest need not erase elementary forms of international societal behaviour.

Not only would Carr have rejected the idea that there could be any genuine common values between states in a hierarchically ordered international political system, he believed that International Relations itself was part of the problem of inequality and not part of the solution. On this point it is significant that Carr turned the realist weapon back on the International Relations academy with the following indictment: 'The study of international relations in English speaking countries is simply the study of the best way to run the world from positions of strength.'[85] Ultimately it is this despair with the discipline that consigns Carr to being a dissident. He was in the English School but the English School was not in him.[86]

NOTES

1. For a comprehensive overview of the idealists' reaction to the book, see Peter Wilson 'Carr and his Critics: Responses to *The Twenty Years' Crisis*', paper given to the 'E.H. Carr: A Critical Reassessment' symposium at the University of Wales, Gregynog, 13–15 July 1997.

2. Hans Morgenthau, 'The Surrender to the Immanence of Power: E.H. Carr' *Dilemmas of Politics*, (Chicago: Chicago University Press, 1962), 350–357. To a lesser extent, and many years later W.T.R. Fox reiterated a realist critique of Carr, see W.T.R. Fox 'E.H. Carr and Political Realism: Vision and Revision', *Review of International Studies* 11 (1985), 1–16.

3. Robert Gilpin, 'The Richness of the Tradition of Political Realism', in Robert Keohane (ed.), *Neorealism and its Critics* (New York: Columbia University Press, 1986), 306.

4. Andrew Linklater has consistently highlighted the centrality of the political community in Carr's work. Linklater notes how Carr's attempt to resolve the antinomy between Realism and Idealism 'was set forth in a defence of national policy which aimed at the extension of moral obligation and the enlargement of political community'. Andrew Linklater, *Beyond Realism and Marxism: Critical Theory and International Relations* (London: Macmillan, 1990), 7. See also his comments on Carr in his essay 'What is a Good International Citizen?' in Paul Keal (ed.), *Ethics and Foreign Policy* (St. Leonards, New South Wales: Allen and Unwin, 1992), 27–28. His fullest exegesis on Carr's critical potential can be found in his memorial lecture to Carr; Andrew Linklater, 'The Transformation of Political Community: E.H. Carr, Critical Theory and International Relations', *Review of International Studies* 23 (1997), 321–38.

5. Even if Carr does not elaborate a full-blown pragmatist epistemology, the anti-empiricism evident in *What is History?* sets him apart from the dominant strand of positivism in International Relations. The idea that there is a family resemblance between Carr and postmodernism is challenged by Keith Jenkins, who argues that 'whilst Carr may well have learnt the late-modernist notion of perspectivism, he hardly seems to have been ready for the postmodernist lesson that perspectivism "goes all the way down"; that it includes everything and everybody – including himself'. See Keith Jenkins, *On 'What is History?': From Carr and Elton to Rorty and White* (London: Routledge, 1995), 62.

6. Justin Rosenberg, *The Empire of Civil Society: A Critique of the Realist Theory of International Relations* (London: Verso, 1994), especially 10–15.

7. The question of the consistency of Carr's international thought is one which scholars are divided on. Whittle Johnson alleges that Carr had 'at least two different theories which he fails to relate to one another in consistent fashion'. See Whittle Johnson, 'E.H. Carr's Theory of International Relations: A Critique' *Journal of Politics*, 39 (1967), 861. Graham Evans responds by suggesting: 'The basic character of his thinking remains the same in the critical period before, during and after the Second World War when international relations was the main focus of his attention'. See Graham Evans, 'E.H. Carr and International Relations', *British Journal of International Studies* 1 (1975), 78. I would argue that the problem of

consistency in Carr's work arises because Carr's audience (and therefore his target) changes, but the arguments remain broadly consistent.

8.   The term 'utopian realism', in its application to Carr's work, belongs to Ken Booth, 'Security in Anarchy: Utopian Realism in Theory and Practice' *International Affairs*, 67 (1991), 527–545. More recently it has been used (although not acknowledged) by Paul Howe in 'The Utopian Realism of E.H. Carr' *Review of International Studies*, 20 (1994), 277–97.

9.   Hedley Bull, '*The Twenty Years' Crisis* Thirty Years On', *International Journal* 24 (1969), 638.

10.   This is Carr's phrase, from E.H. Carr, *The Twenty Years' Crisis 1919–1939: An Introduction to the Study of International Relations* (London: Macmillan, 1 ed., 1939), 7. All references are to the first edition of *The Twenty Years' Crisis* unless stated otherwise. The biographical material has been acquired from a variety of sources; first, the thorough and sensitive obituary by R.W. Davies printed in the *Proceedings of the British Academy* LXIX (1983), 473–511; second, I benefited from listening on two occasions to Carr's former research student, Jonathan Haslam, who is currently preparing for publication a long overdue biography on Carr. For a preview, see Jonathan Haslam, '"We Need a Faith": E.H. Carr, 1892–1982', *History Today* (August 1983), 36–39. Third, there is useful biographical material from Carr's turbulent years as Woodrow Wilson Professor in E.L. Ellis, *The University College of Wales Aberystwyth 1872–1972* (Cardiff: University of Wales Press, 1972). Fourth, Charles Jones's excellent forthcoming work on *Carr and International Relations* (Cambridge: Cambridge University Press, 1997). All of the above writers, and many more, were brought together during the 'E.H. Carr: A Critical Reassessment' symposium held at the University of Wales, Gregynog, 13–15 July 1997.

11.   This led to a number of literary biographies including; E.H. Carr, *Dostoevsky (1821–1881): A New Biography* (London: Allen and Unwin, 1931), and *The Romantic Exiles: A Nineteenth Century Portrait Gallery* (London: Octagon Books, 1933).

12.   See, for example, E.H. Carr, *From Napoleon to Stalin and Other Essays* (London: Macmillan, 1980). This is a collection of essays written primarily for the *Times Literary Supplement*.

13.   Alfred Zimmern, quoted in Michael Joseph Smith, *Realist Thought from Weber to Kissinger* (Louisiana: Louisiana State University Press, 1986), 68.

14.   Marinkovitch at the session of the Commission for European Union in January 1931, quoted in Carr, *The Twenty Years' Crisis*, 74.

15.   In November 1919, David Davies and his family contributed £20 000 as an endowment of a Chair in Aberystwyth, for the study of those aspects of law, politics, economics and ethics 'which are raised by the prospect of a League of Nations and for the truer understanding of civilizations other than our own'. Ieuan John, Moorhead Wright, and John Garnett, 'International Politics at Aberystwyth 1919–1969', in Brian Porter ed., *Aberystwyth Papers* (Oxford: Oxford University Press, 1972), 86.

16.   Ellis, *The University College*, 259.

17.   In correspondence with Professor R.B. McCallum, Pembroke College, Oxford, 24 June 1942. The purpose of the letter was to congratulate McCallum on a damning review of Carr's *Conditions of Peace*, published in

The Oxford Magazine June 18th, 1942, 372–373. I am grateful to Guto
Thomas for bringing this correspondence to my notice.

18. Ellis, *The University College*, 259.
19. In addition to *The Twenty Years' Crisis*, Carr published the following
works: *International Relations since the Peace Treaties* (London:
Macmillan, 1937), reissued as *International Relations Between the Two
World Wars 1919–1939* (London: Macmillan, 1947); *Britain: A Study of
Foreign Policy From the Versailles Treaty to the Outbreak of War* (London:
Longmans, 1939).
20. Many of these ideas can be found in Carr, *Conditions of Peace* (London:
Macmillan, 1943). He also lectured on these themes at Chatham House,
including 'What are we fighting for?' (London: RIIA, August 1940) and
'The Post-War World: Some Pointers Towards Reconstruction' (London:
RIIA, December 1940). For a comprehensive analysis of Carr's work at *The
Times*, see Charles Jones, *Carr on International Relations* (Cambridge:
Cambridge University Press, 1998 forthcoming) especially Ch. 5.
21. Lord Davies was concerned at Carr's continued withdrawal of the Wilson
Professor's stipend. Once again the Wilson Advisory Board did not share
Davies' criticisms of Carr's absence. As one of them put it, 'Professor Carr
on *The Times* is worth several generals in the field, and the brilliant strate-
gist who put him there should be promoted to Field-Marshal of the Home
Guard'. Thomas Jones to Ifor L. Evans, 3 March 1943. Quoted in Ellis, *The
University College*, 259. Carr wrote a detailed response to these charges of
financial irregularity. He began his report by noting that in wartime, 'the
work of the Wilson Professor necessarily takes on an abnormal character'.
Under these unusual circumstances, 'by far the most effective medium open
to me for the dissemination of better and more general understanding of the
"means of promoting peace between nations" is through the columns of *The
Times*, and I propose to continue to avail myself of this fortunate opportunity'. E.H. Carr, Wilson Professor Report to the Advisory Board
(Aberystwyth: University College of Wales archives, 6 April 1943), 52. On
the particular point of the ability of a Wilson Professor to earn an income
outside of his professorial stipend, Carr noted that the 'substantial success'
of *The Twenty Years' Crisis* and the 'spectacular success' of *Conditions of
Peace* led him to 'put the sum of £500 (which exceeded my net income
from the Chair for the year) in a special account with the idea that at the end
of the war I might properly devote this deposit to some purpose associated
with the Chair.' Carr, Wilson Professor Report, 53.
22. According to Norman Stone he was sacked. Stone 'Grim Eminence',
London Review of Books, 20 Jan–3 Feb (1983), 4.
23. The main volumes of E.H. Carr, *A History of Soviet Russia* include the following: *The Bolshevik Revolution, 1917–23*, vols I–III (London: Macmillan,
1950–1953); *The Interregnum, 1923–24* (London: Macmillan, 1954);
Socialism in One Country vols I–III (London: Macmillan, 1958–1964);
Foundations of a Planned Economy, vols I–III (London: Macmillan,
1969–1978), vol. I in collaboration with R.W. Davies.
24. Porter ed., *The Aberystwyth Papers*, appendix 'Holders of the Woodrow
Wilson Chair', 367. There exists a considerable polarisation of academic
opinion on the validity of Carr's interpretation of post-revolutionary Soviet

Russia, with Carr being condemned for evincing an 'unreconstructed Stalinist version' of history on one side and represented as a uniquely gifted historian on the other. In a review of Carr's final volume, *The Twilight of the Comintern*, Norman Stone criticises Carr as a man, as a teacher and as a historian. This is his conclusion: 'Carr's *History* is not a history of the Soviet Union, but effectively of the Communist Party of the Soviet Union. Even then, much of it is the kind of unreconstructed Stalinist version that would not now see the light of day in Russia itself. His world is very much a northern view: cold, Baltic, abstract ... I am nearly tempted to exclaim that no more useless set of volumes has ever masqueraded as a classic. Carr's real talent lay in mathematics.' Stone, 'Grim Eminence', 8. See also the responses by R.W. Davies, Eric Hobsbawm and a number of other senior historians of the Soviet Union, in *London Review of Books*, (5–17 Feb 1983), 4. A similar war of words took place in the *Times Literary Supplement*, cf. Leopold Labedz posthumous review of 'Cominturn', 10 June 1983, and reply by Alex Nove 'E.H. Carr as a Historian', 14 June 1983. Compare also the favourable Chimen Abramsky, (ed.), *Tribute to E.H. Carr* (Macmillan: London, 1974) with the critical Leopold Labedz (ed.), 'The Use and Abuse of Sovietology', special edition of *Survey*, 30 (1988), 95–111. Whatever the legitimate assessment of *A History of Soviet Russia* the important implication for understanding Carr's work on International Relations is that Carr was drawn to the study of the Soviet Union because he believed that 'collectivism' offered a better future than the outdated liberal principles criticised in *The Twenty Years' Crisis*.

25. R.W. Davies lists the Chair of Russian History at the School of Slavonic and East European Studies, the Chair of International Relations at Oxford, a fellowship at St Antony's. Balliol even refused him a fellowship after two years as a Lecturer in Politics. Davies, 'Edward Hallet Carr', 491.

26. Haslam, '"We Need a Faith"', 39.

27. Quoted in Davies, 'Edward Hallett Carr', 477.

28. Carr, *Britain: A Study of Foreign Policy*, v.

29. See Vendulka Kubálková and Albert Cruickshank, *Marxism and International Relations* (Oxford: Oxford University Press, 1989), especially part 2.

30. Carr, *The Twenty Years' Crisis*, preface, 2nd ed., 1946.

31. This imagery was presented in Ken Booth: 'Human Wrongs and International Relations', *International Affairs* 71 (1995), 123.

32. Stanley Hoffmann, 'An American Social Science: International Relations', in Hoffmann *Janus and Minerva: Essays in the Theory and Practice of International Politics* (Boulder Col: Westview Press, 1977), 5.

33. Smith, *Realist Thought*, 68. Christopher Hill also uses the term 'classic' to describe the work, in his, '1939: The Origins of Liberal Realism', *Review of International Studies*, 15 (1989), 324. Martin Griffiths believes the book 'is still rightly regarded as a "classic" in the discipline of International Relations, and rightly so.' *Realism, Idealism and International Politics: A Reinterpretation* (London: Routledge, 1992), 34.

34. W.C. Olson, 'The Growth of a Discipline' in Porter, (ed.), *The Aberystwyth Papers*, 23. There is without doubt a consensus in the discipline that Carr's text is *the* symbolic representation of an hierarchical dualism between

'political realism' and 'utopianism' (in other words, a relationship which imputes power and dominance to the first term in the pairing). In *The Aberystwyth Papers*, the description of the part *The Twenty Years' Crisis* played in the epic inter-war paradigm shift is symptomatic: 'it sounded the death knell for all those writers who had focused their attention on the world as it ought to be rather than as it was'. John, Moorhead Wright, and Garnett, 'International Politics', 96. For a powerful critique of the tendency to view the historiography of the discipline through the prisms of 'great debates', see Brian Schmidt, *The Political Discourse of Anarchy: A Disciplinary History of International Relations* (Albany: New York State University Press, 1997 forthcoming).

35. Booth, 'Security in Anarchy', 530.
36. Carr, *The Twenty Years' Crisis*, preface to the 2 ed., 1946. Emphasis added.
37. Carr, *The Twenty Years' Crisis*, 8 (1939).
38. Carr, *The Twenty Years' Crisis*, 32, note 1.
39. Carr, *The Twenty Years' Crisis*, 38.
40. Cecelia Lynch rightly criticises Carr for taking a broad brush to the canvas of utopianism. Cecilia Lynch, 'E.H. Carr, International Relations Theory, and the Societal Origins of International Legal Norms', *Millennium* 23 (1994), 589–619.
41. This time-frame imputed by Carr begs the question why the prevailing 'harmony of interests' doctrine did not precipitate in the breakdown of the international order sooner. To the contrary, the hegemonic hold of the harmony of interests coincided according to Carr with a century of stability and progress. This contradiction between condition A (harmony of interests prevails, stability results) and B (harmony of prevails, conflict results) is exposed by Johnson, 'E.H. Carr's Theory', 869.
42. Carr, *The Twenty Years' Crisis*, 80.
43. Familiar, but not reducible to Marxism, since Carr did not operate in *The Twenty Years' Crisis* with a notion of a transnational global political economy which existed outside of the structures and actions of states. As Rosenberg argues, from a Marxist perspective Carr's account of agency is too statist. He can conceive of the way in which 'the modern state seeks to mobilise the economy, but not that the economy is also part of a transnational whole which produces important *political* effects independently of the agency of the state'. Rosenberg, *The Empire of Civil Society*, 13. In a later work, Carr argued that '[t]he view that "ideals" are a cloak for "interests" is Marxist, though by no means exclusively Marxist'. Carr, *The Soviet Impact*, 80.
44. Carr, *The Twenty Years' Crisis*, 58.
45. This argument of Carr's is contestable. As Lynch argues, 'the Great Powers have very often *not* been able to use global international organisation to further their interests'. Lynch, 'E.H. Carr', 617.
46. Carr, *The Twenty Years' Crisis*, 77. Emphasis added.
47. Carr, *The Twenty Years' Crisis*, 83. Emphasis added.
48. Carr, *The Twenty Years' Crisis*, 96.
49. In the 'preface to the first edition', Carr lists Mannheim's text *Ideology and Utopia* and Reinhold Niebuhr's *Moral Man and Immoral Society* as two books which have 'illuminated some of the fundamental problems in politics.'
50. Jones, *E.H. Carr and International Relations*, Chapter 6, 2.

51.   Carr, *From Napoleon*, 181.
52.   Morgenthau, 'The Surrender', 350.
53.   Leonard Woolf, in Evans, 'E.H. Carr', 88.
54.   Johnson, 'E.H. Carr', 863.
55.   As Carr put it: 'The state is built up out of these two conflicting aspects of
       human nature. Utopia and reality, the ideal and the institution, morality and
       power, are from the outset inextricably blended in it'. *The Twenty Years'
       Crisis*, 124. At other times, he also flatly contradicts this antinomical
       reading, for example, in his argument that 'Politics are made up of two
       elements – utopia and reality – belonging to two different planes which can
       never meet'. *The Twenty Years' Crisis*, 118.
56.   Knutsen, *A History of International Relations Theory*, 224.
57.   Booth, quoting Joseph S. Nye in 'Security in Anarchy', 536.
58.   E.H. Carr, 'The Moral Foundations for World Order', in E.L. Woodward
       et al., Foundations for World Order (Denver Col.: University of Denver,
       1949), 72. Arguably, the *Conditions of Peace* represented a shift to an 'end-
       point utopia', as Carr's biographical memoir testifies: 'Like a lot of other
       people I took refuge in Utopian visions of a new world after the war; after
       all, it was on the basis of such visions that a lot of real constructive work
       was done, and Churchill lost sympathy by being impatient of them. I began
       to be a bit ashamed of the harsh "realism" of *The Twenty Years' Crisis* and
       in 1940–41 wrote the highly Utopian *Conditions of Peace* – a sort of liberal
       Utopia, mixed with a little socialism ... It was my most popular book to
       date, because it caught the current mood. But it was pretty feeble.' Carr,
       autobiographical memoir, quoted in Davies 'Edward Hallett Carr', 488.
59.   Carr, *The Twenty Years' Crisis*, 265.
60.   For example, A.J. Toynbee's article 'Peaceful Change or War? The Next
       Stage in the International Crisis', *International Affairs* 15 (1936), 26–56.
61.   Carr's discussion of the Munich agreement has variously been described as
       'a brilliant argument in favour of appeasement', A.J.P. Taylor, *The Origins
       of the Second World War* (London: Book Club Associates, 1972), 288; and
       a less fortunate argument for 'accommodation with Hitler', (Stone, 'Grim
       Eminence', 3), depending on which Oxford historian one reads. The level of
       opprobrium was fuelled by the author's editing-out of part of the argument
       from the second edition published in 1946, admitting in the *Preface* only to
       removing 'two or three passages relating to current controversies which
       have been eclipsed or put in a different perspective by the lapse of time'.
       (Carr, *The Twenty Years' Crisis*, preface). His creative editing included the
       removal of the following description of the Munich settlement: 'The negoti-
       ations which led up to the Munich Agreement of September 29, 1938 were
       the nearest approach in recent years to the settlement of a major interna-
       tional issue by a procedure of peaceful change. The element of power was
       present. The element of morality was also present in the form of the
       common recognition by the Powers, who effectively decided the issue, of a
       criterion applicable to the dispute: the principle of self-determination ....
       The change in itself was one which corresponded both to a change in the
       European equilibrium of forces and to accepted canons of international
       morality. Other aspects of it were, however, less reassuring .... There was a
       complete lack of any German readiness to make the smallest sacrifice for

the sake of conciliation. The agreement was violently attacked by a section of British opinion. Recriminations ensued on the German side; and very soon any prospect that the Munich settlement might inaugurate a happier period of international relations in which peaceful change by negotiation would become an effective factor seemed to have disappeared.' Carr, *The Twenty Year's Crisis*, 1st ed., 282–283. Compare with 2 ed., 221–222'. Critics such as W.T.R. Fox reacted strongly to Carr's editing: 'When I discovered which were these two or three deleted passages, I was shocked.' Fox, 'E.H. Carr and Political Realism', 4. Fox could still have read his defence of appeasement in his work on British foreign policy, which expresses the argument in more uncompromisingly realist terms: ' Broadly speaking, British opinion had long ago recognised that the military sanctions, the demilitarization of the Rhineland and the separation of Austria from Germany could not be maintained indefinitely and that the only issue which was the date and manner of their disappearance; and one of the most obvious factors in the crisis of September 1938 was that Britain would not fight to maintain a Czechoslovak state which, in a population of 14 000 000 contained 3 250 000 Germans and other large and disloyal minorities. It cannot be charged to the policy that these concessions were made. The only ground for criticism is that they were not made in other conditions at an earlier date. Carr, *Britain: A Study of Foreign Policy*, 175.

62.   Griffiths, *Realism, Idealism*, 34.
63.   Bull, '*The Twenty Years' Crisis* Thirty Years On', 629.
64.   It is important to note that Carr qualified this comment with the following words: 'it is none the less difficult to pretend that human beings have more than a fitful and faltering knowledge of this absolute good'. Carr, 'The Moral', 66.
65.   Carr, 'The Moral', 71, 74, 75.
66.   Carr, *What is History*, 152–153.
67.   Linklater, 'E.H. Carr'.
68.   Bull, '*The Twenty Years Crisis* Thirty Years On', 629. Emphasis added. Michael Joseph Smith expresses a similar argument: 'His view of morality permits no genuine conception of the moral interest of the international community'. Smith, *Realist Thought*, 52.
69.   Carr, *The Twenty Years' Crisis*, 118 (1939).
70.   Carr, *The Twenty Years' Crisis*, 162. This phenomenological view of the bases of international society is remarkably similar to that held by Charles Manning. See C.A.W.Manning, *The Nature of International Society* (London: Macmillan, ed. 1975), xxxii
71.   Carr, 'The Moral', 56.
72.   Carr, *The Twenty Years' Crisis*, 166. Like Wight, Carr believed that 'effective institutions' in international society required 'the foundation of an accepted common morality: without that foundation no institution can work'. Carr, 'The Moral', 69.
73.   Carr, *The Twenty Years' Crisis*, 272.
74.   This argument is taken up later in the book, but can also be found in Nicholas J. Wheeler and Tim Dunne 'Hedley Bull's Pluralism of the Intellect and Solidarism of the Will', *International Affairs* 72 (1996), 91–108.

75. E.H. Carr to Stanley Hoffmann, 30 September, 1977. Quoted in R.W. Davies, 'Edward Hallet Carr', 486–487. Emphasis added.

76. Carr, 'The Moral', 62.

77. In Carr's words, 'every political act involves considerations of power'. 'The Moral', 62.

78. This is how R.J. Vincent interpreted the change in Carr's thinking from 1939–1945: '"The freedom and equality which the makers of the coming peace must establish is not a freedom and equality of nations, but a freedom and equality which will express themselves in the daily lives of men and women". It is a measure of the impact of Grotianism on the theory and practice of international politics in the twentieth century that these words were written towards the end of the Second World War not by a reformist allowing his vision to distort his interpretation of reality, but by E.H. Carr, the realist destroyer of an earlier reformism.' Vincent, 'Grotius, Human Rights and Intervention' in Hedley Bull, Benedict Kingsbury and Adam Roberts (eds), *Hugo Grotius and International Relations* (Oxford: Clarendon, 1990), 241.

79. Carr, *The Twenty Years' Crisis*, 118.

80. Evident, for example, in Carr's comment that realism is able to reveal 'the relative and pragmatic character of thought itself'. Carr, *The Twenty Years' Crisis*, 87. For a survey of pragmatism, see Steve Smith, 'Positivism and Beyond' in Smith, Booth, Zalewski (eds), *International Theory: Positivism and Beyond* (Cambridge: Cambridge University Press, 1996), 11–46.

81. Carr, *Nationalism and After*, 64. Even in *The Twenty Years' Crisis*, Carr concluded that 'The concept of sovereignty is likely to become in the future even more blurred and indistinct than it is at present'. *The Twenty Years' Crisis*, 295–296. Given this scepticism in the first edition about the capacity of states to deliver security and welfare, it is surprisng that Carr should have reflected in the preface to the second edition that 'the main body of the book too readily and too complacently accepts the existing nation-state, large and small, as the unit of international society'.

82. For example, there are few people today – particularly those that have lived under communism – who could accept Carr's comment that 'Naked and uncontrolled power for the state is no part of Bolshevik doctrine'. Carr, *Soviet Impact*, 86.

83. Martin Wight, 'The Church, Russia and the West', *Ecumenical Review* 1 (1948), 38. Emphasis added.

84. Carr, *The Twenty Years' Crisis*, 7.

85. Letter from E.H. Carr to Stanley Hoffmann, in Davies, 'Edward Hallett Carr', 488.

86. I am indebted to Ken Booth for this formulation.

3 Martin Wight

Wight's contribution to International Relations is a matter of dispute. For those identifying themselves with the English School, Wight is something of a godfather. Such a caricature resonates with both a literal and a symbolic meaning. In the case of the former, Wight maintained throughout his life deeply held religious beliefs, principles which often sat uneasily alongside the body of his work on international theory. The reasons for suggesting that Wight should be accorded this status for his contribution to the English School are twofold; first, his transcendence of the realist / idealist dichotomy and subsequent discovery of a middle way, the 'Grotian' or 'rationalist' tradition; second, his pioneering historical sociology of states systems. The focus for this chapter will mainly be on the former (as Wight's British Committee work is discussed in detail in Chapters 5 and 6).

Outside of the English School, his work has been criticised on two accounts. In the first instance, there is the complicated question of the relationship between Wight's theoretical work and his personal convictions informed by Christianity. It was these fundamental religious beliefs which led him to be a conscientious objector during the Second World War. According to Michael Nicholson, there is a 'problem' with 'reconciling Wight, the power politician with Wight the pacifist.'[1] This relationship will be examined in part one of the chapter, which attempts to unravel the reasons for Wight's decision to be a 'conscientious objector' in the Second World War, and to locate his religious beliefs within his broader understanding of history and politics.

His reputation has been further weakened by the claim that Wight 'steered' International Relations into an intellectual cul-de-sac through his purported separation of 'international theory' from political theory.[2] This critique has emerged in part because the meaning of Wight's inaugural British Committee paper 'Why is there no international theory' has not been sufficiently contextualised; moreover, this reading of a spatial separation between the two realms runs counter to the spirit of Wight's understanding of the social world. Roger Epp's sensitive interpretation of Wight has gone some way to redressing this critique. According to Epp, Martin Wight did not believe in the autonomy of International Relations or even the sub-field of 'international theory'; rather, 'Wight's thought was worked out in the larger, intersecting debates about human history, war and peace, that engaged historians, philosophers, theologians, and others before international relations became the domain of specialists in fragmented universities.'[3]

A striking fact about Martin Wight concerns the inverse correlation between his minimal published output and his influence upon future generations of English School thinkers. Indeed, it is principally because of Hedley Bull's efforts to publish Wight's work posthumously that Wight is now far more widely read and argued about than when he was alive.[4] More recently, the publication of his 'International Theory' lectures by Brian Porter and Gabriele Wight has provided the missing link between the fragments of realism discernible in the 1940s and the more Grotian slant of Wight's essays for the British Committee.[5] These lectures are considered in detail in the second half of the chapter, with a view to critically examining the validity of Wight's approach to the history of ideas. In drawing on Wight's lectures, book reviews, broadcasts and other unpublished sources, a richer picture of the scholar emerges than the one that can been gleaned from a more limited reading of his better known works like *Power Politics* and *Systems of States*.

At the time of his death, a number of Wight's former colleagues expressed regret that he had been unable to produce a great work on International Relations. In the words of his former Chatham House director, Arnold Toynbee, Wight 'missed his chance of giving the world his *magnum opus* through being a perfectionist (a virtue which he conceded was 'inexpedient when carried to extremes).'[6] On this point it is worth quoting a lengthy passage from Wight's academic correspondence with a North American colleague because it reveals the depths of his existential despair provoked by the publishing commitments he had not been able to meet:

> If I die this afternoon, I will leave nothing but some manuscripts too messy for publication, and some publishers faintly annoyed at my unreliability. Great scholars who never wrote their great works are less creditworthy to posterity. I analyze with painful interest the perfectionism which seems to prevent me from being satisfied with anything. . . .
>
> Power Politics thus struggles to be born, like the Age of Nationalism under Metternich. Meanwhile, it has put out a curious shoot, which began as a single chapter. This is the study of the notion of 'International Legitimacy', which has dragged me deeper and deeper (if shoots can drag you deeper), and might make a book. ...
>
> In the background there is the ghostly skeleton of the book on bipolarity. There is also a half-finished book on the development of the idea of

the Balance of Power, accompanied by another book (for which the publisher is waiting) of readings and extracts on the history of the Balance of Power.

Everything you tell me about your own writing programme interests me immensely. I have written the foregoing with distaste, since I think, of all conversation, the least excusable is conversation about the books that you don't get written.[7]

In terms of the history of the English School, the crucial conversation with Wight is not about the list of unpublished and partially completed volumes, but rather, the conversation between realism, rationalism and revolutionism, which represents the symbolic transcendence of realist ideas which informed International Relations theory in Britain in the 1930s and 1940s. These lectures reveal an impressive breadth of erudition, drawing on history, literature, and philosophy. Moreover, they project a sense of history which is not simply about mapping 'recurrence and repetition', but rather one which delights in pointing out the tricks that history plays on those who shape its course, the tragedy which accompanies their ethical choices and the irony of unintended consequences.

Inter-War Pacifism to Post-War Power Politics

After completing a first class Modern History degree at Oxford in 1935,[8] Martin Wight served at Chatham House where he worked closely with Arnold Toynbee, helping to compile the editions of the Institute's *Survey*, to which Wight himself contributed substantially to the 1939/40 edition.[9] It is worthwhile reflecting on the relationship between Martin Wight and Arnold J. Toynbee as they inhabited opposite sides of the realism/idealist divide. (Recall how E.H. Carr baited Toynbee for his 'incessant girding at a reality which refused to conform to utopian prescriptions.'[10]) How then, is one to explain this co-operation across the great intellectual divide?

Whilst at Chatham House,[11] Toynbee wrote his ten volume *The Study of History*, which documented the transformations of civilisations and the links between them. In a glowing review in the *Observer*, Wight predicted that '... it will probably be regarded as the greatest historical work of the present century.'[12] Toynbee appreciated Wight's criticisms of *The Study of History* and frequently inserted Wight's comments into the text as footnotes. A particularly lengthy commentary by Wight on Christianity is included as an appendix to volume seven.[13] This is one of the earliest indications of his penchant for 'dialogue', which finds its apotheosis in the lectures on the traditions.

Apart from being professional colleagues, Wight shared Toynbee's interest in universal history. This is evident from Martin Wight's description of Toynbee's method which could equally apply to Wight himself:

> What I believe to be Toynbee's unique quality among historians is the insight which comes when the mind is freed as far as possible from attachment to its own time and place. He has insisted, against the established tradition of academic specialisation, that *the historian is implicitly concerned with the entirety of human history*; and, furthermore, that the standpoints of other civilisations are as valid, and their influence is in the long run as powerful, as those of our own.[14]

A more substantive convergence of opinion between Toynbee and Wight concerns their enthusiasm for the League of Nations. Donald Mackinnon, a colleague of Wight's at Oxford in 1935–6 and later on a fellow member of the British Committee, recalled how Wight had been 'among those who passionately believed in the old League of Nations'.[15] In this respect, Wight's 'turn' to power politics after the war grows out of the experience of the failure of the League and the liberal-cum-idealist principles it was seen to embody.

The significant event in Wight's life in the inter-war period, which has important implications for his understanding of International Relations, was his conscientious objection to the Second World War. His first published article was on 'Christian Pacifism', with defines pacifism in the following manner:[16]

> The core of pacifism is the belief that it is never right to take human life. It is nothing to do with quietism in the sense of immoral apathy and passivity. It is not the organization of mass-cowardice. It does not condemn all use of force. It does not assert that there is nothing worth fighting for. It does not make an unconditional surrender to evil. It does not believe in peace at any price. Its basis is not utilitarian.[17]

Wight provides theological reasons to justify the argument that a Christian may sacrifice no life: 'Above all' he argues, 'he must condemn, in opposition to the Roman Church and the tradition of Augustine and Aquinas, the *immorality* of war.'[18]

Despite some inconsistencies in the article[19] (he was, after all, only twenty-three when he wrote it) the theory that lies behind Wight's argument is that of 'pessimistic pacifism'. This position bridges the divide between a realist understanding of the minimal influence an individual's pacifism will have on the course of the war (allied potentially to a recognition of the inevitability of conflict), yet still refusing to participate in a conflict which is alien to that persons ethical/religious views.[20] In an interesting passage, Wight argues that the political implications of the doctrine of pacifism require 'a complete reorientation of social and political values'. At the domestic level, opposition to capital punishment, abortion and euthanasia. At the international level, peace requires,

> [U]nilateral disarmament pending a disarmament conference, surrender of the Crown Colonies and Mandates to international administration by the League, abolition of tariff barriers, and unqualified co-operation with the ILO and the League's organization of the international law of peace. The Christian pacifist who is not insistent in furthering these aims has no right to the name.[21]

This clearly underscores Wight's enthusiasm for the League in the mid-1930s. Indeed he seems to be entering the very 'kingdom of the fairies' that he later castigated others for inhabiting.[22]

A number of the arguments made in 'Christian Pacifism' appear in Wight's application to register as a conscientious objector in May 1940.[23] The tribunal rejected Wight's application on the surprising grounds that 'his answers disclosed that he had no deep-seated and definite conscientious conviction that he would be doing wrong to participate in military service'. Wight successfully appealed against the decision in October 1940, and was permitted to do 'full time social research' in view of his chronic asthma.[24] Wight was helped in his appeal by Margery Perham, a Reader in Colonial Administration at Oxford University.[25] Perham recalls her role in the proceedings: '[h]earing that he was in trouble over being a conscientious objector, I brought him into the small team I was running during the war to write on Colonial Constitution.'[26] Interest in the governing of colonial territories was heightened in the 1930s when it was decided to develop them economically and administratively. This was the impetus behind the colonial social research institutes that flourished during and after the war. It would be a mistake to presume that Wight's work on the colonial project stood outside of his international theory. Indeed, he argued in one of the most interesting of his lectures, that 'the "Theory of Mankind", for want of a better name, verges upon a theory of colonial administration.'[27] Apart from stimulating an interest in colonial encounters, perhaps the most important intellectual lesson Wight acquired in this period was the discipline of empirical history after the grand theoretical history of the Toynbee years.

Wight returned for a second spell at Chatham House in 1946. This was soon interrupted by Wight's correspondence for the *Observer* covering the United Nations sessions at Lake Success in 1946/7. Charles Manning noted how he 'read them with much profit at the time.'[28] It was Manning who approached Wight with the offer of a Readership in International Relations at the London School of Economics 1949, in order to strengthen the 'philosophical' and the 'scientific' basis of the teaching of International Relations.[29] Clearly Wight made a massive contribution to the former, but completely undermined the latter. He did not empathise with Manning's efforts to establish International Relations as a rigorous academic and social *scientific* discipline. Manning mused how Wight 'lowered his spirits' at a conference when he 'seemed to question – and this in a school of the social sciences – the very propitiousness of our having, or indeed envisaging, such a subject at all.'[30] For his part, Wight disliked 'the Byzantine subtlety of Manning's philosophical approach' which he thought tended to obscure the central points in a maze of linguistic analysis.[31]

Wight's more analytical approach to international relations is in evidence in the first edition of *Power Politics* published in 1946.[32] It is perhaps not surprising that a work with this title should prompt the interpretation of Wight as a realist. Bull regarded the *geist* of the work to be, 'in a loose sense, a realist one.'[33] Other writers have mistakenly projected this interpretation of *Power Politics* as being representative of the body of Wight's thinking. For example, Alan James argues that, 'As a teacher and writer Wight falls unambiguously into the category which is widely termed, not least by himself, realist.'[34]

Power Politics approximates to realism in three respects. First, Wight argues that we should start out with the assumption that international relations 'are always approximating to "power politics" in the immoral sense', even if there are occasions when state leaders are influenced by considerations of right and law and justice.[35] Second, there is the discursive prominence of power throughout the work. For example, states are frequently referred to as 'powers', and Wight was instrumental in defining and grading states according to terms such as 'dominant powers', 'great powers', 'world powers', 'minor powers', and so on. Crucially, the management of international relations takes place within this hierarchy of powers, to which Wight adds, '[t]his is the system which has always obtained hitherto in power politics, and which the League of Nations failed to supersede.'[36] The third realist argument evident in the original

Power Politics follows from the anarchy problematic, where states 'are in a state of potential enmity.'[37] For this reason, war remains 'the only means by which each of them can in the last resort defend its vital interests.'[38] According to Wight, war is an in-built dynamic of the international system. As he put it rather hauntingly in a radio broadcast, 'war is inevitable, but particular wars can be avoided.'[39]

Despite these undoubted expressions of realism in Wight's Chatham House pamphlet, perhaps the clearest exposition of Wight's early realism can be found in an article entitled 'The Church, Russia and the West'.[40] Written in 1948, it provides an insight into his view of the Cold War as the final phase of the death of Christendom.[41] The following passage demonstrates Wight's graphic description of the fallen international system:

> It is in the international sphere that the demonic concentrations of power of the modern neo-pagan world have their clearest expression. Russia and America are the last two Great Powers within the Westernized system of sovereign states. And the characteristic of that system, after centuries in which the Church has had no influence upon its development, *is the emancipation of power from moral restraints.* Leviathan is a simple beast; his law is self-preservation, his appetite is for power. The process of international politics that has followed from this is equally simple: the effective Powers in the world have decreased in number and increased in size, and the method has been war.[42]

This argument is vital to our understanding of Wight's thinking on International Relations since it is an occasion where his two worlds of religion and politics collide. The above passage illustrates his belief in the Christian meaning of history, which identifies a movement towards 'the divine act of judgement that will bring it to an end.'[43] Driving this eschatological philosophy of history is the doctrine of original sin. In a powerful passage, Wight argued that: 'We are not well-meaning people doing our best; we are miserable sinners, living under judgement, with a heritage of sin to expiate.'[44]

Although religion and politics were intimately connected in Wight's mind, there is an obvious difficulty in interpreting the nature of their relationship for the reason that, in his early writings in particular, the balance shifts markedly in different contexts. In his article on the balance of power in 1939, and in the original *Power Politics*, there is no hint of a Christian view of history. However, in his article on 'Christian Pacifism' and the 1948 essay on 'The Church, Russia and the West', worldly history is subordinate to the will of God. The fusion of the sacred and the secular is a constant problem in interpreting Wight's international theory. It seems, in the last instance, that he believed that the City of God and the City of Man were 'always mixed up in this world, but *there is a rhythm in their inter-action.*'[45] However, as we will see in the following section, Wight's 'International Theory' lectures concerned themselves with the rhythms and patterns in the history of European international society.

Beyond Power Politics: International Society and the 'Three Rs'

The first course that Wight taught at the London School of Economics was on 'International Institutions', a subject which 'did not greatly interest him.'[46] From 1957 onwards, Wight lectured on 'International Theory'.[47] Hedley Bull recalls how the lectures 'made a profound impression' on him.[48] T.B. Millar described the lectures as 'brilliant', elevating Wight to the status of 'the best academic lecturer' he had heard. Other members of Wight's audience included Brian Porter, Maurice Keens-Soper, Alan James, Peter Lyon, and Jack Spence. Although Alan James agrees that Wight's lectures were 'impressive', he nevertheless believes that the three traditions were of limited value in understanding international relations. 'Neither he nor his approach is, so far as I can see, much treated as an exemplar.' Moreover, James adds, those scholars who identify with a 'classical approach' but do not invoke the three traditions should not be labelled as 'second class'. In this, James is surely correct. But to claim that Wight's approach to the history of ideas has not been enormously influential is a questionable one, judging by the number of recent publications about the three traditions and the various thinkers who represent them.[50]

The origins of the thinking behind the lectures can be traced to Wight's increasing dissatisfaction with the 'two schools' analysis immanent within Carr's *Twenty Years' Crisis* and appropriated by the emerging discipline as its founding dualism.[51] Although profoundly influenced by Carr's work,[52] Wight was the first theorist to reject the bifurcation of international thought into realism and idealism, as he believed it to be 'the reflection of a diseased situation.'[53] The essential weakness of this dualism is that it engenders the unfortunate tendency of interpreting different ideas as necessarily mutually exclusive (even when, as in the case of Carr, this was not the author's intention). Wight's additional category of rationalism, therefore, usefully serves the function of a *via media* between the two diametrically opposite traditions of realism and idealism. Rationalism, as we will see below, is the stream of thought most closely associated with the vindication of international society as both a description of how states *do* behave, and how they *ought* to behave. Before dwelling on this question, it is important to deal with the meta-theoretical status of traditions. What purpose does the act of tradition-building serve? Where are traditions found? What criteria are there for membership? Finally, which tradition did Wight belong to (or most closely identify with)?

Traditions as an Approach to the History of Ideas

All intellectual traditions share, to varying degrees, the following four attributes: classification, continuity, abstraction and exclusion. The need for classification is common to all academic subjects. At a minimum, it is a way of imposing order upon a complex and protean reality. Indeed, Wight suggests that his lectures are primarily 'an experiment in classification'.[54] Wight's use of traditions as instruments of classification differs sharply from the tendency within the study of International Relations to use 'paradigms' as containers for ideas. A paradigm denotes the practices of a particular scientific (or social scientific) community, one which presents the researcher with a set of precedents and acts as a guide to the possible answers. For this reason, paradigms compete with each other implying a degree of incommensurability.[55] This is in sharp contrast with Wight's description of the nature of traditions:

> Thus, the three traditions are not like three railroad tracks running into infinity. They are not philosophically constant and pure like three stately, tranquil and independent streams flowing first from Vitoria and Suarez to J.L. Brierly, secondly from Machiavelli to E.H. Carr, and lastly from Ignatius Loyola to Eric Hobsbawm and Palme Dutt. They are streams, with eddies and cross-currents, sometimes interlacing and never for long confined to their own river bed. They are, to vary the metaphor, interwoven in the tapestry of Western civilization. They both influence and cross-fertilize one another, and they change, although without, I think, losing their inner identity.[56]

At this point traditions enter the debate as a form of classification which thrives on the cross-over between traditions. Indeed, Wight goes a stage further when he argues that '[c]lassification becomes valuable, in humane studies, only at the point where it breaks down.'[57]

Related to the element of classification is the belief that there is some pedagogical value to be derived from the classification of the history of ideas into traditions. According to James Der Derian, the value of a tradition lies, 'in its ability to condense and simplify this complexity into uniform, comprehensive, teachable expressions.'[58] In connection with

Martin Wight's three traditions, Roy Jones has cast doubt on their pedagogical utility: how could 'an undergraduate deploy Wight's historical
learning?'[59] Reading through the thickets of Wight's prose, one is
reminded of Bull's comment that 'the branches of the tree are so weighted
down with historical foliage that it is difficult to find the trunk.'[60]
Certainly it is easy to imagine a divergence of opinion in Wight's lecture
theatre between his academic audience quite content not to see the trunk,
and finals students praying for autumn.

An inevitable part of this classificatory process is the abstraction of
ideas from their historical context. However, the degree to which 'traditions' can engage in abstraction is hotly contested. As will be argued
below, in the process of the discovery of traditions the core ideas are
abstracted and distilled into a coherent form, albeit one which is not representative of any one thinker. In sharp contrast, a number of contemporary
political theorists argue for the recovery of more genuinely historical traditions, in order to reveal the ideologies which the idea in question was
endorsing or challenging.[61]

A derivative attribute of traditions is that they define the limits (either
historical or philosophical) of a particular discourse. By participating in
the tradition itself, the theorist enters into a debate framed by common
assumptions and a common language. This language is given and trans-
mitted by the discursive practices that intimate the central texts, the
appropriate analogies and the limits of criticism. In this sense, traditions
are self-regulating, defining 'insiders' and 'outsiders' through an act of
naming.

The fourth and final defining element of a tradition is the assumption of
continuity. Recall how one of the central claims of Bull's critique of the
scientists was their 'lack of any sense of inquiry into international politics
as *a continuing tradition*'.[62] The effect of this emphasis on continuity was
to shift the parameters of International Relations back from 1919, to an
earlier mythic marker of 1648 and the Treaties of Westphalia. Here the
influence of Wight on Bull is most evident. Wight's lectures are infused
with the importance of historical perspective, and the need to transcend the
specific problems and the latest formulas driven by political agendas. The
following passage is illustrative in this regard:

> One of the main purposes of a university education it to escape from the
> *Zeitgeist*, from the mean, narrow, provincial spirit which is constantly
> assuring us that we are at the peak of human achievement, that we stand
> on the edge of unprecedented prosperity or an unparalleled catastrophe;
> that the next summit conference is going to be the most fateful in

history or that the leader of the day is either the greatest, or the most disastrous, of all time. It is a liberation of the spirit to acquire perspective, to recognize that every generation is confronted by problems of the utmost subjective urgency, but that an objective grading is probably impossible; to learn that the same moral predicaments and the same ideas have been explored before. One need read very little in political theory to become aware of recurrence and repetitions.[63]

It is not just Wight's belief in perspective that is conducive to traditions, but also his methodological assumption that there are discernible patterns in the history of ideas. These patterns are more easily identified given the lack of progress in the history of international relations.[64]

How then are traditions discovered? Where are they found? The orthodox answer, proffered by Meinecke, is that the classical texts are the laboratory for historians of ideas.[65] Whilst Martin Wight would have partially endorsed Meinecke's defence of the classics as the source of historical ideas, he put more emphasis on the force of events acting upon the minds of great thinkers. As mentioned above, what is interesting about Wight's traditions is that he does not confine himself to constructing a canon out of classical texts in political philosophy. This is just one of the narratives he relied upon. In addition to 'internationally minded political philosophers', Wight drew upon 'the philosophically minded international lawyers', beginning with the Spanish theologians from the Catholic Universities of Europe.[66] The third of his 'scattered sources' is to be found in 'the statements and policies of politicians'.[67] A fourth source is literature. As he argued in the conclusion to his lecture on ethics, the judgement of ethical principles 'is not a process of scientific analysis; it is more akin to literary criticism.'[68] In this process of sifting, selecting and simplifying ideas from the theory and practice of international relations, Martin Wight is *discovering* traditions.

The aforementioned focus on the sources of Wight's traditions runs the risk of suggesting that the three traditions were abstractions from history. In contrast to the 'paradigms' or 'models' which accompanied the scientific phase in International Relations, Wight's traditions represented doctrines in history in which people have believed. For example, he referred to realism and rationalism as 'self-conscious' traditions.[69] Wight discovered realism, rationalism and revolutionism *in* history and not independently of history. Despite the general historical orientation of Wight's traditions, it is necessary to consider the criticism that the traditions discovered by Wight, and endorsed by later English School scholars such as Bull and Vincent, are not historical enough. By showing how philosophers, diplomats, strategists and state leaders conform to a particular pattern, Wight and the English School are in danger of imposing a 'mythology of coherence' in their act of discovering realism, rationalism, and revolutionism. This warning is well articulated by Richard Tuck:

> It is sometimes tempting to think that the heroes of the various histories of philosophy or ethics ... were all in some sense engaged on a common enterprise, and would have recognized one another as fellow workers. But a moment's reflection reminds us that it is we who have made a unity of their task.[70]

In place of the discovery of traditions, contextualists like Tuck and Skinner present a radically different interpretation of key classical thinkers and their respective traditions. For example, according to Tuck, Hobbes's thinking is the culmination of a medieval natural rights thinking articulated by Grotius. And Rousseau, far from inhabiting the same tradition as Hobbes, was a radical critic of this tradition which he regarded as conservative.[71]

An inevitable question provoked by all the variations of contending patterns of thought is whether there is a danger that 'traditions' relativise knowledge, and therefore, judgement? In short, *which* tradition? The question of relativism is one which both Wight and Bull's use of traditions must confront. By interpreting realism, rationalism and revolutionism as cardinal elements of international relations, the traditions evade the epistemological imperative of examining the truth or falsity of their claims.[72] Wight's response would be to claim that at different periods in history, the traditions vary in strength. For example, Wight noted that between 1914 and 1939, 'Kantianism and Machiavellism destroy supreme Grotian experiment.'[73] This demonstrates that the dialectical movement of the traditions provides a benchmark by which different epochs can be compared, and by implication, judged.[74]

Assessing the Rationalist Tradition

The principal innovation of Wight's traditions was his invention of a third category. This begs the question whether rationalism is intended to inhabit the space between realism and idealism, or whether it is an attempt to subdivide 'idealist' thinking into a liberal reformist wing which accepts the ontology of international society, and a revolutionary wing which seeks to transcend it? In which case, does rationalism succeed in being something other than not-realism, and not-revolutionist, thereby becoming a meaningful category it itself?

It is somewhat of a surprise to discover that in his opening lecture, Wight argues that it is the revolutionists 'who concentrate upon the element of the society of states, or international society.'[75] The rationalists were relegated to 'those who emphasize and concentrate on the element of international intercourse.'[76] However, in the course of the lectures, rationalism is restored as the principal defender of the society of states against the revolutionist attempt to establish a single world state or the realist aim of aggrandizement. The rather protean character of the traditions throughout the course of the lectures serves as a reminder that Wight never elaborated the three traditions in a final published form.

The starting point for Wight's rationalism is its assumption of the social nature of humankind in the pre-contractual state of nature. Therefore, on the basis of this analogy, international society is a site for co-operation as well as conflict. Given these rationalist assumptions, it is apparent that states are not merely tied together by legal contracts. There are laws of nature governing the universe in addition to the positive international law contrived by states themselves. In addition to law, institutions such as diplomacy, alliances, the balance of power, arbitration, war, and great power concerts, serve to regulate the customs of international society in the absence of a common sovereign.[77] Even when the habit of co-operation breaks down and conflict ensues, states are still subject to the doctrine of the just war concerning both the reason for war and the conduct of war. The task then for rationalist statecraft is to mediate between the national interest and the interests of international society as a whole.[78]

We must now move from the principles common to rationalism to its source: where did Wight discover rationalism? This question is crucial for an understanding of the limits of rationalism. In Wight's thinking, the origins of rationalism lies in the view that reason is the source of knowledge. One interpretation took the form of secular political philosophy, with its analogy between the rights of individuals and the rights of states. The older strand in rationalism represents a 'thicker' notion of international society as 'a cosmic, moral constitution'. According to Wight, it is at this stage in the evolution of international society that the 'upkeep' was 'taken over by the Catholic Church.'[79] (However, we should note here the inappropriate use of the term rationalism for a theistic approach given the opposition of philosophical rationalism to religion.)[80]

This brief overview underlines how deeply embedded rationalist thought is in the development of European civilisation (and its bedrock of 'western values'), from ancient Greece to modern liberalism, embracing Catholicism on route. For this reason, Wight concedes that rationalism is 'the broad middle road of European thinking' which includes Aquinas,

Vitoria, Suarez, Grotius, Locke, Hooker, Washington, Hamilton, Jefferson, Kant, Mill and Cobden. Also included are statesmen such as Burke, Gladstone, Wilson and Churchill. But the most surprising of all is the inclusion of Hegel and Mazzini.[81] The cast list of rationalism highlights its diversity *and* indeterminacy.

It is significant here that Wight should describe rationalism as '*potentially* universal to mankind'.[82] This opens the door to what Wight regarded as the complementary question to 'What is International Society?', namely, 'How far does international society (supposing there be one) extend?'[83] Part of the answer to this question can be found in Wight's most innovative lecture on the 'theory of mankind: barbarians'. Realists deny that the other has any rights and consequently, the use of force is a legitimate means of securing ones interests. At the other end of the spectrum, revolutionism maintains that 'barbarians have equal rights.'[84] This is the doctrine of assimilation; indeed, Wight poses the penetrating questions, do 'barbarians' have 'the right *not* to be assimilated.'[85] Rationalism recognises that the other has rights, but crucially, they are not the same as those enjoyed by civilised states. According to Wight, rationalists, from Vitoria to Gladstone have fought against the realist doctrine of a right of conquest, but have not been able to treat the other as different *and* equal. This would seem to be Wight's own position, being an opponent of colonialism but at the same time doubtful about the resilience of the norms of international society in the face of rampant anti-colonial ideology.[86]

Locating Wight in the Three Traditions
An unresolved question, and one which has provoked considerable debate, concerns Wight's own position within the 'three Rs'. The lectures provide important clues to his intellectual orientation. To begin with, there is a telling passage where Wight explains how pacifism may be reconciled with realism:

> Inverted Revolutionism in its classic form is fed by a pessimistic estimate of human nature, not an optimistic one. This bleak view of mankind explains why pacifists, if they descend from being above the battle to entering the fray, tend to adopt a Realist stance.[87]

But perhaps this interpretation is not entirely satisfactory. There is a strong under-current of rationalism in the lectures. As Wight cautiously suggests in the opening lecture, rationalism 'is a road on which I suppose all of us, in certain moods, feel we really belong.'[88] This position is given further support in the concluding chapter: 'I find my own position shifting round the circle. You will have guessed that my prejudices are Rationalist, but I find I have become more Rationalist and less Realist through rethinking this question during the course of these lectures.'[89] The frequency with which he refers to the ideas of Grotius and Burke adds weight to Wight's 'prejudice' for rationalism. Later in the book we will see how Wight's British Committee paper on 'Western Values in International Relations', presented a few years after the lectures, signifies a growing alignment with rationalism and its emphasis upon the twin principles of 'constitutional government' and the desire to find the 'golden mean'.[90]

Finally, it could be argued that these lectures qualify the interpretation of Wight as a pessimist, a view which is shared by both Wight's critics and his disciples. Bull suggested it was the 'central characteristic' of Wight's International Relations.[91] Michael Nicholson viewed this characteristic as something of a vice: 'My real complaint against Martin Wight is that he made pessimism respectable in British international relations.'[92] Wight's lectures do not communicate the sense of doom evident in his pre-1950 writings. Rather, they can be interpreted as a relentless search for an escape from the narrow intellectual focus of the present. In this sense, there is an apparent tension between Wight's argument in 1948 that the day of judgement was approaching and the view expressed in his introductory 'International Theory' lecture that the purpose of education was to transcend the idea that 'we stand on the edge of unprecedented prosperity or an unparalleled catastrophe.'[93]

Conclusion

As noted in the preceding chapter, E.H. Carr is a pivotal figure in the historiography of the English School in so far as he set the stage for engaging with International Relations through the medium of political theory and the philosophy of history. The figure who occupies the centre of the stage is Martin Wight. He built upon Carr's insights into power, analysed more clearly the causes of conflict, and recognised like Carr the paucity of realism in the absence of normative ideals. Indeed, Wight's conclusion to the original *Power Politics* bears a remarkable resemblance to Carr's process utopianism: 'Powers will continue to seek security without reference to justice', argued Wight, 'and to pursue their vital interests irrespective of common interests, but in the fraction that they may be deflected lies the difference between the jungle and the traditions of Europe.'[94] It is Wight's elaboration of the 'traditions of Europe' in his international theory lectures of the late 1950s which is his distinctive contribution to the English School. The continued importance of the three traditions lies not only in the recognition that three perspectives on international thought are more convincingly able to represent the plurality of threads woven into the tapestry of international relations, but also in the acceptance of traditions as a medium for interrogating theory *and* practice. It is this profound anti-positivism which continues to mark out the approach of the English School from the mainstream American approach to international theory.

Wight's use of the three traditions raises a number of questions about the way in which history is interpreted. Important as these are, perhaps the central issue concerns the relationship between the three traditions. Do they represent three metaphorical pieces in the jigsaw of world politics, in other words, co-existing and interdependent elements? Without all three pieces, the scholar can only possess a partial knowledge of the subject. The hermeneutic version would add to this position the idea that these patterns reflect elements in human consciousness, for instance, in our capacity to show solidarity and indifference, treat each other alternately as friends, strangers and enemies, and in our ability to invent weapons for the mass destruction of human life alongside the creation of institutions for the preservation of individual and collective welfare.[95] Perhaps a more convincing metaphor for the three traditions is not to treat them as partial truths which can be cumulative (that is, add the 'three Rs' and 'stir'), but to view them as three voices in a conversation about global politics. As a contemporary English School theorist put it: 'The conversation is what matters.'[96]

Earlier in the chapter, it was shown how Wight's intellectual journey represents a conversation between the three traditions. In the case of Wight's pacifism, his defence of the doctrine itself is confused, but there is no necessary contradiction between realism and pacifism (just as in the case of E.H. Carr, there was no contradiction between realism and appeasement). Indeed, Wight convincingly argued that Christianity and the realist tradition of despair are fully compatible.[97] At times, this outlook translates into an extremely harsh view of human nature, evident in his Augustinian denunciation of the idealist belief in the perfectibility of humanity. From the early 1950s onwards, Wight increasingly turned away from the narrow realist pursuit of interpreting the causes of the present predicament, and the fatalism of 'inverted revolutionism', and chose instead to think about the social and historical construction of modern international society initially through the medium of the three traditions and latterly in his comparative sociology of historic states systems.

This process of discovering the interplay of theory and practice continued during the early period of the British Committee, although increasingly the focus centred on the rules and institutions which underpinned international society, viewed primarily through rationalist lenses. In this sense, there is an unambiguous link between the theoretical investigations by Wight in the 1950s, and the work of the British Committee in the 1960s. The early work of the Committee was framed by Wight's central question for international theory: what is international society? Later, the Committee oriented itself around the subsidiary question: how far does it extend? With their responses to these questions, the British Committee papers by Wight, Butterfield, Bull and Watson brought culture and identity into the mainstream of International Relations.

NOTES

1. Michael Nicholson, 'The Enigma of Martin Wight', *Review of International Studies*, 7 (1981), 18. See also the dialogue which ensued between Alan James, 'Michael Nicholson on Martin Wight: A Mind Passing in the Night', *Review of International Studies*, 8 (1982), 117–123; and Nicholson, 'Martin Wight: Enigma or Error', *Review of International Studies*, 8 (1982), 125–128. Part of the justification for engaging with the biographical material at the beginning of the chapter is to counter arguments made by both scholars.
2. R.B.J. Walker, *Inside/Outside: International Relations as Political Theory* (Cambridge: Cambridge University Press, 1993).
3. Roger Epp, 'Martin Wight: International Relations as Realm of Persuasion', in Francis A.Beer and Robert Hariman (eds), *Post-Realism: The Rhetorical Turn in International Relations* (East Lansing: Michigan Stage University Press, 1996), 123.
4. Hedley Bull explains in his correspondence why he chose to devote so much time to editing Wight's work: 'I believe that Martin Wight had one of the most distinguished minds ever applied to the study of International Relations. He was a perfectionist who published only a tiny fraction of his work, and it is of great importance to the subject that more of what he wrote should be brought to the light of day'. Letter from Hedley Bull to Adam Watson (16 January, 1976). The life and work of Wight is known to students of International Relations because of Bull's considered introductions to *Systems of States* and the revised edition of *Power Politics* (with Carsten Holbraad) and also his memorial lecture for Martin Wight. Hedley Bull and Carsten Holbraad, 'Introduction', in Martin Wight, *Power Politics* (London: Penguin, 2 ed., 1978), 9–22. Although the introduction to the above work was attributed to both Carsten Holbraad and Hedley Bull, it was Bull who wrote it and Holbraad who edited it. See also Hedley Bull, 'Introduction: Martin Wight and the Study of International Relations' in Martin Wight, *Systems of States* (Leicester: Leicester University Press, 1977), 1–20; and

'Martin Wight and the Theory of International Relations', in Martin Wight, *International Theory: The Three Traditions* (Leicester: Leicester University Press, ix–xxiii.

5. However, the idea that there is a linear progression in Wight's thinking must be partly qualified by the recognition that realist arguments are maintained in his later work just as more idealist arguments are evident in his early writing; evident in, for example, Wight, 'Beyond Power Politics', *Power Politics* (London: Royal Institute of International Affairs Pamphlet, 1946), 62–68.

6. Letter from A.J. Toynbee to Hedley Bull (18 April 1974).

7. Letter from Martin Wight to Matt Melko, (1 November 1971).

8. Herbert Butterfield, who became Wight's closest academic colleague in the early years of the British Committee, was one of his examiners. Letter from Donald Mackinnon to Hedley Bull (5 February 1974). See also Bull 'Introduction: Martin Wight and the Study of International Relations', 2.

9. A.J. Toynbee and F.T. Ashton-Gwatkin (eds), *The World in March 1939*, (London: Oxford University Press, 1952). Martin Wight wrote three lengthy sections on 'Eastern Europe', 'Germany', and 'The Balance of Power', 206–286, 293–349, 508–531.

10. E.H. Carr, The *Twenty Years' Crisis* (London: Macmillan, 1 ed., 1939), 52.

11. Arnold Toynbee was Director of Studies at Chatham House from 1924 to 1954.

12. Martin Wight, 'The March of History', review of Arnold J. Toynbee, *A Study of History*, Abridgement of Volumes I–VI by D.C. Somervell, (London: Oxford University Press, 1947), *Observer* (5 January 1947).

13. A.J. Toynbee, *A Study of History* (London: Oxford University Press/RIIA, 1954), 'Universal States Universal Churches', Vol. VII. See especially, Martin Wight, 'The Crux of for an Historian Brought up in the Christian Tradition', Annex III, 373–748. The key point of difference between Toynbee and Wight was over the role of religion in the rise and fall of civilisations. Wight believed that Toynbee underestimated the 'exclusiveness and universality of Christianity'. Martin Wight in Toynbee, *A Study* VII, 739.

14. Martin Wight, 'Arnold Toynbee: Personal Portrait', *London Calling London*, (26 February 1955). Emphasis added. Epp relates this endorsement of Toynbee to the wider dispute which raged over Toynbee's Reith lectures on 'The World and the West'. Accused by conservative critics of betraying Christian Civilization, Wight argued in Toynbee's defence of the need to see the aggressive and exploitative side of Western Civilization. See Epp, 'Martin Wight', 128.

15. Letter from Donald Mackinnon to Hedley Bull (5 February 1974).

16. Martin Wight, 'Christian Pacifism', *Theology*, 33 (1936), 12–21.

17. Wight, 'Christian Pacifism', 13. Emphasis added.

18. Wight, 'Christian Pacifism', 16. Emphasis added.

19. Wight's argument in 'Christian Pacifism' is internally inconsistent. In the first instance, the opening sentence in the above passage is straight forwardly pacifist, i.e., it is wrong to take human life; later Wight argues that pacifism 'does not condemn all use of force'. But if Wight's brand of pacifism does not condemn all uses of force then the question must be

asked, what kind of cause is worth fighting for? Later in the article he addresses more directly the coming of war: 'The amount of evil in the world remains pretty constant; and my refusal to fight will not obliterate the doctrines of Mein Kampf nor change the state of mind of its author'. Wight, 'Christian Pacifism', 21. This is clearly at odds with the earlier statement that the basis of pacifism 'is not utilitarianism'. There is no principle here, only fatalism. In addition, the second part of the passage is a rather weak tautology. Obviously, a decision whether to fight will not change the doctrine, but it may help to defeat it.

20.	There is no logical incompatibility between recognising that international politics is power politics but at the same time refusing to participate in its violent practices. Brian Porter makes this argument clearly in 'Patterns of Thought and Practice: Martin Wight's "International Theory"', in Michael Donelan (ed.), The Reason of States (London: Allen and Unwin, 1978), 68

21.	Wight, 'Christian Pacifism', 15, 20.

22.	Martin Wight, 'War and International Politics', *Listener* (13 October 1955), 584–585.

23.	This is an extract from his defence:

1. That the War is the convulsion of a civilisation that has forsaken its Christian origins, and become increasingly enslaved to secularism and materialism. It is divine judgement upon European civilization for the corporate Sin (in which all share without distinction or religion or nations) which is the cause of the War: a judgement which is the consequence and punishment of past sin, itself taking the form of a more violent abandonment thereto.

2. That the method of War can do nothing towards solving this fundamental problem of spiritual apostasy: it is one of the worst symptoms of that apostasy, and is utterly opposed to the Kingdom of God as shown in the life of Christ. The only method that can fully overcome the irrational and demonic forces of evil that have their fullest expression in Nazi Germany, is that of Calvary [sic] and the catacombs.

3. That the Christian who believes this, cannot avoid a refusal to take part in war, and must seek by other means to prepare the foundations of a new civilization that will be less in conflict with the Kingdom of God.

I have outlined these beliefs in an article published in "Theology" in June 1936 and they led me to join the Peace Pledge Union in 1936, the Anglican Pacifist Fellowship in 1936 .... I therefore ask to be placed on the register of conscientious objectors, but will gladly undertake any occupation under civilian control when the Authorities decide that I can be of more use to the community than in my present reserved occupation'. Martin Wight, 'Application to Local Tribunal by a Person Provisionally Registered in the Register of Conscientious Objectors' (Case Number E.1561A, 11 May 1940), in accordance with the National Service (Armed Forces) Act, 1939.

24.	Letter from the 'Clerk to the Appellate Tribunal' to Martin Wight (20 May 1941).

25. Martin Wight to the 'Chairman of the Appellate Tribunal' (5 May 1941).

26. Letter from Margery Perham to Hedley Bull (5 February 1974). Perham continues, 'I think – only think – that by this I was able to help to prevent him being sent to prison, but I am not sure how real this threat was.' Wight's publications in this area were: Wight, *The Development of the Legislative Council 1606–1945* edited by Margery Perham (London: Faber, 1946); Wight, *The Gold Coast Legislative Council* edited by Margery Perham (London: Faber, 1947); Wight, *British Colonial Constitutions 1947* (Oxford: Clarendon, 1952).

27. Wight, *International Theory*, 50.

28. Letter from C.A.W. Manning to Hedley Bull (5 February 1974).

29. Letter from C.A.W. Manning to Hedley Bull, (second letter not dated).

30. Letter from C.A.W. Manning to Hedley Bull (5 February 1974). This is not to suggest that Manning did not hold his Reader in high regard, admitting in the same correspondence to being 'rather proud' of bringing him to the London School of Economics, and clearly saw him as his successor. This was, Manning recalled, 'an option that, in the event, he never chose to exercise.' Wight decided to leave the School in 1961 to become Dean of the School of European Studies, joining a select group of academics whose objective was to establish a new type of university. His motives for participating in this venture have been recorded in his contribution to an edited volume on *The Idea of a New University*. Martin Wight 'European Studies' in David Daiches (ed.), *The Idea of A New University: An Experiment at Sussex* (Andre Deutsch: London, 1964) The programme was innovative in that every student had to study a European language (other than English), and that the degree was composed of a 'major' (for example, in European literature or philosophy) and a 'minor' (for example, European politics or history). I would argue that, apart from demonstrating Wight's commitment to progressive education, the School of European Studies highlighted Wight's dedication to European civilisation and Western values, and also his belief in intellectual history being the master-subject of the humanities. This latter point is apparent from the following passage on the inter-disciplinary nature of the programme: 'If one is to look, in the School of European Studies, for a common thread, a centre of gravity, it might be found in intellectual history, the region where literature, philosophy, history and the social studies meet and cross-fertilize'. Wight, 'European Studies', 105.

31. Letter from Geoffrey Goodwin to Hedley Bull (30 May 1974).

32. It was appropriately labelled a pamphlet as it is only sixty-eight pages long. Wight, *Power Politics*, 1st edition.

33. Although his use of a small 'r' here is significant. Bull, 'Introduction: Martin Wight and the Study of International Relations', 8. Note also that in the introduction to the revised edition of *Power Politics*, Bull and Holbraad argue that 'it may be doubted whether Martin Wight's position is properly described as realist'. See Bull and Holbraad, 'Introduction', 18.

34. Alan James, 'Michael Nicholson on Martin Wight', 118.

35. Wight, *Power Politics* (1946), 11. In a rather positivistic tone, Wight adds that this assumption of power politics enables us to 'more usefully assess the moral problem'.

36. Wight, *Power Politics* (1946), 58–60. See also, Wight, 'The Balance of Power' in Toynbee and Ashton-Gwatkin (eds), *The World in March 1939*, 508–9.
37. In the revised edition, Wight makes a clearer distinction between the structural antinomy between domestic and international politics: 'This indeed' argues Wight 'is the main justification for calling international politics "power politics" *par excellence.*' Wight, *Power Politics* (1978), 102.
38. Wight, *Power Politics* (1946), 34.
39. Wight, *The Listener* Vol. LIV No. 1389 (1955), 584–5. A reprint of the broadcast can be found as the Chapter 13, on 'War' in Wight, *Power Politics* (1978), 136–143.
40. Wight, 'The Church, Russia and the West', 25–45.
41. Wight, 'The Church, Russia and the West', 26.
42. Wight, 'The Church, Russia and the West', 30. Emphasis added.
43. Wight, 'The Church, Russia and the West', 30. In the original *Power Politics* Wight refers to this process as 'world unification'. Wight, *Power Politics* (1946), 33.
44. Wight, 'The Church, Russia and the West', 36.
45. Wight, 'The Church, Russia and the West', 34.
46. Bull, 'Introduction: Martin Wight and the Study of International Relations', 6.
47. The summer term of the academic year 1956/7 is the first time that Wight's 'International Theory' lectures are recorded in the London School of Economics 'Calendar'.
48. Bull, 'Martin Wight and the Theory of International Relations', ix.
49. T.B. Millar, 'Academics and Practitioners in Foreign Affairs', *Paradigms* 2 (1988/9), 98.
50. Porter, 'Martin Wight's International Theory'; Tim Dunne, 'Mythology or Methodology? Traditions in International Theory', *Review of International Studies* 19, (1993), 305–318; Ian Clark, 'Traditions of Thought and Classical Theories of International Relations', in Ian Clark and Iver B.Neumann (eds), *Classical Theories of International Relations* (London: Macmillan, 1996), 1–19.
51. Wight, *International Theory*, 267.
52. The influence of Carr on Wight is noted in Bull's introduction to, Wight *Power Politics* (1978), 19.
53. For the reason that, according to Wight, 'the more it [the two schools analysis] is made the basis for a general international theory the more untrue it seems to become'. Wight, *International Theory*, 267.
54. Wight, *International Theory*, 5.
55. As Steve Smith argues, 'the proponents of each paradigm literally do not see the same world'. Steve Smith 'Paradigm Dominance in International Relations: The Development of International Relations as a Social Science', in Hugh C.Dyer and Leon Mangasarian (eds), *The Study of International Relations: The State of the Art* (London: Macmillan, 1989), 20.
56. Wight, *International Theory*, 260.
57. Wight, *International Theory*, 259.
58. James Der Derian, 'Introducing Philosophical Traditions', *Millennium* 17 (1988), 190.

59. R.E. Jones 'The English School of International Relations: a case for closure', *Review of International Studies*, 7 (1981), 9. This is not a good argument against traditions since other approaches may be more comprehensible but simply wrong.

60. Hedley Bull, 'Martin Wight and the Theory of International Relations', in Wight, *International Theory*, xxii.

61. See Quentin Skinner, 'Meaning and Understanding in the History of Ideas' in James Tully (ed.), *Meaning and Context: Quentin Skinner and his Critics* (Cambridge: Polity Press, 1988), 29–67.

62. Hedley Bull, 'International Theory: The Case for a Classical Approach', in Klaus Knorr and James N.Rosenau (eds), *Contenting Approaches to International Relations* (Princeton: Princeton University Press, 1969), 37. Emphasis added.

63. Wight, *International Theory*, 6.

64. Martin Wight, 'Why is there no International Theory?', in Herbert Butterfield and Martin Wight (eds), *Diplomatic Investigations: Essay in the Theory of International Politics* (London: Allen and Unwin, 1966).

65. '[The] ideas which guide historical life, do certainly not indeed spring solely from the intellectual workshop of the great thinkers; on the contrary, they have a much broader and deeper origin. But it is in this workshop that they are condensed and solidified; it is there, in many cases, that they first assume the form which will have an effect on the progress of events and the actions of men.' Friedrich Meinecke, *Machiavellism: The Doctrine of Raison d'Etat and Its Place in Modern History* (London: Routledge, 1957), 21.

66. Wight, *International Theory*, 3.

67. Wight, *International Theory*, 4. In whose number Wight ranks: Machiavelli, Bismarck, Lenin, Burke, Hamilton, Gladstone, Wilson, Churchill and Nehru.

68. Wight, *International Theory*, 258. Elsewhere in his lectures, Martin Wight frequently quotes Tolstoy, whose *War and Peace* Wight described as 'the world's greatest novel'; Camus's, *The Rebel* he considered 'the best modern analysis of Revolutionism'. Other novelists mentioned include Dostoevsky, E.M. Forster, Thomas Mann, Somerset Maugham and George Orwell.

69. Wight, *International Theory*, 16. Also, Wight, 'An Anatomy of International Thought', *Review of International Studies*, 13 (1987), 222.

70. Richard Tuck, *Hobbes* (Oxford: Oxford University Press, 1989), 1.

71. Richard Tuck, *Natural Rights Theories: Their Origin and Development* (Cambridge: Cambridge University Press, 1979), 3.

72. E.B.F. Midgley makes this point. See Midgley, 'Natural Law and the "Anglo-Saxons" – Some Reflections in Response to Hedley Bull', British *Journal of International Studies*, 5 (1979), 260–272.

73. By Kantianism, in this context, Wight is referring to the Russian Revolution of 1917. Machiavellism denotes the *Realpolitik* of Nazi Germany, and the Grotian experiment, is of course, a reference to the League of Nations. Wight, *International Theory*, 163.

74. In his critique of this attempt to distinguish historical and ethical relativism, Smith argues that each tradition has its own 'distinctive, evaluative criteria, with no foundation for evaluating truth claims outside each tradition'. Steve Smith, 'The Self-Images of a Discipline: A Genealogy of International Relations Theory', in Ken Booth and Steve Smith (eds),

International Relations Today (Cambridge: Polity Press, 1995), 13. Arguably, the charge of relativism is one which the 'contexualists' must respond to, given their argument that 'the classic texts cannot be concerned with our questions and answers, but only their own'. Skinner, 'Meaning and Understanding', 65. In his concluding lecture, Martin Wight produces a useful counter-argument to the effect that the great moral debates of the past articulated in the classic texts 'are in essence our debates.' Wight, *International Theory*, 268.

75. Wight, *International Theory*, 8.
76. Wight, *International Theory*, 7.
77. Wight, *International Theory*, 141–151.
78. Wight, *International Theory*, 126.
79. These rationalist themes can be found in Wight, *International Theory*, 13–14.
80. Midgley, 'Natural Law', 266.
81. In Wight's words: 'It is a *broad* middle road, but just as it seems to become rather uncertainly wide; its edges are difficult to discern and the road itself seems sometimes disconcertingly narrow. Hamilton, for instance, seems to be on the road, but look again and he is to be found well away from it, on the turf towards the marshes. Burke is apparently marching sturdily along the road, but his movements are erratic. Kant one would like to think is on it, but he shows a disquieting tendency to dart away, to the other side from Hamilton, towards the crags and precipices. A little later there looms up a pocket of fog, called Hegel, which makes it difficult for some time to know where the road is and who is on it.' Wight, *International Theory*, 15. Although this is an amusing characterisation of the different figures in the rationalist pattern, it does beg the question whether rationalism is itself surrounded by a 'pocket of fog'.
82. Wight, *International Theory*, 14. Emphasis added.
83. Wight, *International Theory*, 49.
84. Wight, *International Theory*, 83.
85. Wight, *International Theory*, 96.
86. For a recent attempt to apply Wight's three trading in this context see Tim Dunne 'Colonial Encounters in International Relations: Reading Wight, Writing Australia', *Australian Journal of International Affairs*, 51 (1997), 309–23.
87. Wight, *International Theory*, 110. Wight's interest in 'Inverted Revolutionism' is underscored by the fact that 'The Gandhian Tradition' is the fourth tradition in Wight's 'select bibliography on international theory' prepared for the European Studies Department at the University of Sussex, (February 1965).
88. Wight, *International Theory*, 14.
89. Wight, *International Theory*, 268.
90. Martin Wight, 'Western Values', British Committee paper (October 1961) published in Butterfield and Wight (eds), *Diplomatic Investigations*, 91.
91. Bull, 'Introduction: Martin Wight and the Study of International Relations', 11.
92. Michael Nicholson, 'The Enigma of Martin Wight', 22.
93. Wight, *International Theory*, 6.

94.   Wight, *Power Politics* (1946), 68.
95.   An illustration of an existential version of the three traditions is provided
       in Pierre Hassner, 'Beyond the Three Traditions: The Philosophy of War
       and Peace in Historical Perspective', *International Affairs* 70 (1994),
       737–56.
96.   Robert Jackson, 'Pluralism in International Political Theory', *Review of
       International Studies* 18 (1992), 272. Roger Epp, a fellow English School
       'émigré' in Canada, builds on this point; '[w]hatever the limits of Wight's
       own work, the idea of theory as dialogue is open to other interlocutors'.
       Epp, 'Martin Wight', 135.
97.   In Wight's words, 'it is with agnosticism verging on despair that
       Christianity can work best'. Wight, 'The Church, Russia and the West',
       37.

4 Herbert Butterfield

In terms of his association with particular disciplines, Herbert Butterfield travelled in the opposite direction to E.H. Carr. Beginning his academic career as an historian, he became increasingly drawn to international relations theory, and in particular the nexus between religion and international politics. Indeed, his interest in international politics can be traced back to one of his earliest works, *The Statecraft of Machiavelli* first published in 1940.[1] What interested him most about international relations was that it was a 'field' where there was an obvious imperative 'to learn from experience' yet seemed to be 'a realm in which it is peculiarly difficult to transmit experience from one generation to another'.[2] Given that the dilemmas of international politics occupied his mind from the early 1950s onwards, it is surprising that his contribution to International Relations has not been given more prominence. This is particularly the case in Britain where there has been no article or book reviewing his contribution to the discipline.[3]

An obvious reason why Butterfield has hitherto been seen as marginal to International Relations in Britain is because of his identity as an historian. He published works of narrative history,[4] on historical method,[5] and on diplomatic history.[6] His academic career began at Peterhouse, Cambridge in 1923, where he was to become Master (1955 to 1968) and Professor of the Faculty of History. Butterfield's association with Peterhouse has recently been linked to the revival of conservative thinking in British politics in the 1970s and 1980s. According to a leading intellectual historian of British society:

> He organised in and from Peterhouse a kind of militant conservatism, distinct from the establishment conservatism of most Cambridge colleagues. It was radical, reverent towards Christianity, irreverent towards liberals and scornful of socialists. His adjutant was Brian Wormald, his young lieutenant Maurice Cowling, a devoted tutor whose school of right-wing iconoclasts was to make an impression in the eighties.[7]

From the point of view of his influence over the development of International Relations, it is important to note the extremely high regard in which he was held by other realists in the United States. Unlike Carr and Wight in particular, Butterfield's reputation resonated more widely in America than in Britain.[8] His influence on International Relations in the

United States can be traced back to his close friendship with Kenneth Thompson who wrote a number of pieces on Butterfield[9] and worked closely with him in setting up a parallel 'Rockefeller Committee' in Britain (discussed in more detail at the end of the chapter). Indeed, correspondence from Thompson to Butterfield reveals the gravitas Buttterfield was accorded in the US. 'We are well aware from your writings', Thompson wrote, 'what a deep contribution you are making to this field of thought.'[10]

We should perhaps not be surprised that Butterfield found intellectual allies among Christian realists in America during the 1950s. By the mid-1960s however, their voices were being silenced by the forces of secularism and science. Even within the American Rockefeller Committee, where traditionalism continued to reign, the balance of power was shifting from Niebuhr to Waltz, whose 'third image' view of the discipline inevitably marginalised theological thinking.[11] Butterfield had to wait until the neo-conservative revival in the 1980s before his star began to rise once more.[12]

Beyond the orbit of the academy, Butterfield caused a stir in the United States with the publication of his *Christianity, Diplomacy and War*. The editor of *Life* magazine took exception to Butterfield's preference for co-operating with communism over 'ideological diplomacy' which dominated US foreign policy in the 1950s.[13] To an American audience, this looked like a return to the bad old days of managing power rather than saving the world from the tyranny of communism.

Although of interest in terms of political culture, the extent to which Butterfield's thinking was appropriated by Conservatives in Britain and Republicans in America is not the focus for this chapter. Instead, a case will be made for Butterfield's re-integration into the internal disciplinary history of the English School. There are two important reasons for this, each dealt with at length in part one of the chapter. First, like Carr, Butterfield mounted a polemical attack against progressivism, initially against the history academy but later against 'moralism' in international relations theory and practice. In addition to conforming to the realist critique of idealism, Butterfield's work in the 1940s and early 1950s converges with Wight's Christian pessimism; indeed, Butterfield's application of Augustinian principles to politics is arguably more developed and more consistently applied than in the case of Wight, particularly Butterfield's use of 'original sin', 'providence' and his hostility to 'moralism' in foreign policy.

A second reason for bringing Butterfield back in to the English School should be located in his attempt to moderate the 'tragic predicament' of international relations by prudential statecraft (discussed in part two of the chapter). His interest in outlining the principles of a rationalist international order led him, in the 1950s, to engage in discussions with Kenneth Thompson about the possibility of organising a parallel 'institution' to the American Rockefeller Committee. More than any substantive intellectual contribution, it is this pivotal role in organising The British Committee on the Theory of International Politics which marks out Herbert Butterfield as one of the founder members of the English School.

Butterfield's Augustinian Realism

In his first major work of historiography entitled *The Whig Interpretation of History* Butterfield constructed a powerful critique of liberal progressivism. His target was the kind of moral absolutism of Lord Acton, who understood history as the progressive realisation of liberty.[14] Butterfield alleges that Whig history 'studies the past with reference to the present', when the rightful approach 'is the elucidation of the *unlikenesses* between past and present.'[15] He railed against the presumption that history unfolds according to a grand master-plan, with a mythical origin and a triumphant *telos*. By way of an example, he argues that parliamentary democracy evolved out of contestations, in which right and wrong, corruption and propriety, good and evil, existed on all sides. At its core, *The Whig Interpretation* was a warning shot fired by Butterfield across the bows of fellow historians who had allowed progressivism to infiltrate their narratives.

A related concern of Butterfield's was the widespread tendency among historians to write like hanging judges rather than recording angels. He referred to this penchant for dispensing moral judgements as 'useless' and 'unproductive'. Contextualism led him to argue that judgements about right and wrong should be dispensed in accordance with our own standards.[16] Ultimately, morality is a matter for individuals and their conscience, hence the historian does not have the need (or the right) to judge the past. The following excerpt from *The Whig Interpretation* provides a good illustration of this position:

> When all historical explanations of character and conduct have been exhausted, it must be remembered that the real moral question is still waiting to be solved; and what can the historian do about the secret recesses of the personality where a man's final moral responsibility resides?[17]

As Butterfield later wrote, the fight between good and evil is something that happens 'inside every one of us'.[18] There is an important parallel here with Martin Wight's early writings on Christian pacifism, which also argue that morality lies in the realm of the individual and their conscience.

The question of judgement is treated at length in Butterfield's lectures on 'Christianity and History' given in 1948. Here Butterfield argues that 'the judgement which lies in the structure of history gives none of us the right to act as judges over others.'[19] He gives the example of how one of the causes of the First World War was the German tradition of militarism, but adds the following qualification: 'I know, however, that I have no *right* to say any such thing, and I very much doubt whether it would be within the competence of the technical historian to assert it.'[20] Worldly judgement is an occasion for self-righteousness and is therefore sinful.

In place of the 'Whig' approach, Butterfield adumbrated what he called 'technical history'. He describes a technical historian as someone who 'performs an act of self-emptying in order to seek the kind of truths which do not go further than the tangible evidence warrants.'[21] Butterfield's strictures on technical history are in some respects remarkably prescient – given the prevailing current of methodology in intellectual history[22] – but they beg a number of questions. First, how much technical history did Butterfield engage in? It would not be unreasonable to argue that the body of Butterfield's intellectual production was general history, with only a few articles based on documentary sources of a technical historical kind.[23] A more important charge than whether or not Butterfield conformed to his own methodological canon, is the question whether it is possible to isolate history from political questions. As Martin Wight put it in a review of *History and Human Relations*: 'For Butterfield, technical history precludes moral judgement. It might be asked whether you can describe sin without implicitly denouncing it.'[24] The implication of Butterfield's attempt to cleanse history of judgement is well put by Alberto Coll:

> The question was not whether Bismarck was more virtuous than Napoleon but whether, assuming both men to be sinful and prone to cupidity, a historian could go on to discover how and why one of them had embarked on a course of absolute mastery and the other on a course of political self-restraint.[25]

At times it seems that Butterfield is himself unsure of the validity of the distinction, when he suggests that the historian 'deals with morality in so far as it is part of history.'[26] A third question provoked by technical history is the tension between Butterfield's commandment to look at historical conflicts for their own sake,[27] and his studies on diplomacy which assume that relevant lessons can be drawn from the experience of past centuries.

This tension is particularly evident in Butterfield's discussion of the eighteenth century international order, whose 'rules and predictions', he noted, 'have shown a remarkable applicability to modern cases.'[28]

The second background assumption maintained by Butterfield, which has an important bearing on his realism, is his Christian theology. In probably his most famous work, *Christianity and History*, Butterfield adumbrated the same Augustinian view of original sin which we came across in Wight: 'all men are', according to Butterfield, 'and men have always been, sinners.'[29] The religious notion of worldly sin is often equated in International Relations with a rapacious view of human nature as the ultimate cause of war.[30] The term sin is not meant to imply evil, rather humankind's pride and will-to-power which lead to anxiety, insecurity and corruption. The other important theological aspect of Butterfield's thought is his notion of providence; the implication of this other-worldly force turning the wheels of history is that statecraft must be oriented towards the preservation of the *status quo*. It requires, as Butterfield put it, a strategy of 'co-operation with Providence'.[31]

From the earlier discussion of original sin, one could be forgiven for assuming that the world of (international) politics was no place for a Christian. (This was the view which Martin Wight took in the inter-war period, as we saw in Chapter 3.) As Butterfield put it early on in *Christianity, Diplomacy and War*: 'It might be thought, therefore, that the Christian should withdraw from the tumult of international affairs, the whole sorry story of power, diplomacy, armaments, and war.'[32] But it was to these very themes of the 'sorry story' that Butterfield devoted his academic work from the early 1950s onwards. The post-war context of the Cold War and the threat that nuclear weapons posed for human civilisation was the principal motivation for his increasing interest in international politics.[33]

Relations between states, were, according to Butterfield, even more prone to suffer 'from the cupidities of the wicked, the anxieties of the strong, and the unwisdom of the virtuous.'[34] Moreover, the regularity of conflict is such that international politics can be amenable to intellectual analysis. As Butterfield put it: 'the problems and paradoxes of nations show such *constancies* of fundamental pattern *throughout the ages*, it is the realm where man ought to learn most (though in reality he refuses to learn) from the accumulated experience of the human race.'[35]

Against 'Moralism'

The idealists (or what he more often called 'moralists') in the inter-war period failed dismally to draw from the well of diplomatic experience.[36]

According to Butterfield, the League era was 'one of the most unfortunate periods in the history of modern diplomacy.'[37] The exclusive focus on international morality led to 'colossal blunders'. Here Butterfield has in mind the 'relative disarmament' in Britain during the inter-war period which 'was bound to be almost an invitation to misconduct.' The upshot is that the *status quo* powers bear 'partial responsibility' for Hitler's aggression.[38] Therefore, the flight from realism in the inter-war period was, in Butterfield's mind, a contributory cause of the Second World War.

One particular aspect of idealism which concerned him was the prevalence of 'war for righteousness' thinking in the legal discourse of the inter-war period. Butterfield applies the same argument to the Cold War, recognising the dangers of judging Communism as evil and then fighting a 'war for righteousness' against it.[39] This point is sharply made in *Christianity, Diplomacy and War*:

> But the greatest menace to civilization is liable to be the conflict between giant organized systems of self-righteousness .... If man arrogates to himself the right which he is not fit to possess, and which Christianity withholds from him – namely, the right to judge actual wickedness, to adjudicate on sinners and to punish the sin itself – then there can be no end to the atrocities.[40]

In a tribute to Hans Morgenthau, Butterfield underlined his argument against self-righteousness with the claim that it 'sometimes produces more terrible results than *Realpolitik*.'[41]

A further aspect of Butterfield's critique of the League era relates to its artificial construction, in contrast to the organic order of post-Westphalian Europe. The problem with international organisations is that they are not sustained by a feeling that they are all 'members of the same club'. Here Butterfield invokes a peculiarly Burkean notion of club as 'the sentimental bonds between nations . . . all this is a matter of time and slow growth, and it needs considerable intervals of peace and normal, settled relationships.' The belief in 'loyalty through law' was a clear departure from the practice of the European states-system where, according to Butterfield, the 'fundamental prescription was loyalty to the "states-system" itself.'[42] However, as we shall see in the final section, Butterfield believed that mature statecraft combined loyalty to the state *and* loyalty to the states-system.

What was needed in place of this moralistic approach, Butterfield argued, was a 'scientific' approach. By science, Butterfield means two things. First, he is invoking the strictures of technical history, meaning an analysis of the structure of the international order – in particular the elements of an international system – rather than judging the decisions of particular statesmen. Second, he identifies a scientific approach with the eighteenth century balance of power system. In his view, the new world order of 1919 turned its back on the accumulated wisdom of the European states-system. Butterfield gives the example of how the 'older diplomatic science' would have preferred to keep an ancient (though imperfect) border rather than suppose that it was in their power to redraw the map of Europe in the manner of the Versailles settlement.[43]

The 'Hobbesian Fear'

It is less his critique of idealism which marks out Butterfield as a key thinker in British International Relations than his analysis of the causes of wars. According to Booth and Wheeler, Butterfield provides the earliest account of the security dilemma in the literature.[44] This fact about international politics constituted the condition of 'absolute predicament' which 'lies at the very geometry of human conflict'. Mutual fear lies at the heart of Butterfield's conception of the tragic nature of international conflict. The following passage clearly captures the essence of Butterfield's conception of the security dilemma:

> It is the peculiar characteristic of the situation I am describing – the situation of what I shall call *Hobbesian fear* – that you yourself may vividly feel the terrible fear that you have of the other party, but you cannot enter into the other man's counter-fear, or even understand why he should be particularly nervous. For you know that you yourself mean him no harm, and that you want nothing from him save guarantees for your own safety; and it is never possible to realise or remember properly that since he cannot see the inside of your mind, he can never have the same assurance of your intentions that you have.[45]

There is an important link here between his conception of the security dilemma and his critique of 'moralism', in that the dynamics of the 'Hobbesian fear' are exaggerated when state leaders 'read' aggressive intentions into the minds of their adversary. According to Kenneth Thompson, Butterfield's sermon against the dangers of self-righteous statecraft had an impact on American foreign policy during the Cold War. Indeed, Thompson referred to these warnings as Butterfield's 'most lasting and valuable contribution.'[46]

Was there a way out of the Hobbesian fear? Butterfield argues at one point that the predicament would not exist, 'if all the world were like St Francis of Assisi.'[47] But in the absence of universal Christian love, the power of the predicament is such that it presents itself irrespective of the morality of individual statesmen or the disposition of a particular state. Butterfield makes this point categorically:

> The predicament would not be removed even if there were no Communism in the world at all .... Even supposing Russia were liberal and democratic – supposing the great Powers on either side were so situated that their populations could put pressure on the government in the very matter of foreign policy – still the populations would be just as fearful or suspicious.[48]

Butterfield, therefore, rejects the liberal notion that the international system can be transformed by 'second-image' domestic reform. Indeed, Butterfield argued that democracies have historically 'been more generally bellicose than kings.'[49]

As further evidence for his structural view of conflict, Butterfield notes the curious law that good states in one century become bad states in another – he cites the examples of Spain in the sixteenth century, France in the early nineteenth century and Germany in the twentieth century. As he put it, 'even if a state has been virtuous hitherto, a certain position of power ... will in fact produce a corrupting effect.'[50] This structural account of international conflict links back to his belief in the importance of technical history which he thought could 'lay bare the essential geometry of the problem.'[51] Therefore, in the case of Communism, he counselled against viewing it as a monolithic threat in favour of treating it as an object of science in order to reveal precisely what aspects of Communism were a threat to the states system.[52] By rigorously applying ancient maxims, the analyst will see that the Soviet Union is behaving like all great powers have behaved hitherto.

Statecraft and the Containment of the 'Hobbesian Fear'

Herbert Butterfield's diagnosis of the international predicament ex-emplified by the Cold War led him to examine the periods of international stability when power politics was 'chastened'.[53] The period which Butterfield most frequently drew upon in order to demonstrate the poss-ibilities for taming power politics was the eighteenth century balance of power system. This is how Butterfield described the relationship between diplomacy, the balance of power and the states-system:

> The theory noted the limits to which a state could safely go either in egotism or altruism and insisted that the diplomat can never afford to

ignore the distribution of power, that indeed the virtuous conduct of states might depend on this. And the pattern of the system became printed on the minds of practising diplomats – reinforcing the tendency to constant vigilance and perpetual negotiation – reinforcing also the need for farsightedness, because, once the predominance of a state is a *fait accompli*, the situation is liable to be irreversible.[54]

Two important insights can be drawn from Butterfield's analysis of the evolution of the European states-system. The first is that he sees a duality in the 'moderating effect' where the system acts as a constraint upon the freedom of states, but there is also a significant role to play for virtuous statesmen. A second theme which can be drawn from Butterfield's view of the eighteenth century states-system is his preference for diplomatic practice over political theory or international law. For Butterfield, diplomacy was the filter through which 'so much of the world's past experience' flowed.[55]

What is to be made of Butterfield's view that the eighteenth century states-system provided a historical example of an era where cupidity was successfully curbed? The core of Butterfield's argument for the stability of the eighteenth century states-system is the claim that states acted according to their own interests *and* the interests of the system as a whole. For example, in *Christianity, Diplomacy and War*, Butterfield describes it as a time when 'governments knew that they were vitally interested in the preservation of the international system.' But isn't this synthesis between the interests of state and the interests of the system an instance of the progressivist doctrine of the harmony of interests which Butterfield had earlier deplored?

From a more empirical point of view, Butterfield is open to the charge of romanticising a century which witnessed thirty-six inter-state conflicts, one every 2.85 years.[56] Martin Wight argued that Butterfield's view of the eighteenth century as an age of balance and liberty was 'so extravagant a description ... that it discredits the particle of truth it may contain.'[57] Although certain of Butterfield's arguments about the eighteenth century are valid (such as the change in the perception of what reasons for war were legitimate), Butterfield's key argument about the loyalty of statesmen to the system itself must be questioned. As Holsti has recently argued, diplomacy and mediation 'did not reflect the consciousness of a common interest.'[58] What is surprising is that Butterfield seldom used the early nineteenth century Concert of Europe as an example of statecraft guided by a set of norms designed to preserve the system.[59]

A further criticism of Butterfield's analogy between stability and the eighteenth century system concerns his lack of clarity over the precise maxims which constitute diplomatic wisdom. He frequently adumbrates vague notions regarding the creative nature of diplomacy, or the ubiquity of power in the diplomatic game, the dangers of 'crude moralism' in international relations, or the 'imponderables' of international order. But what is striking about his diplomatic investigations is that he never systematically outlines the 'maxims' by which power politics can be contained, nor provides examples in history where specific diplomatic wisdom has prevailed.

Although the content of the diplomatic moral code remains underdeveloped in Butterfield, it is perhaps more important to dwell on the rationalist moment immanent his thinking. The following lengthy extract from *Christianity, Diplomacy and War* symbolises the rationalist search for international order emerging from beneath the shadow of the 'Hobbesian fear':

> Short of the conversion of all men and the harnessing of human cupidity itself, what is required of us is that we should tame the lion, and steal a march on Power as we can, so that human reason encroaches on the jungle, if only inch by inch. And all this is itself involved in the progress of advancing civilization; it needs peace, perhaps the better part of it can only be achieved when the lion is asleep. Steady conditions, historical continuity, and the healing effects of time – these are historical factors the force of which we greatly under-estimate when we try to play Providence for ourselves. It is through these that the process is encouraged by which power gives way to diplomacy, diplomacy in turn becomes more urbane, *the diplomatic profession develops into an international society*, and morality itself comes to have its place amongst the recognized conditions of the intercourse between states.[60]

Although it would be a mistake to construe this as evidence for Butterfield's conversion from realism to rationalism, there are nevertheless clear signs that Butterfield was following Wight 'beyond realism'. Notice, for example, the same linguistic distinction between 'civilization' and 'the jungle' that Wight used in his conclusion to the original *Power Politics*. More substantively, the passage underscores the way in which, within certain limits (seemingly determined by providence), there is some space for moral learning in international relations. For Butterfield, this was in evidence in the classical European international society, but was something that the twentieth century 'so often forgot – that civilisation is a precarious thing, a constructed thing, built on the side of a volcano, and requiring much thought even for its simple maintenance'.[61]

Lurking behind Butterfield's ideas about how the international state of nature might be tamed lies a 'domestic analogy'.[62] As he adumbrated in

Christianity and History, government cannot cure humankind of its sinful nature, but evil can be 'mitigated by institutions which are the gift of God.'[63] Projecting this argument onto the international realm, Butterfield was drawn to consider the habits and practices which could mitigate international 'fear' and 'pride' (the two faces of sin), such as the balance of power, diplomacy, and limited war.[64] It is through these instruments that 'cupidity itself would be curbed.'[65]

Increasingly, Butterfield believed he could make an impact on academic International Relations by providing an institutional forum for the self-conscious investigation into the historical and sociological elements of international society. In 1954, the year after *Christianity, Diplomacy and War* was published, Kenneth Thompson invited him to attend one of the meetings of the recently formed American Rockefeller Committee.[66] Butterfield's answer is worth quoting at length as it provides the strongest indication of his heightened interest in international relations theory:

> I am most interested indeed to hear about the little group who are discussing international politics, because though I am not primarily concerned about contemporary affairs, or really well-informed about them (indeed I am essentially an historian), I am quite obsessed with the view that our theoretical approach to international politics requires very severe analysis, and that the frontiers of thought itself can be enlarged by this genuinely fundamental approach.[67]

Butterfield added that he was unable to join the American group in the near future owing to his responsibilities at Cambridge. Two years later, however, Butterfield finally made it to the 'Theory of International Relations Meeting' of June 1956. Apart from Butterfield, the minutes noted those in attendance: 'Present: W.T.R. Fox, Louis Halle, Reinhold Niebuhr, Paul Nitze, Kenneth Thompson, Arnold Wolfers, Kenneth Waltz (rapporteur).' In order ensure that the discussions about great powers remained the domain of great men, the group met at the 'Men's Faculty Club, Columbia University'. The title of Butterfield's talk was 'Morality and the Historical Process'. The talk was not fully minuted although the notes from the meeting reveal Butterfield's justification for an historian adopting a 'theoretical' position. First, he cites the need to develop generalisations based on historical study, 'an important activity for statesmen themselves to engage in and that the historian can, in turn, learn much from the study of the actions and writings of statesmen'. Second, Butterfield noted how an interest in theory had developed out of his 'concern with ethical questions'.

Although Herbert Butterfield later admitted to being somewhat 'heckled' by his audience,[68] the experience of the meeting prompted him to reconsider the possibility of a parallel international theory group in Britain. In a long letter to Thompson in October of that year, the Master of Peterhouse raised a number of doubts concerning the depth of International Relations thinking in Britain. He also noted the strong presence of diplomatic historians but thought they would be resistant to the theoretical nature of the project. A further conjecture concerned the appropriate 'home' for the Committee. Clearly the London School of Economics was the obvious choice for the Committee, although Butterfield noted a 'curious vagueness and ineffectuality' about Charles Manning.[69] If it had to be the London School of Economics, Butterfield added that 'Martin Wight would be more suitable than Manning, if it is possible to go over the head of a Professor to his Reader.' Thompson agreed that Wight 'would be eminently suited' to serve on a British Committee.[70] He was also keen for the Committee to be based around Butterfield in Cambridge, despite the absence of a Department of International Relations, noting that 'existing departments of International Relations appear to have made rather modest contributions to this field.'[71]

Conclusion

The assumption with which this chapter opened was that Butterfield's thinking on history, politics and international relations is indivisible. His contribution to academe and to political practice more broadly was undergirded by his fundamentalist Christian principles. His views found many disciples in the 1950s, as intellectuals sought to grapple with the darker side of modernity. This point is nicely articulated by Michael Howard, a fellow member of the British Committee:

> The Christian eschatology, long disdained by liberal humanists even within the Church itself, once again became terrifyingly relevant to human affairs .... And the teachers who best provided an adequate framework for understanding were the philosophers and theologians Niebuhr, Bonhoeffer, Karl Barth, Tillich ... men for whom the march of humanitarian, utilitarian liberalism, including its change of gear into Marxism socialism, had simply been a long excursion into the desert in search of a mirage.[72]

Just as Carr jumped from the deck of liberalism and boarded socialism, Butterfield found Christian realism an accommodating resting place in the early post-war period. The background assumptions of Augustinian thought enabled him to study 'the rules of the grammar of power'[73] without having to make moral judgements.

One of the constitutive rules of the grammar of power politics was, according to Butterfield, the 'Hobbesian fear' or 'predicament'. In their quest for security, states create an irreducible fear and enmity in other states, even if their intentions are benign. This is a classical realist argument, shared by the American theorists of the early post-war era, in particular Niebuhr, Morgenthau and Herz In the case of Morgenthau, the element of predicament is echoed in his first principle of political realism, namely, the ceaseless struggle for power driven by man's rapacious human nature.[74] The Cold War was a classic example of the 'absolute predicament'. For this reason Butterfield recommended that the Soviet Union should be treated as a great power rather than an ideological threat. In a veiled attack upon idealism, he added that only in the twentieth century 'did there come to prevail that kind of naïveté which expected Russia to be nonaggressive when her accumulated power had given her the predominance?'[75]

Butterfield was not solely interested in the grammar of power. He recognised that although Christianity cannot make the world virtuous, it can make it prudent and stable. As he expressed it in *Christianity and History*, '[b]y organising our cupidities, society tames them, exacts its toll from them, curbs them and even conceals a considerable part of their operation.'[76] Likewise, he thought that the practices of international society could potentially deliver order and balance to international politics. In the case of the European states system, 'wise and moderate statesman' had succeeded in making 'the path of self-interest coincide with the path of virtue.'[77] The excessive moralism which has become the daily round of foreign policy in the twentieth century has effectively cut international relations loose from the civilising habits and practices of an earlier age.

It is interesting that Kenneth Thompson attached great importance to Butterfield's writings on European statecraft. It was here, he argued, that 'Butterfield's realism' was 'tempered by his profession as an historian and by Britain's ancient tradition in foreign policy.'[78] The regulation of conflict, and the preservation of the independence of states, demonstrates how international order can be morally worthy without falling into the righteous moralism of the idealists, or the despair of the pure realists. This desire to turn back the wheels of history from the tragic predicament of the inter-war period and the early Cold War, led Butterfield to his mission to recover a classical conception of prudential statecraft. He saw the British Committee as the institutional forum for realising this growing 'obsession' with the need to enlarge 'the frontiers of knowledge' about international society.

NOTES

1. Herbert Butterfield, *The Statecraft of Machiavelli* (London: Macmillan, 1940).

2. Letter from Herbert Butterfield to Peter Savigear (16 February 1970).

3. There are signs that there may be a growing interest in Butterfield and International Relations. See Roger Epp 'The "Augustinian Moment" in International Politics: Niebuhr, Butterfield, Wight and the Reclaiming of a Tradition', International Politics Research Occasional Paper No.10, University of Wales, Aberystwyth, 1991. Also, Cornelia Navari 'English Machiavellism', European International Studies Conference paper, Heidelberg, September 1992.

4. Herbert Butterfield, *George III and the Historians* (London: Collins, 1957); *George III, Lord North and the People, 1779–1780* (London: George Bell, 1949).

5. Included under this rubric are: Herbert Butterfield, *The Whig Interpretation of History* (London: George Bell, 1950); *The Englishman and His History* (Cambridge: Cambridge University Press, 1944); *Christianity and History* (London: George Bell, 1949); *Christianity, Diplomacy and War* (London: Epworth, 1953); 'Historiography' *The Dictionary of the History of Ideas, Vol.1* (New York: Scribner's, 1973), 464–98; *History and Human Relations* (London: Collins, 1951). *Man on His Past: The Study of History of Historical Scholarship* (Cambridge: Cambridge University Press, 1955).

6. Diplomatic history includes: Herbert Butterfield, *The Peace Tactics of Napoleon 1806–1808* (Cambridge: Cambridge University Press, 1929); and *The Statecraft of Machiavelli* (London: George Bell, 1940); 'The Scientific versus the Moralistic Approach in International Affairs', *International Affairs*, (27, 1951), 411–422; *International Conflict in the Twentieth Century: A Christian View* (New York: Harper and Brothers, 1960); 'Sir Edward Grey in July 1914', *Historical Studies* 5, (1965), 1–25; 'Morality and an International Order', in Brian Porter (ed.), *The Aberystwyth Papers: International Politics, 1919–1969* (London: Oxford University Press, 1972), 336–57; 'Raison d'Etat: The Relations between Morality and Government', The First Martin Wight Memorial Lecture, (University of Sussex, April 23, 1975); 'The Balance of Power' and 'The New Diplomacy and Historical Diplomacy', in Herbert Butterfield and Martin Wight (eds), *Diplomatic Investigations* (London: Allen and Unwin, 1966), 132–48, 181–91.

7. Noel Annan, *Our Age: The Generation that made Post-war Britain* (Fontana: London, 1991), 365–366. Maurice Cowling casts doubt on this view. In an obituary he wrote: 'Butterfield was never a party Conservative, though he voted in the course of his life for all three parties'. 'Herbert Butterfield: 1900–1979', *Proceedings of the British Academy*, LXV (1979), 600.

8. Here of course I am referring to scholars working in Britain not identified with the English School.

9. Kenneth W. Thompson, *Masters of International Thought* (Baton Rouge: Louisiana State University Press, 1980) and Kenneth W. Thompson (ed.), *Herbert Butterfield: The Ethics of History and Politics* (Washington: University Press of America, 1980).

10. The remainder of the paragraph is also worthy of note: 'I am taking the liberty of showing your letter to Professors Niebuhr and Morgenthau who have been especially interested in your writings.' Letter from Thompson to Butterfield, 30 April 1954. In addition to earning the respect of Kenneth Thompson, Hans Morgenthau described Butterfield as 'an ally', and Butterfield reciprocated the compliment by contributing a chapter to a collection of essays in honour of Morgenthau. Herbert Butterfield, 'Global Good and Evil' in Kenneth W. Thompson and Robert J. Myers (eds), *A Tribute to Hans Morgenthau* (Washington: The New Republic Book Company, 1977), 199–202.

11. Epp, 'The "Augustianian Moment"', 20.

12. Alberto Coll, *The Wisdom of Statecraft: Sir Herbert Butterfield and the Philosophy of International Politics* (Durham: Duke University Press, 1985). In a foreword, Adam Watson describes the work as 'the best and most accurate exposition' of the man and his contribution to history, politics and theology' (xiv).

13. This vignette is discussed in Epp, 'The "Augustianian Moment"', 15.

14. As William H. McNeill put it, 'Lord Acton was the first Englishman to view British, American, and Continental European history as a common whole, and to imprint upon the synthesis what Herbert Butterfield has aptly termed the Whig interpretation of history, that is, the notion that all mankind has been toiling onward and upward through time towards the pinnacle of English (and/or American) constitutional liberty'. See W.H. McNeill, *Essays in the Liberal Interpretation of History* (Chicago: University of Chicago Press, 1967), xviii.

15. Butterfield, *The Whig Interpretation*, 10–11. Emphasis added.

16. Butterfield, *The Whig Interpretation*, 36. Although undoubtedly an important work, I am persuaded by Geoffrey Elton's view that '*The Whig Interpretation* proves on re-reading to be really perilously thin – truly an essay, lacking in substance, and in particular lacking in history. The range of examples used is surprisingly narrow, even for a man of thirty-one; one gets very tired of Martin Luther popping up on page after page, with nothing said about him that indicates serious study.' Geoffry Elton, 'Herbert Butterfield and the Study of History', *The History Journal* 27 (1984), 729–743. For a recent defence of *The Whig Interpretation*, see Bernard Bailyn, 'Context in History' *Quadrant* (March 1996), 9–15.

17. Butterfield, *The Whig Interpretation*, 115.

18. Butterfield, 'Global Good and Evil', 202.

19. Herbert Butterfield, *Christianity and History*, 62.

20. Butterfield, *Christianity and History*, 63. Arguments such as these provoked the following rebuttal: 'Is God alone to pass judgement on Belsen?' Keith Feiling, 'The Function of a Historian', *The Spectator* 187 (21 September 1951). Quoted in Epp, The "Augustianian Moment"', 25.

21. Butterfield, *History and Human Relations*, 102.

22. For an overview of the new history approach, see James Tully (ed.), *Meaning and Context: Quentin Skinner and his Critics* (Cambridge: Polity Press, 1988).

23. The most 'technical' of Butterfield's works is the detailed study embodied in *The Peace Tactics of Napoleon*.

24. Martin Wight, 'The Tragedy of History', *Observer* (2 September 1951), review of Butterfield, *History and Human Relations*. A similar argument is made by Maurice Cowling: 'his conclusion should have been not that "technical historical study has its place" but that "technical historical study" insulated from religion or culture is an impossibility.' See Cowling, 'Herbert Butterfield', 609.

25. Coll, *The Wisdom*, 46.

26. Butterfield, *The Whig Interpretation*, 126.

27. As Butterfield put it, such an approach means 'that we try to see each generation in its own context'. Butterfield adds, '[i]t is the discontinuities between the generations that more definitely concern us'. See Herbert Butterfield, *The Discontinuities between the Generations in History: Their Effect on the Transmission of Political Experience*, The 1971 Rede lecture, (Cambridge: Cambridge University Press, 1972), 4–5

28. Butterfield, *Christianity, Diplomacy and War*, 100.

29. Butterfield, *Christianity and History*, 106. For a lucid exegesis of Augustinian thought, see Epp, 'The "Augustinian Moment"'.

30. See Kenneth Waltz's 'first image pessimism' in *Man, the State and War* (New York: Columbia University Press, 1959), 40–41.

31. Herbert Butterfield, *The Englishman and his History* (Cambridge: Cambridge University Press, 1944), 83.

32. Butterfield, *Christianity, Diplomacy and War*, 11.

33. Butterfield, *International Conflict*, 30.

34. Butterfield, 'Morality and an International Order', 343.

35. Butterfield, 'Morality and an International Order', 343. Emphasis added.

36. His description of 'moralists' as 'specialists in wishful thinking' draws from Carr's realist language game; Butterfield, *History and Human Relations*, 31.

37. Butterfield, 'Morality and an International Order', 343.

38. Butterfield, *Christianity, Diplomacy and War*, 61, 64, 64.

39. There is an interesting parallel with Carr in that Butterfield believed there was a degree of ideological convergence after 1945. In Butterfield's words, 'we are all nearer to communism than we imagine – for in regard to our social arrangements we have been moving in some respects in the same direction, however unwilling we may be to move quite so far.' Butterfield, *Christianity, Diplomacy and War*, 122.

40. Butterfield, *Christianity, Diplomacy and War*, 43.

41. Butterfield, 'Global Good and Evil', 202.

42. Butterfield, *Christianity, Diplomacy and War*, 345, 338.

43. Butterfield, *Christianity and History*, 102.

44. See Ken Booth and Nicholas J. Wheeler, *The Security Dilemma* (London: Macmillan, forthcoming, 1999). In America, the father of the security dilemma is John Herz. See J. Herz, *Political Realism and Political Idealism* (Chicago: University of Chicago Press, 1951).

45. Butterfield, *History and Human Relations*, 20, 21.

46. Thompson (ed.), *Herbert Butterfield*, 52.

47. Butterfield, *History and Human Relations*, 22.

48. Butterfield, *History and Human Relations*, 25–26.

49. Butterfield, *Christianity, Diplomacy and War*, 55.

50. Butterfield, *Christianity, Diplomacy and War*, 56. Clearly, the implication here is that power in international politics corrupts absolutely. It is interesting that Butterfield should import Acton's law of power into the international arena, whilst at the same time being highly critical of Acton's liberal progressivism.
51. Butterfield, *History and Human Relations*, 27.
52. Butterfield, *Christianity, Diplomacy and War*, 107.
53. Butterfield, *Christianity, Diplomacy and War*, 79.
54. Herbert Butterfield, 'Diplomacy', in Ragnhild Hatton and M.S. Anderson (eds), *Studies in Diplomatic History: Essays in Memory of David Bayne Horn* (London: Longman, 1970), 370.
55. Butterfield, *Christianity, Diplomacy and War*, 186.
56. K.J. Holsti, *Peace and War: Armed Conflicts and International Order 1648–1989* (Cambridge: Cambridge University Press, 1991), 84. These figures are for the period 1715–1814.
57. Martin Wight, 'Morals and Warfare', review of *Christianity, Diplomacy and War*, *Observer* 16 August 1953.
58. Holsti, *Peace and War*, 112–113.
59. Holbraad argues that the idea of a Concert with informal norms, and common assumptions remained a feature of European international relations until the end of the nineteenth century. Carsten Holbraad, *The Concert of Europe* (London: Longman, 1970), 3.
60. Butterfield, *Christianity, Diplomacy and War*, 76. Emphasis added.
61. Butterfield, *Christianity, Diplomacy and War*, 82.
62. Epp makes this argument. See Epp, 'Augustinian Moment', 14.
63. Butterfield, *Christianity and History*, 34. Emphasis added.
64. Butterfield, *Christianity, Diplomacy and War*, 23.
65. Butterfield, 'Morality and an International Order', 337.
66. Letter from K.W. Thompson to Herbert Butterfield (12 April 1954). The letter begins rather modestly: 'I am writing at the suggestion of a small group of scholars, including Reinhold Niebuhr, Hans Morgenthau and Arnold Wolfers. They have been the nucleus of a little group who have been meeting to discuss theoretical approaches to international politics.'
67. Letter from Herbert Butterfield to Kenneth W. Thompson (26 April 1954).
68. Letter from Herbert Butterfield to Martin Wight (6 May 1958).
69. The paragraph from which this phrase has been quoted provides an interesting 'window' into International Relations in Britain in the 1950s at least from Butterfield's view-point: 'I think you will easily realise what the snags are in this country. On the one side, we have a number of diplomatic historians, many of whom are purely interested in the concrete aspect of research and on the whole refractory to any idea of general thinking or scientific analysis. On the other hand I am a little afraid of Professor Manning, because, although his is one of the nicest men in the world and his department would naturally be very interested in the matter, there is a curious vagueness and ineffectuality about him, and he provides some pretext for those people who object to the more general study of international relations. Between these two dangers it would need rather a strong hand to make an English committee follow anything like the lines of the American one, and I would rather like to know whether in your view, I ought to take the matter

up with the idea of pursuing the kind of line of enquiry that you and I have talked about.' Letter from Herbert Butterfield to K.W. Thompson (17 October 1956).

70. Thompson went on to add: 'He [Wight] has after all done more with theory than others one might mention and in this light it is no affront to choose him over Manning.' Letter from K.W. Thompson to Herbert Butterfield (14 December 1956).

71. Letter from K.W. Thompson to Herbert Butterfield (14 December 1956).

72. Michael Howard, 'Ethics and Power in International Policy', Martin Wight Memorial Lecture, reprinted in *The Causes of War and Other Essays* (Cambridge, Mass.: Harvard University Press, 1984), 51–52.

73. Coll, *The Wisdom*, 28. Emphasis added.

74. Hans Morgenthau, *Politics Among Nations: The Struggle for Power and Peace* (New York: McGraw Hill, 1993), 4–16.

75. Butterfield, *Conflict in the Twentieth Century*, 34.

76. Butterfield, *Christianity and History*, 34.

77. Butterfield, *Conflict in the Twentieth Century*, 35.

78. Thompson (ed.), *Herbert Butterfield*, 51.

5 The British Committee I

In his introduction to Martin Wight's posthumously published British Committee papers on historical states-systems, Hedley Bull acknowledges that the essays 'are part of a collective enquiry', therefore 'the reader coming fresh to these essays will occasionally have the impression that he is eavesdropping on a conversation.'[1] The published essays of the Committee,[2] however, only tell part of the story. By piecing together a narrative history of the Committee, from the correspondence between the members and the transcripts of their discussions, a context unfolds in which it becomes possible to locate the 'community of assumptions' that guided their theoretical investigations.[3]

The absence of an authoritative account of the British Committee in the history of the discipline is surprising given its symbolic significance as the first self-conscious attempt to organise a community of scholars working in Britain for the purpose of generating a deeper understanding of the 'big questions' in International Relations. For this reason, one of the general aims in this first of two chapters on the British Committee is to narrow the gap which currently exists between the general familiarity with key ideas associated with the Committee and the relative paucity of knowledge concerning how and why the Committee was set up, who the members were, and the overall purpose of the group. In addition to filling a void in the discipline's history, the second important contention of the following two chapters is that our understanding of a number of key essays such as Martin Wight's 'Why is there no International Theory?' and Hedley Bull's 'International Theory: the Case for a Classical Approach' is heightened by a knowledge of the history of the British Committee and the principles and prejudices upon which it was founded.

The first part of this chapter retraces the origins of the Committee, from the initial prompting of Kenneth W. Thompson of the Rockefeller Foundation in the early 1950s through to the group's inaugural meeting of the 'British committee on the Theory of International Politics' held at Peterhouse, Cambridge, in January 1959. Part two will examine the agenda which developed in the early years (1959–62), in particular the central meta-questions of the English School such as: What is international theory, and what is the nature of international society?

The founding of the British Committee

It is somewhat ironic that the British Committee on the Theory of International Politics was dependent upon both American motivation and financial support. The reason for the generous support of the Rockefeller Foundation was due principally to the interest of Kenneth Thompson who, as noted in the previous chapter, was 'sympathetic' to Butterfield in particular and to traditionalist approaches in general at a time when they were under siege in the American academy.

Kenneth Thompson began his career at the Rockefeller Foundation in 1955 becoming Vice-President to Dean Rusk between 1961 and 1973, thereby holding considerable power within the Foundation during the heyday of the British Committee. Aside from his work at the Foundation, Thompson was one of the leading realist thinkers on international politics in the postwar era, writing numerous works on politics, diplomacy and ethics.[4] However, he is perhaps best known for being a former pupil and long time colleague of Hans Morgenthau, for co-editing with him *Principles and Problems of International Politics* and for preparing the sixth edition of Morgenthau's *Politics Among Nations*.[5] As we saw at the end of Chapter 4, Thompson was Butterfield's 'closest friend and warmest admirer' in the US.[6]

The American Committee first met in 1954 under the auspices of Dean Rusk and Kenneth Thompson of the Rockefeller Foundation. The group consisted of the most prominent figures in modern American realist thought: Reinhold Niebuhr, Hans Morgenthau, Arnold Wolfers, Paul Nitze, W.T.R. Fox and Kenneth Waltz. Columbia University was the institutional home of the American Committee. In the foreword to their collaborative publication, the editor states the objectives of the American Committee: 'In the course of this work we have come to recognize the importance of developing a theory to comprehend, explain, and guide the study of international relations and the formulation of foreign policy.'[7] The centrality of foreign policy to the American Committee's agenda (and the concomitant view that 'theory' was to serve 'practice') was a crucial difference between the two Rockefeller groups. It is also a principal reason for the failure of the American Committee whose 'deep divisions' between theorists and practitioners, recalls Kenneth Thompson, 'meant it faded away after a couple of meetings.' In contrast to the American group, Butterfield and the British Committee remained detached from policy issues. According to Thompson, Butterfield was 'scrupulous about maintaining the "quiet" nature of the project.'[8]

Between 1954 and 1958, Butterfield and Thompson continued their correspondence about the possibility of setting up a parallel Committee in

Britain in order to extend 'the frontiers of thought' about international politics.[9] Following his visit to Columbia to give a paper to the American
Committee in June 1956, their discussions shifted from the question
whether it made sense to have a British Committee at all, to the more
definitive issue of *where* it should be located and who should be invited to
participate. The decision to attach the Committee to the University of
Cambridge came about, as we saw in the previous chapter, largely because
of Thompson's insistence that Butterfield should be the 'anchor'.[10]

The Composition of the Committee
The first to be asked to join was Desmond Williams, a diplomatic historian
from University College, Dublin, and long-term academic contact of
Butterfield's. Martin Wight was asked to join in May 1958. In a long
letter, Butterfield outlined the activities of the American Committee and
proposed that Wight be involved in the parallel group, noting that without
Wight's participation the venture would not be possible.[11] Butterfield also
anticipated that they should proceed cautiously in issuing invitations to
join the group.[12] At the time, Wight was Reader in International Relations
at the London School of Economics, although soon to become Professor of
History and Dean of the School of European Studies at the University of
Sussex. Wight insisted on the inclusion of a philosopher in order to
strengthen the 'ethical dimension.' He chose a colleague from his Oxford
years, Professor Donald Mackinnon, then Professor of Divinity at
Aberdeen. Michael Howard, then a lecturer in War Studies at the
University of London, was brought in to 'balance him by filling in on the
military side.'[13]

Given the academic backgrounds of Wight and Butterfield, it is perhaps
not surprising that the original cell of the Committee was composed
mainly of philosophers and historians, although the two founder members
differed on the balance of the committee (as we will see below). More
surprising is the inclusion of practitioners, reflecting perhaps the influence
that policy-makers held in the American Rockefeller Committee.[14] Adam
Watson was suggested by Butterfield because he felt 'it is desirable to
have somebody from the Foreign Office.'[15] They also brought in a representative from the Treasury, William Armstrong, with expertise in economic affairs and the functioning of government. Michael Howard usefully
characterises the purpose of the practitioners, which was 'to provide pragmatic input into our theorising, not as channels to feed our theories into
the real world.'[16]

After a couple of the early meetings, Wight became concerned about the
direction and composition of the Committee. Butterfield had raised the

possibility of bringing a scientist into the discussions, no doubt reflecting his interest in the history of science. This suggestion provoked an exasperated reply: 'Is there any argument for admitting a physicist to our group, which would not be equally or more cogent in respect of a biologist, a demographer, an agronomist, an expert in international economics, a social psychologist, and so on? *I should very much regret it if we developed into a collection of distinguished amateurs*, rather than a body of people having the *same language* and frame of reference.' Wight went on to contrast the composition of the British Committee with the group based in Columbia. The passage is worth quoting in its entirety:

> Perhaps I may carry this line of thought further and ask what kind of Committee we are aiming to become. When you took the initiative in convening the Committee it delighted me personally because I hoped that here was a group where international relationists and historians might meet to mutual advantage. And I was thinking of course of the American Committee, the vast majority of whom are teachers of the subject ... with a leavening of philosophers like Niebuhr and ex-officials like Nitze. We however are moving so far in a different direction, not necessarily a bad thing, but interesting to observe. It is difficult to avoid analysing our composition as follows: 2 general historians ... [Butterfield and Desmond Williams], 2 historians whose field embraces contemporary history ... [Michael Howard and Geoffrey Hudson],[17] 1 philosopher [Donald Mackinnon], 1 Treasury official [William Armstrong], 1 Foreign Office man [Adam Watson], 1 student of international politics [Wight himself]. You know, I think, that I have always kept out of the arguments about the merits of International Relations, and that I do not have any prejudice against historians, rather the other way. All the same, the question does obtrude itself whether we are not a little lop-sided.[18]

This sentiment expressed by Wight explains why his protégé Hedley Bull was drafted into the Committee in 1961.[19] At that time Bull was a lecturer in International Relations at the London School of Economics. This group of nine remained the core of the Committee during the 1960s although the Committee received a number of guests throughout this period. The procedure for selecting members usually took the form of inviting a speaker to participate in one of the weekends – a kind of informal interview to see whether they were culturally and intellectually suitable.

An important consideration concerning the membership of the Committee was why certain other important International Relations scholars working in

Britain were not invited to participate. The two most obvious omissions were scholars F.H. Hinsley and E.H. Carr.[20] On this point the correspondence between Butterfield, Mackinnon and Wight is revealing. Mackinnon suggested Carr's name in late 1958, to which Wight replied,

> I should like to express the view that we should do better to establish a tradition of discussion between a few of us, some six to eight at most, than to expand rapidly. It might put a strain upon us individually at first in the matter of preparing papers or opening discussions, but it would allow us to develop some corporate purpose without being swamped. I wonder if you would agree.

> Rather for this reason, I hesitate about E.H. Carr. On personal grounds I would welcome his being invited, but *he is himself so much a Great Power in this region* that I should have misgivings lest he might deflect our discussions into channels opened up by his own work. For this same reason again, I should prefer not to coopt any St Antony's people before we have established our own line of enquiry.[21]

As we saw in Chapter 1, by this stage Carr had parted company with International Relations and devoted himself to his history of the Soviet Union. Apart from this shift in his political and intellectual interests, it is unlikely he would have been partial to the 'gentleman's club' *gestalt* of the Committee. Wielding the weapon of the relativity of thought in the direction of the Committee would surely have exposed the way in which the idea of international society served to mask over the interests of European imperial powers in general, and the declining prestige of a once hegemonic power in particular.

A perhaps more surprising omission from the proceedings of the British Committee was F.H. Hinsley, who was then a lecturer in history at the University of Cambridge. Adam Watson suggests a convincing explanation, that Hinsley 'sees Europe, and the world, as more of an anarchy and less of a society than Bull or myself.'[22] As we shall see in the following section, the exclusion of Hinsley from the British Committee exacted a price when the group eventually sought to publish a collection of papers. Another absentee was Charles Manning. Michael Howard suggests that 'Manning was too idiosyncratic (I don't think that Wight and Bull had much time for him anyway).'[23]

The location of the Committee at Peterhouse, Cambridge, and the rather tortuous discussions about the group's 'constitution', who was 'in' and who was 'out', suggests that cultural factors were built into the very foundations of the Committee. It was a close-knit community of scholars who were almost as interested in the occasion as the content of the papers. They met three times a year to hear a series of papers written specifically for the Committee (and usually circulated in advance) around a particular theme. After a paper had been presented, the Committee would engage in lengthy discussions concerning questions or issues raised. Herbert Butterfield placed more importance on these than Wight;[24] he originally intended to publish both the discussions and the papers, but eventually found this to be too demanding a task.[25] The transcripts tend to reinforce Wight's view that the discussions were too general for publication. One culprit in particular was Donald Mackinnon who, as Michael Howard recalled, 'sometimes talked at great length, very obscurely and a long way off the point, but he was such a delightful and amusing man that none of us really minded.'[26] Howard also paints a vivid picture of the ambience of the meetings: 'we simply sat around the table in the dining-room in the Master's Lodge at Peterhouse, with the chairman, a cigarette permanently in the corner of his mouth, endlessly taking notes and occasionally asking questions and making contributions.'[27]

Aims of the Committee

Martin Wight's essay 'Why is there no International Theory?' was presented at the inaugural meeting of the British Committee in January 1959. For Wight, the most obvious point about the history of international theory was its talk of a canon of classical texts. 'It may seem puzzling' mused Wight, 'that, while the acknowledged classics of political study are the political philosophers, the only acknowledged counterpart in the study of international relations is Thucydides, a work of history.'[28] Wight advances two reasons for the poverty of (international) theory. The first is 'the intellectual prejudice imposed by the sovereign state' as a result of the simple fact of the organisation of individuals into states. Wight argues that this 'has absorbed all the intellectual energy devoted to political study.'[29] The second explanation for the poverty of (international) theory is due to the historical fact that the freedom of states is conditioned by the necessity of the system. In a sentence which has 'launched a thousand exam questions,'[30] Wight hauntingly argues that: 'International politics is the realm of *recurrence* and *repetition*; it is the field in which political action is most regularly necessitous.' These fragments have been seized upon by critics of the English School as evidence of an ontological break in their thinking between the 'domestic' and the 'international.'[31]

At this point, Wight's colleagues could have been forgiven for thinking that the Committee might as well 'shut up shop' since he seemed to be undermining their very reason for existing. Such a literal act of closure would have been too hasty. The intention behind Wight's paper was to shape the Committee's theoretical investigations in the direction of discovering patterns of theory and practice in international relations, rather than focusing (as a good deal of political philosophy does) on questions of justice which take the existence of order for granted. There is no doubt that Wight succeeded in persuading the Committee of the urgent need for international theory, although subsequent papers on this question did little more than rehearse his argument.[32]

The way in which Wight framed the question about the nature of international theory has been the subject of considerable contention. Those sympathetic to natural law insist that by privileging a world of independent states, international theory is bound to be marginal to political theory. This objection is neatly articulated by Michael Donelan, who argued that if we do not begin 'with this assumption of separate states, there is all the international theory in the world to be done. For there is now a primordial community of mankind; separate states are but an arrangement of it.'[33] A related objection comes from political theorists who do not start out from the assumption of a latent cosmopolitanism but rather, recognise that sovereign states represent the will of a particular community. For them, Wight's representation of political theory in terms of speculation about the state commits him to making the 'basic mistake' of treating international relations and political theory as separate discourses. As Chris Brown argues, a more compelling definition of political theory would be framed in terms of a 'discourse on justice', thereby transforming the inside /outside relationship, in which case '[i]t would be no longer either possible or necessary to specify in advance a distinction between domestic and international political theory.'[34]

Whilst these criticisms are well founded, there is sense in which they obscure the principal motivation behind the paper. 'Why is there no International Theory?' should be understood in terms of his overriding intention to stimulate a debate on the nature of theory within the British Committee. This was the main message Wight conveyed to his British Committee colleagues, and their subsequent papers must be interpreted as a response to this challenge. That said, even allowing for the context to explain Wight's rather polemical dismissal of the 'paucity' of international theory, 'Why is there no International Theory' contained within it the kernel of an important argument about the constraints imposed by practice on theory. Some of the most influential great political theorists of out time, such as John Rawls, agree with his contention that whilst it is possible to debate competing conceptions of the 'good' within states, between the members of international society there is no consensus on the ends of political life.

After the third meeting, the Committee decided to review the aims of the organisation. These minutes provide perhaps the clearest statement of their intention to transcend the main assumptions and preoccupations of political realism. The lengthy extract below highlights how Herbert Butterfield and Martin Wight articulated a new agenda for the English School:

Herbert Butterfield mentioned the Committee that had sat for a few years in New York, and said that he was interested primarily as an historian, concerned to make past history continuous with present experience, and to see how far the more long-term views or surveys of the historian might affect one's appreciation of the present day. The intention had been that the Committee should not devote itself merely to diplomatic history and should avoid mere journalistic discussion of contemporary affairs, but should try to go rather deeper in its analyses and move in the direction of fundamental principles. Butterfield declared that, for his part, his interest in this field was stimulated by certain ethical obsessions and a desire to relate political conduct to ethics. Also he had the feeling that a lot of current assumptions concerning international politics ought to be re-examined. He did not think that it was the intention of the Committee to discuss the issue of the hydrogen-bomb.

Wight in general agreed with this statement, and expressed his interest in seeing events not only against a background of history but also in relation to ethical principles. He thought that the Committee would be helpful in the field of Political Science since the purpose was not merely to exchange factual information but to discover whether any forms of generalisation were possible. Also, it implied an attempt to *analyse the nature and the structure of that 'international society'* which had existed since the age of Machiavelli. At the same time he thought that the Committee, by tackling fundamental questions, might be valuable from the point of view of Political Philosophy.[35]

These passages underscore the way in which the two leading players in the Committee wished to orient the group around a normative theoretical agenda, rather than being conditioned by 'events' in the contemporary international system. Indeed, given the presence of practitioners in the organisation it is surprising how the Committee insulated themselves from the issues which dominated the global political environment in their day; questions such as the end of empire, Suez, the Cuban Missile Crisis, and the arms race. Their real interest did not lay in the present, but rather in the structure of international society, the rules by which it was constituted and the meanings that diplomats and state leaders gave to their actions.

Ontological Investigations

In the preface to *Diplomatic Investigations*, the editors describe international society as their 'frame of reference.'[36] It is certainly true that it was the referent object for their most significant papers, but it must also be said that the idea of a society of states barely figured in the majority of them. William Armstrong's papers concentrated on aspects of government such as decision-making,[37] Adam Watson on foreign and security policy,[38] Butterfield[39] and Desmond Williams[40] concentrated on diplomatic history in the main, and Michael Howard[41] and Geoffrey Hudson[42] presented papers on strategic studies. Although many of Donald Mackinnon's papers did concern themselves with the ethical basis of international society, they did not make an effective contribution to this debate.[43]

The main impetus to interrogate international society came from Martin Wight and Hedley Bull. Three of their papers stand out as being particularly influential: Wight's 'Western Values in International Relations'[44,] Bull's 'Society and Anarchy in International Relations', both given in October 1961, and Bull's 'The Grotian Conception of International Relations', presented in April the following year. These were Bull's only two papers given in the first period of the Committee, effectively vindicating Wight's earlier argument that the composition of the Committee needed to be strengthened by specialists in International Relations.[45]

Written when he was only 29 years old, 'Society and Anarchy' contains within it a formidable argument (and one which Bull was to hold fast to for the rest of his life). 'Society and Anarchy' clearly builds on Wight's attempt in his 'international theory' lectures to reveal the existence of a tradition of thought that was not adequately captured by either realism or idealism. 'The salient fact of international relations', Bull argued, was not eternal anarchy or immanent transformation, 'but co-operation among sovereign states in a society without government.'[46] According to Bull, two particular bodies of thinking have advanced a theory of international society; international law and the balance of power. Whilst the founding members of the committee had both written lengthy papers on the balance of power, the contribution of international law to international society had been neglected by the Committee. Below I will draw out their thinking on these two streams and how they filtered into their interpretation of international society.

Herbert Butterfield's essay on the balance of power was given at the Committee's second meeting in April 1959.[47] His narrative account relates the theory to three developments in seventeenth century history of ideas: the emergence of scientific ideas of mechanical forces in equilibrium; the notion of the balance of trade; and 'the theory of equipoise in the British constitution.'[48] By the eighteenth century, the balance of power had become a 'general theory of international politics'.[49] In a later essay, Butterfield makes more explicit the Burkean basis of the balance of power:

> It came to be understood that the system of states depended in fact on an underlying unity of culture, *a common sense of values and a pre-existing community of tradition and custom*. The international order itself, and the balance within it, depended on the assumption that all the participants were like members of the same club. A theory that was far from denying the egotism of states, called at times therefore for loyalty to the club itself and asked that egotism should stop short of a threat to the international order.[50]

Although Butterfield could be justly rebuked for not providing – consistent with he professed methodology – a detailed contextual recovery of instances where obligations generated by the balance of power shaped the interests and actions of state leaders, his account is interesting for the principal reason that it sees the balance of power as evidence of a collective European identity.

Two years after Butterfield's paper, Martin Wight presented a quite different approach to the balance of power.[51] Wight's essay complemented Butterfield's study by concentrating on the different possible meanings of the term, as opposed to tracing the history of the idea. From the point of view of the Committee as a whole, the importance of Wight's paper was not the multiplicity of meanings but rather the claim that from the Treaty of Utrecht to the First World War, 'the balance of power was generally spoken of as if it were the constituent principle of international society, and legal writers described it as the indispensable condition of international law.'[52] Bull clarified this position somewhat, by arguing that it was only with the positive lawyers of the eighteenth century that 'the two streams converged.'

Both the balance of power and international law also come together in a different sense. They are institutions – habits and practices as Bull was to call them later on – which require an obligation to act in the interests of international society as a whole. The source of the obligation is the sense of belonging, being a sovereign member, being bound by the rules. Herein lies the essence of international society. It exists in the activities of state leaders, and is reproduced in the treaties they sign, friendships they form, customs they observe, and laws they comply with. And crucially, it continues to exist even when treaties are torn up, and diplomatic relations are broken off. This point is well made by Bull: 'International action which, although it is contrary to recognized principles ... is accompanied by pretexts stated in terms of those principles, attests the force in international relations of right and wrong, just as does action which conforms to them.'[53]

'Western Values', Martin Wight's key paper on the society of states, recapitulates a number of these themes. But the question he is addressing is not whether international society exists, but whether the principles and practices which underpin it are distinctively European. Wight recognised the importance of this line of thinking, noting in correspondence that the paper contained the 'most substantial argument' he had contributed to the early years of the Committee. In order to answer the question, Wight turns to the history of ideas, and finds evidence of a distinctive set of Western values in the 'quality of a *via media*.' 'The cultivation of this middle ground' argues Wight, 'and the discovery of political morality, seem peculiarly related to Western values.'[54] By middle ground, Wight means 'a permissible accommodation between moral necessity and practical demands':

> And it assumes that moral standards can be upheld without the heavens falling. And it assumes that the fabric of social and political life will be maintained, without accepting the doctrine that to preserve it any measures are permissible. For it assumes that the upholding of moral standards will in itself tend to strengthen the fabric of political life. These assumptions seem to lie within the province of philosophy of history, or belief in Providence, whither it is not the purpose of this paper to pursue them.[55]

Although Wight seeks to defend 'moral standards', it is significant that he does not furnish a theory of knowledge on which to base moral claims. In which case, how did he respond to Carr's argument that the problem with morality in international politics was not due to any inadequacy on the part of the 'standard bearers', but rather the more profound question about whether a disinterested standard existed at all. Note how Wight extricated himself from this epistemological dilemma by assigning these questions to historicism and theology.

The subsidiary question Wight examines, which we find recurring in later English School thinking, is the extent to which Western values are able to withstand challenges to their ideological hegemony from the non-Western world. His discussion of Burke and the French revolution is instructive here. Wight argues that 'European society was more resilient' than Burke had feared. But how resilient is international society to changes in its constitution? 'Is it', asks Wight, 'indefinitely modifiable?' This is one of key questions Bull and Watson put before the British Committee in their final phase, in relation to the challenge posed by post-colonial states to the rules and institutions of international society.

Their understanding of the ontology of international society begins to unfold in the course of these discussions. Key institutions such as diplomacy and the balance of power were examined, and the background assumption of Western values considered. The one key institution which remained under-theorised was international law. Given the absence of an international lawyer from the Committee, it fell to Hedley Bull to fill this gap. His second paper to the British Committee 'The Grotian Conception of International Society' triggered an important discussion about the role of law, and the type of obligations generated by different forms of international society.

Bull sets up the paper in terms of a tension between the nineteenth century legal positivists or 'pluralists' (such as Oppenheim) and 'neo-Grotians' or 'solidarists' (such as Lauterpacht).[56] Bull defined the pluralist conception of international society as one in which states are capable of agreement only for certain minimum purposes, the most crucial being reciprocal recognition of sovereignty and the norm of non-intervention. For pluralists, the society of states is based primarily on a procedural conception of common values: this is neatly encapsulated by the thought that 'states are able to agree on the need for order despite their competing views of justice.'[57] In other words, whilst states do not share substantive goals and values, they nevertheless recognise that they are legally and morally bound by a common code of co-existence.

Against the pluralist conception stands solidarism with its central assumption of 'solidarity, or potential solidarity, of the states comprising international society, with respect to the enforcement of the law.'[58] Bull argues that the solidarist conception is a purposive one in that it seeks to subordinate the use of force in international politics to 'the collective will of the society of states'.[59] It is possible to identify two different manifestations of this collective will in Bull's early writings. The first concerns what he calls 'police action', where states exhibit solidarity in their response to law-breaking states which violate the cardinal rules and norms of the society of states. This is the collective security conception of solidarism which underpinned the League of Nations Covenant and influenced the framers of the United Nations Charter. But crucially, Bull's solidarism is not reducible to collective security. Even in his early discussion of the question, he indicated that a solidarist society of states had a responsibility to monitor the way in which particular states treated their own citizens. If a state failed to provide for the security of its citizens, then the society of states would have to consider suspending the non-intervention principle. In this respect, according to the solidarist theory, state leaders 'are burdened with the guardianship of human rights everywhere.'[60] In contrast to the pluralist emphasis upon the rights and duties of states, this deeper level of solidarism places the rights and duties of individuals at the centre of its ethical code.

Despite his fragmentary articulation of solidarist international society theory, the young Bull offered a trenchant critique of solidarism on both descriptive and normative grounds. According to Bull, the conception of international relations embodied in the League of Nations, the United Nations and more generally 'in Western thinking about international relations' should not only be condemned on the grounds that it was impractical but also that it was '*morally unsound...* constituting too simple a view of the moral dilemmas of international politics, and as being a system which it may be dangerous even to attempt to put into practice.'[61] By implementing solidarist grand designs, Bull thought that there was a danger of undermining the traditional devices for the maintenance of inter-state order.[62]

One could argue that the 'pluralism-solidarism' debate constructed in Bull's essay is considerably more important than the dubious methodology which underpinned it. By relying on Hersch Lauterpacht's commentary published in 1946,[63] Bull infers that the 'central Grotian assumption' of solidarity *is* the central assumption of Grotius.[64] Such a distortion flows easily from Bull's attempt to read the tension between the power political order and the normative legal order in terms of a dialogue between Oppenheim and Grotius. His instrumental approach to the history of ideas is evident in the discussion that followed: 'I had in mind', Bull reflected, 'to criticise the conception of international relations embodied in the League and United Nations and to some extent in Western thinking about international relations.'[65] If Bull's target was the League of Nations (and the internationalist ideas that underpinned it)[66] then why take the labyrinthine route of associating it with the work of Grotius? Moreover, all this was in the name of inventing a 'pluralist doctrine', which in turn required the resurrection of Oppenheim.

Hedley Bull's approach to the 'neo-Grotian' tradition contrasts sharply with the contextual account of Grotius provided by contemporary political theorists. According to Richard Tuck, Grotius believed that there were two essential natural rights (of dominion and of property) which are distilled into the general maxim, 'respect one another's rights.'[67] The important point about the 'rights' based interpretation of Grotius is that it transcends the natural law theory that Lauterpacht (and to a lesser extent, Bull) regard as central to the Grotian legacy.[68] According to the rights based interpretation, the link from 'rights' to international law is given by the domestic analogy between individuals and sovereign states.[69] In sum, the contextual recovery of Grotius's thinking challenges the international society argument for a Grotian tradition on two grounds: on a narrow point of interpretation and on a broader question of general methodology. In the case of the former, the international society focus on Grotius's insistence on restraint in war and resort to war, Bull's interpretation is on surest ground.[70] However, the degree to which this affords a 'solidarist' view of international society is contested by the contextual interpretation of Grotius, which argues that the only obligation for nation-states was not to harm each other – they were under no obligation to help each other.[71] This is an international society of self-interest not of solidarism.[72]

Not only is Bull's paper on the 'Grotian Conception of International Society' suspect on grounds of intellectual history, his defence of pluralism is open to the objection that it is little more than a diluted form of realism. The representation of 'pluralism' as a theory of state practice (advocating positive international law subordinated to the requirements of the balance of power, where war is a legitimate instrument of state policy) furnishes no effective moral code by which it is possible to judge the actions of states, the very argument which Bull mobilised so powerfully against Carr's political realism. The discussion which followed Bull's paper provides further evidence for the influence that Carr exerted over Bull. 'It generally seems to me', Bull reflected, 'that the League of Nations picture of the world is criticised on grounds that it is impracticable, but not on the grounds that it is morally unsound ...'[73] Bull explained in more depth his motives for presenting the paper in the discussion which followed:

> [Lauterpacht] argues that the Grotian conception of international society is a sound one and a morally admirable one .... Whereas *I want to take an unfavourable view of Grotius*, and to try and rehabilitate the nineteenth century positivist international lawyers and the view particularly of Oppenheim, who, given that he had the limitations of a lawyer thinking about international politics, seems to me to have written more sensibly about international relations than certainly many other international lawyers and many other thinkers.[74]

He concludes the discussion by reiterating his ethical critique of the Grotian conception of international society for assuming universality in international society: 'The doctrine of Natural Law is an anti-historical doctrine, and it really simply posits a moral unanimity irrespective of what the history of a particular society is, irrespective of whether people in fact form a moral community.'[75] This is the first sign of a recurring tension in Bull's thinking due to his simultaneous critique of ethical universalism in solidarist-cum-idealist thinking *and* realism for not recognising 'the good of international society as a whole.'[76]

The two principal members of the Committee lined up on opposite sides of Bull's argument. Wight criticised his junior colleague on methodological grounds, for his 'cavalier use of evidence.'[77] As the passage below highlights, Wight was critical of the conservative undercurrent of 'pluralism' and its toleration of war as an instrument of statecraft:

> The stand point from which the Grotian conception is criticised is one which erects certain historical institutions on international society – the laws of war, neutrality, alliances, sovereignty and the obligations of citizens to bear arms in defence of their country – into something like idols. Ought the world to be so attached to these institutions that it should consider no modification in them? Or to put the question in a more fundamental way, are there no aspects of International Relations which urge the sensitive and intelligent man to strive for their amelioration? The Grotian premise, explicit both in Grotius and his 20th century followers, is that war is an intolerable evil. H.B.'s alternative position is that war is a tolerable and necessary evil.[78]

Bull's argument prompted a more sympathetic response from Herbert Butterfield.[79]

> The real implication of Hedley Bull's lucid paper then – and I think it is a profound implication – is that the Grotian conception of international society gets in the way of a realistic view of the world situation. It leaves statesmen to think in terms of punishing unjust enemies rather than in terms of setting up a viable balance or distribution of power. The Grotian system sets nations to thinking about international morality in an epoch when international morality may not be sufficient by itself to guarantee peace and stability. The Grotian conception sets statesmen and scholars thinking about the justice of the world order rather than the workability of the world order. And Hedley Bull is surely right in thinking that we are in such an early stage in the evolution of world society that the most we can hope for now is workability.[80]

What we see here in the British Committee's early discussions on international law is two rival conceptions of the relationship between the management of power, the autonomy of states, and their obligations to international society. Both Hedley Bull and Herbert Butterfield feared law and morality running ahead of state practice, thereby endangering stability. Martin Wight, on the other hand, was critical of their complacency and the 'sorry comfort' they gave to state practice. In his later thinking, Bull became far more critical of Vattel, who unlike Grotius, 'never gave the impression of having looked over into the abyss of international anarchy.'[81] Although Bull's thinking on the relative merits of pluralism and solidarism shifted, as we shall see in Chapter 7, these rival conceptions of international society remained his anchor.

Publishing the Early British Committee Papers
By the autumn of 1962, the Committee was coming to the end of the three year period that the Rockefeller Foundation had initially agreed to fund. It was the prospect of having to ask for additional support that concentrated Butterfield's mind on the issue of publishing some of the early papers. In fact, in his letter requesting (in a roundabout way) further funding, Butterfield tried to head off any criticism with the following confession: '[t]he chief snag has been that we haven't published anything, and I don't know how far that would affect the attitude of the Foundation.'[82] He hastily added that a proposed 'table of contents' was at the top of the agenda for the next meeting.

The original title for the volume was to be 'Essays on International Theory'. Wight thought that this was too sober, and suggested *Diplomatic Investigations*.[83] Although the work was published in 1966, all of the essays were given to the Committee before the end of 1962. The delay was caused in part because of Herbert Butterfield's rather ambitious plans to synthesise both the essays and the discussions into a single volume. Given how sought after copies of the collection are today, it might come as a surprise to many that the original submission was not considered to be worthy of publication. In August 1965, Butterfield received a letter from Cambridge University Press expressing regret at not being able to publish the work as they felt that 'the contributions were very much "occasional papers"'.[84] Butterfield's reaction, expressed in a letter to Wight, gives an insight into the personal politics at the University and within the Committee:

> Though one can never be absolutely sure, I am pretty sure, from one or two very concrete points, that Hinsley is the author of this. He is in a curious state at the moment. I learn from the Chairman of the History Board that he has given serious trouble because he has not been

nominated for a Chair – he has long been more impatient about this than anybody else. Also, he will be very conscious of the fact that we have not made him a member of the Committee.[85]

Irrespective of the identity of the referee, the two main criticisms of the volume are of interest. In the first instance, the papers were out of date.[86] As one of the referees commented: 'In a book list of 60 selected references, recently prepared for students, more than half the books had been published in the last two years. All would have been published since these essays were first written.' Second, the contributions failed to consider properly the emerging literature on International Relations coming out of America which, argued the referee, 'cannot be pushed aside as passing fashions.'

In view of his concern about 'the effect of this rebuff on the whole future of the Committee,'[87] Martin Wight decided to try Allen and Unwin[88] who were in favour on condition that the editors cut the contributions from seventeen to twelve. Although the completed *Diplomatic Investigations* was nominally a co-edited volume, it is apparent from the correspondence that it was Wight who was the principal editor. He wrote the important 'preface' for the original version which was rewritten to take account of the changes in the composition of the book.[89] The final version was expanded to include 'more about the way in which we have understood the term International Theory' and 'to make clearer our position as against the contemporary school of International Theory'.[90] Although the preface does indeed contain fragments about the distinctive approach taken by the British Committee, the full-blown assault on behaviouralism did not emerge until the second phase of their proceedings (considered in the next chapter).

Conclusion

The historical narrative on the organisational aspects of the Committee sheds light on a number of previously unanswered questions concerning the involvement of the Rockefeller Foundation and the criteria for membership of the Committee. What emerges from this institutional history is a view of the Committee as an élite 'club' drawing from the senior ranks of the traditional universities and the civil service. Added to this, the extraordinary counter-factual thought that this very British Committee would not have existed without the $4000 grant from one of America's leading social science foundations.[91]

In terms of academic International Relations, what is interesting about the early years of the Committee is the members' collective belief that the discipline was far broader than the debate between realism and idealism had allowed for. As a result, their agenda was not restricted to the vindication of international organisations or the subordination of politics to the principle of original sin. Neither did the committee intend to tilt before the imperatives of policy-makers, a tendency which signalled the demise of the original Rockefeller Committee in the United States. Rather, their purpose was to 'analyse the nature and the structure of that "international society"' and the 'principles of prudence and moral obligation' which held it together.

The Committee's point of departure was Martin Wight's 'Why is there no International Theory?' presented at the inaugural meeting in January 1959. Wight's polemical essay opened the way to a construction of international theory as historical interpretation, thereby reaffirming the approach to international theory he had taken in his lectures at the London School of Economics. Perhaps a more sober guide to the view of theory maintained by the Committee can be found in Wight's preface to *Diplomatic Investigations* in which the notion of theory emerges in the form of principles arrived at inductively from philosophical and historical experience. As Wight put it in a letter to Butterfield, 'to a large extent we are rediscovering and restating truths and views which have been traditional in the European diplomatic community.'[92] Therefore, the Committee's view of theory was one that was driven *and* constrained by practice. It was not until after the papers for *Diplomatic Investigations* had been completed, that the Committee became self-conscious of the growing bifurcation in British and American approaches to International Relations.

In the most important of the early Committee papers, the 'truths' that they were 'rediscovering and restating' included the practices of the balance of power, the diplomatic dialogue, and international law. Crucially, none of these institutions were self-regulating, not even the balance of power. In Butterfield's words, order in international society 'is not a thing bestowed upon by nature, but is a matter of refined thought, careful contrivance and elaborate artifice.'[93] This position is distinct from modern forms of realism which tend to regard order either as an unintended consequence of the pursuit of self-interest, or as a deliberate imprint made by power. Therefore, for Butterfield and his Committee, a rationalist approach to statecraft required balancing the interests of the state with the wider interests of the society as a whole.

In a number of the Committee papers, the balance of power is likened to the first article in the 'constitution' of international society. Here we see an interesting tension emerge between this tentative constitutional analogy and Hedley Bull's attempt to impose an ontological break between society inside the state and the society shared by states. Moreover, the distinction between the domestic and the international, inside and outside, is blurred by the solidarist theory of international legitimacy which refuses to leave the question of compliance to 'moral standards' to the consent of individual states alone. The norm of non-intervention, on this account, may be suspended (in exceptional circumstances) to maintain civilised standards of behaviour. This argument of Wight's raises a number of key issues addressed in subsequent British Committee papers and taken up by more contemporary English School thinkers like R.J. Vincent. What, for instance, is to count as civilised practices both within the state and in relations between states, and what actions are legitimate (and by whom) in response to a breach of these moral standards? How can Butterfield's concern that solidarism 'gets in the way of a better system of international practice' be assuaged?[94] These two stories about international society, with a solidarist theory grounded in cosmopolitan ethics at one end of the continuum, advocated (albeit cautiously) by Wight, and the legal positivist side defended by the Bull and Butterfield at the other, resurface in Bull's more mature work on justice and Vincent's path-breaking study of human rights in international relations.

NOTES

1. Hedley Bull, 'Introduction: Martin Wight and the Study of International Relations', in Martin Wight, *Systems of States* (Leicester: Leicester University Press, 1977), 15.
2. Herbert Butterfield and Martin Wight (eds), *Diplomatic Investigations: Essays in the Theory of International Politics* (London: Allen and Unwin, 1966); Wight, *Systems of States*; Hedley Bull and Adam Watson (eds), *The Expansion of International Society* (Oxford: Clarendon, 1984).
3. Biographical sources include the following: Herbert Butterfield, private papers, Cambridge University Library; Martin Wight, private papers, maintained by Gabriele Wight; Hedley Bull, private papers, Nuffield College, Oxford; British Committee papers held at the Royal Institute of International Affairs, London. The only 'secondary' source on the British Committee is the Introduction to the Italian edition of *The Expansion of International Society*, with the new subtitle 'Europe and the rest of the world from the end of the Middle Ages to Today'. See Brunello Vigezzi, 'The British Committee on the Theory of International Politics' (1958–1985), Introduction to *L'Espansione Della Societa Internazionale: L'Europa e il Mondo della fine del Medioevo ai tempi nostri* (Milan: Jaca Book, 1994, trans. Roberta Guerrina). Whilst Vigezzi's 'introduction' has

been meticulously researched, and contains a good deal of important material, it borders on hagiography. For example, he illustrates the origins of the British Committee with phrases about how it gave Butterfield (then 'at the peak of his career') the opportunity to 'reunite' with colleagues and friends at his 'beloved' Peterhouse. Vigezzi, 'The British Committee', 7.

4.   Kenneth W. Thompson's works include the following: *Political Realism and the Crisis of World Politics: An American Approach to Foreign Policy* (Princeton: Princeton University Press, 1960); 'Idealism and Realism: Beyond the Great Debate', *British Journal of International Studies*, 3 (1977), 159–180; *Ethics, Functionalism and Power in International Politics* (Baton Rouge: Louisiana State University Press, 1979); (ed.), *Masters of International Thought* (Baton Rouge: Louisiana State University Press, 1980).

5.   Hans J. Morgenthau and Kenneth W. Thompson (eds), *Principles and Problems of International Politics: Selected Readings* (Alfred Knopf: University Press of America: Washington, 1950); Hans J. Morgenthau, *Politics Among Nations: The Struggle for Power and Peace* (New York: McGraw-Hill, 6 ed., 1985).

6.   This is Coll's description. See Alberto Coll, *The Wisdom of Statecraft: Sir Herbert Butterfield and the Philosophy of International Politics* (Durham: Duke University Press, 1985), 10.

7.   W.T.R. Fox (ed.), *Theoretical Aspects of International Relations* (Notre Dame: University of Notre Dame Press, 1959).

8.   Letter from Kenneth W. Thompson to the author (7 June 1993).

9.   Letter from Herbert Butterfield to Kenneth W. Thompson (26 April 1954).

10.   This judgement was made against the backdrop of a rather unfavourable portrait of Manning painted by Butterfield. Letter from Herbert Butterfield to Kenneth W. Thompson (17 October 1956).

11.   In the letter sent to Houghton St, the background to the Committee and the importance of Wight's prospective contribution is outlined by Butterfield. 'For some time now Kenneth Thompson has been suggesting to me that it would be nice to have a similar committee with its centre in Cambridge, and when I saw him again this Easter, he asked me once more if I would see whether this was possible, though he has not put the matter formally to his corporation, he gives it as his opinion that the Rockefeller Foundation would support the committee in the way it has supported the Columbia committee. I have in fact been hesitating about this for a year or two, partly because in this country there is a greater leaning to the concrete study of diplomatic history or the more topical discussion of current affairs, both of which might be calculated to carry discussion far from the main purpose. I hesitated also because I heard first that you were going to Australia, and then that you were unwell, and if you were not available I don't know that the thing would be possible at all. I have been talking the matter over with Professor Desmond Williams of Dublin, who is interested in very much the same kind of thing and who was with Kenneth Thompson in New York shortly before my visit. We all feel that a moment has come when fundamental discussions might be more relevant than ever before, and all of us – i.e. including Kenneth Thompson – feel that your attitude to the matter would be important.' Butterfield to Wight (6 May 1958).

12. Letter from Herbert Butterfield to Martin Wight (12 April 1954). A preliminary meeting took place between Butterfield, Wight, Mackinnon and Williams in September 1959. See Vigezzi, 'The British Committee', 7.

13. Letter from Michael Howard to the author (7 January 1992).

14. Butterfield was keenly aware of the presence of intellectuals who were high-ranking 'professionals' in the American Committee. In earlier correspondence with Thompson, Butterfield noted: 'We are unfortunate in one respect here. We haven't a class of people corresponding to George Kennan and Halle. On the other hand, I do know one to two people in the middle ranks of the Foreign Office who are greatly interested in talking about just the kind of thing that I am concerned with.' Herbert Butterfield to Kenneth W. Thompson (17 October 1956).

15. Letter from Herbert Butterfield to Martin Wight (10 March 1959). Watson, like Williams, was a former pupil of Butterfield's.

16. Letter from Sir Michael Howard to the author, (7 January 1992).

17. Geoffrey Hudson was a fellow of St Antony's College and an expert on China and 'international communism'. Wight was concerned initially not to invite anyone from St Antony's in case they deflected the discussions into 'area studies' rather than 'international theory'. Wight to Butterfield (30 December 1958).

18. Wight to Butterfield, 2nd February 1960. Emphasis added.

19. Although Wight had suggested his membership as early as December 1958. Letter from Martin Wight to Herbert Butterfield (30 December 1958). In correspondence with Wight, Butterfield reflected on the wise decision to bring Bull into the Committee: 'All of you know that I did not suggest Bull's membership, because I did not know him, but I understood right away that he was the right man for us. He appears to know exactly what I think about the structural problems in International Relations.' Quoted in Vigezzi, 'The British Committee', 21.

20. Perhaps surprisingly, Michael Howard wrote that 'I don't think that any of the three figures you mention [Manning, Carr, Hinsley] were felt to have anything specific to contribute.' Letter from Michael Howard to the author, (7 January 1992).

21. Letter from Martin Wight to Herbert Butterfield (30 December 1958). Emphasis added.

22. Watson, *The Evolution*, 8. Michael Howard added that 'Hinsley had not yet written very much (and it is possible that his relations with Butterfield were not very close).'

23. Clearly, Manning's work *was* highly idiosyncratic, although it is worth noting that one of Bull's most influential papers on 'Society and Anarchy' acknowledges his intellectual debt to Manning. Hedley Bull, 'Society and Anarchy in International Relations', (October 1961). Letter from Michael Howard to the author, (7 January 1992).

24. In correspondence with Butterfield, Martin Wight noted that he had 'always thought the discussions more discursive and less constructive than you did – though none the less valuable and enjoyable.' Letter from Martin Wight to Herbert Butterfield (10 August 1965).

25. Letter from Herbert Butterfield to Kenneth W. Thompson (October 5 1962).

26. Letter from Sir Michael Howard to the author, (7 January 1992). Mackinnon's idiosyncratic style, and imperialist predisposition, can be inferred from his contribution to the discussion on the cultural bases of international society: 'is it ever possible to tolerate those with whom we cannot communicate?' Mackinnon, in British Committee discussion on 'international society', (8 October 1961).

27. He adds that the discussions were taken quite seriously and were 'intellectually absorbing'. Many of the Committee's *alumni* testify to the seriousness of the discussions and the impact they had on their later work. According to Geoffrey Best, the British Committee influenced 'everything I've done in IR or near to it'. Letter to the author, (20 December 1992).

28. Wight, 'Why is there no International Theory?', 32. This distinction between the fertility of the political theory of domestic society versus the paucity of the political theory of international society is one which has been repeated in the discipline. For example, W.B. Gallie argues 'that there is no tradition of philosophy of international or inter-state relations', but he adds: 'There are at least certain threads which could be regarded as materials for, or harbingers of, such a tradition.' W.B. Gallie, 'Wanted: A Philosophy of International Relations', *Political Studies*, 27 (1979), 484

29. Wight, 'Why is there no International Theory?', 20, 21.

30. Chris Brown, 'Sorry Comfort? The Case Against "International Theory"', in Frank R. Pfetsch (ed.), *International Relations and Pan-Europe: Theoretical Approaches and Empirical Findings* (Lit Verlag: Hamburg, 1993), 89

31. See, for example, R.B.J. Walker, *Inside/Outside: International Relations as Political Theory* (Cambridge: Cambridge University Press, 1993), 33–34.

32. The impact of Wight's argument can be seen in Donald Mackinnon's paper, given to the second Committee meeting where Mackinnon argued that: 'While it is perfectly true that most political theorists have largely neglected the issues raised by the involvement of individual human societies in an international community, the same is certainly not true of some of those who have essayed what may be comprehended under the term 'philosophy of history'.' Donald Mackinnon, "Philosophy of History and the Problems of International Relations"', (April, 1959). In a much later discussion, Butterfield recalls how 'Why?' informed their understanding of theory: 'Martin Wight, in the first of his papers, drew attention to the fact that there has been so little fine literature on the theory of international politics ... I remember telling the Committee, in the course of the discussion of that paper, how, for many years, I had made it my slogan that "Political Theory is the enemy"'. Butterfield, 'Notes for a Discussion on the Theory of International Politics', (January 1964).

33. Michael Donelan, 'The Political Theorists and International Theory', in Donelan (ed.), *The Reason of States* (London: Allen and Unwin, 1978), 90.

34. Brown, 'Sorry Comfort?', 92–93.

35. Desmond Williams contributed the following to the discussion: 'In my view the Committee did not come together either for the purpose of arranging an agreed outlook on international relations in general or for the purpose of merely discussing current affairs. Its real function was to bring together a group of people with a common, though not a similar, interest in international

relations from an historical and a theoretical viewpoint. ... It is also important that the phrase 'historical', as used above, should be interpreted as widely as possible, it would be unwise to tie ourselves to a fixed programme or to attempt to achieve any definition of our aims except in the widest and vaguest terms.' Donald Mackinnon reiterated Wight's concern that 'international theory' was underdeveloped, and added that 'as a philosopher' he found the Committee 'useful in that it gave him an association with those who had much of the relevant factual knowledge.' He also confessed to being an 'amateur internationalist' with some sympathy for the Campaign for Nuclear Disarmament 'though he had a horror of campaigns'. The objective of the Committee, according to Michael Howard, 'could not be achieved by just introducing any member of the Foreign Office or a military historian, and that what united us was the interest in a certain kind of analysis and in the discussion of underlying principles.' Adam Watson 'said he came to the Committee as a student or observer of events who wanted to examine the patterns that were produced, and the correlations that could be made. He added that there were two worlds of international relations, the theorists and the practitioners, and that 'in the U.S. there had been an interesting attempt to bring the two together. This kind of thing has been rather lacking in England.' This theme was followed up by Robert Armstrong, who 'found himself repeatedly reflecting on the relations between theory and practice' and thought that 'it was useful to exchange ideas with those who had made a more academic study of these things – particularly with those who tried to deal systematically with events in their historical context.' 'Discussion on the Objects of the Committee' (September, 1959). Emphasis added.

36.   Butterfield and Wight (eds); *Diplomatic Investigations*, 12. Emphasis added.
37.   His two papers in this first period (1959–1962) were 'The Nature of the Decision-Making Process' (January 1960) and 'Working Together' (September 1960).
38.   'The Methods used by Governments to suborn or influence the Subjects of Another State' (April 1959), 'Interests of States other than Vital Interests' (September 1959), 'The Foreign Policy of Newly Independent States (October 1961), 'The Problems facing the Newly Independent States of West Africa' (October 1962).
39.   Butterfield's opening paper, 'Misgivings about the Western Attitude to World Affairs' re-iterated his objections to a 'moralistic approach' to international relations. His other papers in this period were: 'Crowe's Memorandum of 1st January 1907' (September 1960), 'The New Diplomacy and Historical Diplomacy' (September 1960). His most theoretical contribution, with relevance to the ontology of international society, was 'The Balance of Power' (April 1959). These last two papers were published in Butterfield and Wight, (eds), *Diplomatic Investigations*.
40.   'Aspects of the Role of Strategy in International Relations' (April 1959); 'The Primacy of Foreign Policy' (September 1959), 'The Role of National Prejudice in the Formation of Foreign Policy' (January 1960), 'Machiavellianism in Twentieth Century Diplomacy' (July 1961). His main theoretical contribution to the Committee's thinking on international society was a talk he gave on 'International Morality' (October 1961), of which there is no written paper.

41. 'Vital Interests' (April 1959), 'Scientific Developments in International Relations' (January 1960), 'Sovereignty in the Nuclear Age' (April 1961), 'War as an Instrument of Policy' (July 1960), 'Problems of a Disarmed World' (October 1962) – both published in *Diplomatic Investigations*.

42. 'Threats of Force in International Relations' (April 1961), and 'Collective Security and Military Alliances' (April 1962), 'The Communist Theory of International Relations' (October 1962). The first two were published in *Diplomatic Investigations*.

43. Martin Wight clearly recognised this. In their discussions about which papers should be published in *Diplomatic Investigations*, Butterfield proposed Mackinnon's paper on 'The Philosophy of History', which provoked the following response from Wight: 'After getting your letter, I took the opportunity to read Mackinnon's paper again. I entirely agree with your own judgement of it. It is deeply interesting, and pregnant with hints and insights for which I at least am deeply grateful. But I think it is irrelevant to our main concern. There is virtually nothing in it relating directly to international theory.' Wight to Butterfield, 29 April 1963. Mackinnon's papers between 1959 and 1962 included: 'What is the Attraction of Communism Today?' (January 1959), 'Philosophy of History and the Problems of International Relationships' (April 1959), 'What is the real Persona of the Community?' (September 1959), 'Natural Law' (January 1960, published in *Diplomatic Investigations*, 'Freewill and Determinism in Relation to International Theory' (July 1960), 'Western Values' (September 1960), 'Some Notes on the Notion of a Christian Statesman' (July 1962). For a more favourable evaluation of Mackinnon's work, see Vigezzi, 'The British Committee', 11.

44. Wight's other papers in this period were: 'Why is there no international theory?' (January 1959), 'Has scientific development transformed International Relations' (January 1960), 'The balance of power' (April 1961), 'Western Values in International Relations' (October 1961). All but his second paper were published in *Diplomatic Investigations*.

45. Later correspondence shows that Butterfield was persuaded by Wight's arguments on the need for a core of International Relations theorists. This is evident from the advice Butterfield gave to Peter Savigear from Leicester University who expressed an interest in forming a parallel theory group. In Butterfield's words, 'My own view would be that a similar group in Leicester would be an excellent thing – I mean a group recruited from appropriate people in universities in the British Isles, but reinforced if possible e.g. by one man from the Foreign Office, one from the Treasury, but with a nucleus of people from departments of International Relations in universities. Although one feels that there are people in varied realms who would make a contribution (e.g. the military historian, the expert on armaments, the expert on Pacific studies etc.) my own personal view (but a very strong one) would be that the students of International Politics generally should have the real lead and should envisage a Theory of International Politics as the end – taking care that the group should not merely turn to the discussion of Current Affairs.' Letter from Herbert Butterfield to Peter Savigear (16 February 1970)

46. Bull, 'Society and Anarchy', in Butterfield and Wight, *Diplomatic Investigations*, 38.

47. Herbert Butterfield, 'The Balance of Power', (April 1959), in Butterfield and Wight (eds), *Diplomatic Investigations*.
48. Butterfield, 'The Balance of Power', 141.
49. Herbert Butterfield, 'Balance of Power', *Dictionary of the History of Ideas – Vol. 1* (New York: Scribners, 1973), 179–188.
50. Butterfield, 'Balance of Power', *Dictionary*, 185. Emphasis added. Note how Butterfield's conception of the balance of power and its function in the European Commonwealth is remarkably Burkean in character. For an exposition of Burke's ideas, see Jennifer M. Welsh 'Edmund Burke and the Commonwealth of Europe: The Cultural Bases of International Order', in Ian Clark and Iver B. Neumann (eds), *Classical Theories of International Relations* (London: Macmillan, 1996), 173–92. Other writers on diplomatic history see homogeneity as an *a priori* condition for a successful balance of power. See V.Gulick, *Europe's Classical Balance of Power: A Case History of the Theory and Practice of One of the Great Concepts of European Statecraft* (New York: Norton, 1955), 19–24.
51. Martin Wight, 'The Balance of Power', (April 1961), published in Butterfield and Wight (eds), *Diplomatic Investigations*.
52. Wight, 'The Balance of Power', 153. Within the Committee, this normative theory of the balance of power did not command widespread agreement. For example, in response to Wight's question of whether the balance of power 'is the guarantee of the independence of nations? or is it the occasion of war?' (174–175), Michael Howard argues that 'the balance of power may be the only *modus vivendi* among sovereign states, but its operation seems to lead to war with monotonous regularity.' Michael Howard, 'Vital Interests', (April, 1959).
53. Bull, 'Society and Anarchy', 42.
54. Wight, 'Western Values', 128.
55. Wight, 'Western Values', 131.
56. Hedley Bull, 'The Grotian Conception of International Society', (April 1962) published in Butterfield and Wight (eds), *Diplomatic Investigations*.
57. Andrew Linklater, *Beyond Realism and Marxism: Critical Theory and International Relations* (London: Macmillan, 1990), 20.
58. Bull, 'The Grotian Conception', 52.
59. Hedley Bull, *The Anarchical Society* (London: Macmillan, 1997), 238.
60. Bull, 'The Grotian Conception', 63.
61. Discussion, 'The Grotian Conception of International Society', (April 1962).
62. Bull, 'The Grotian Conception', 72.
63. Hersch Lauterpacht, 'The Grotian Tradition in International Law', *British Yearbook of International Law* (1946), 1–53.
64. Bull's later writings on Grotius do not repeat so definitively the argument made in his British Committee paper that 'the central Grotian assumption is that of the solidarity of states' in international society. In his essay on 'The Importance of Grotius' written more than two decades later, Bull argues that the core of the Grotian tradition is to be found in the broad range of agreement on the rules of international society. See Hedley Bull, 'The Importance of Grotius', in Hedley Bull, Benedict Kingsbury and Adam Roberts (eds), *Hugo Grotius and International Relations* (Oxford: Clarendon, 1990), 72–73.

65. Hedley Bull, in the discussion on 'The Grotian Conception of International Society', (15 April 1962). In his later work, Oppenheim took a favourable view of both Grotius and the League of Nations. For example, in 1921 Oppenheim referred to *De Jure Belli ac Pacis* as an 'immortal work' whose author 'stands on the shoulders of his predecessors'. It is interesting that Oppenheim put forward a limited 'constitution' for the 'international community' which included a 'permanent institution' of peace conferences. Lassa Oppenheim, *The Future of International Law* (Oxford: Clarendon, 1921), 1, 3, 18–19.

66. See, for example, Lauterpacht, *The Function of Law in the International Community* (Oxford: Clarendon, 1933).

67. Richard Tuck, *Natural Rights Theories: Their Origin and Development* (Cambridge: Cambridge University Press, 1979), 67.

68. See 'Introduction' to Bull, Kingsbury and Roberts (eds), *Hugo Grotius*, 30.

69. As Tuck put it, 'private individuals and states were interchangeable with respect to property, and a state's boundaries were the same kind of thing as the boundaries of a private estate'. Tuck, *Natural Rights Theories*, 63.

70. Introduction to Bull, Kingsbury and Roberts (eds), *Hugo Grotius*, 28. Also, Lauterpacht, 'The Grotian Tradition in International Law', 19.

71. Richard Tuck, *Hobbes* (Oxford: Oxford University Press, 1989), 21.

72. See Michael Donelan, 'Grotius and the Image of War', *Millennium* 12 (1983), 241.

73. Discussion, 'The Grotian Conception of International Society', (April 1962).

74. Bull partly qualifies his criticism of Grotius by noting that he was 'not trying to object to the whole Grotian system', but that the main thrust of his argument against Grotius is aimed at the Just War tradition. Discussion, 'The Grotian Conception of International Society', (April 1962).

75. Discussion, 'The Grotian Conception of International Society' (April 1962).

76. Hedley Bull, '*The Twenty Years' Crisis* Thirty Years On', *International Journal*, 24 (1969), 629.

77. Martin Wight, 'Comment on Hedley Bull's Paper "The Grotian Conception of International Society"', (paper not dated but postmarked 12. 8. 1962). Wight concludes that '[t]here are no clear criteria for detecting Grotian influences in practice'. But there is an inconsistency here. In 'Western Values', Wight explicitly links the League with Grotianism: 'After 1919, the Grotians discovered, with a kind of messianic wonder, that the doctrines of the master had at last, after three hundred years, been embodied in the first written constitution of international society.' Martin Wight, 'Western Values', 105.

78. Wight, 'Comment on Hedley Bull's Paper', 2.

79. Herbert Butterfield, 'Alternative Conceptions of International Law', (July 1962).

80. Butterfield, 'Alternative Conceptions of International Law', 3.

81. Andrew Hurrell, 'Vattel: Pluralism and its Limits', in Clark and Neumann (eds), *Classical Theories*, 250.

82. Letter from Butterfield to Thompson (5 October 1962).

83. Letter from Martin Wight to Herbert Butterfield (13 May 1965).

84. Letter from R. David to Herbert Butterfield (4 August 1965).

85. Letter from Herbert Butterfield to Martin Wight, (13 August 1965).
86. Herbert Butterfield's paper 'The New Diplomacy' came in for particularly severe criticism: 'This essay suffers, like most of them, from being out of date. It was originally written in 1960. It will not be published for at least another year, and the "new diplomacy" will appear to be very old.' Cambridge University Press, referee's comments, (11 August 1965). Even in the published version there remained some glaring examples of intellectual antiquity. For example, Geoffrey Hudson's second paper 'Threats of Force in International Relations' was reprinted without reference to the Cuban Missile Crisis of October 1962. The footnote after the title reads: 'This paper was written in April 1961. We have printed it without alteration, so that the reader may test it against subsequent events.-Ed.' Herbert Butterfield and Martin Wight (eds), *Diplomatic Investigations*, 201.
87. Letter from Martin Wight to Herbert Butterfield (10 August 1965).
88. Oxford University Press was considered by Wight, but he decided against it on the grounds that it had recently accepted a *Festschrift* for Charles Manning, which Wight described as 'altogether a less distinguished collection than our Rockefeller book.' Letter from Martin Wight to Herbert Butterfield (10 August 1965).
89. Letter from Martin Wight to Herbert Butterfield (13 May 1965).
90. Letters from Martin Wight to Herbert Butterfield (1 October 1965; 11 January 1966).
91. In January of 1959, the assistant secretary of the Rockefeller Foundation, wrote to Butterfield confirming that the Committee had been awarded a sum of $4000 'for use by the British Committee on the Theory of International Politics for research and conferences'. This sum was for the first three years. Janet M. Paine to Herbert Butterfield (21 January 1959).
92. Letter from Martin Wight to Herbert Butterfield (15 October 1965).
93. Butterfield, 'The Balance of Power', 147.
94. Butterfield, 'Alternative Conceptions of International Law', (July 1962).

6 The British Committee II

As the first stage of the Rockefeller funding was coming to an end, Butterfield wrote to Thompson noting with missionary-like enthusiasm his intention to lead the Committee into the next stage, subject of course to further Rockefeller support:

> I must confess that the last two or three meetings have been so good – the discussions, in my view, so much better than ever – that I have been deterred from taking any step that would end the Committee. It is quite a wonderful thing that these Professors etc. from various Universities are passionately keen on continuing the Committee, if that is possible at all. Our Foreign Office representative, who has been Ambassador in Dakar, has kept a great interest in the Committee, and, now that he is back in England, wants very much to continue. Our Treasury man, William Armstrong was pulled up to the top in Macmillan's July coup d'état (you may have read the interesting profile of him in last Sunday's *Observer*). I feared he would say he was too busy for our Committee. But he, too, is as keen as ever.[1]

Although the original cell of the Committee remained, they lost the services of Bull for most of the 1960s and early 1970s. In 1963, Bull went to Princeton for the year to work with (among others) the 'salvationist' Richard Falk; in early 1965 he was drafted into the Arms Control and Disarmament Research Unit and by June 1967 he was back in Australia taking up a Professorship at the Australia National University. During this time, Donald McLachlan became an occasional member of the Committee.[2] They also hosted a number of guest speakers, the most high-profile being Thomas Schelling, whose visit was the catalyst for some frantic cramming on recent American contributions to International Relations.

After a year long respite in 1963, the Committee resumed with a new agenda centred upon two particular themes.[3] The first was their growing awareness of a distinction between their approach to International Relations in comparison to American 'behaviouralism'. Hedley Bull's 'International Theory: The Case for a Classical Approach'[4] is, of course, the paradigmatic English School assault on the wave of scientism sweeping through American International Relations in the 1950s and 1960s. From the analysis below, it is clear that Bull's essay developed in the context of the British Committee's proceedings, suggesting a need to revise the view that Bull was the only traditionalist participating in the so-called 'new great debate'.[5] More importantly, the argument presented below counters the revisionist reading of the 'second great debate' (prominent in the 1980s) which argued that the British and American approaches shared fundamental background assumptions about international relations. This claim underestimates the ontological and normative differences between traditional realists and the work being done by the likes of Wight and Bull; moreover, it is precisely these substantive differences which dictate the use of alternative methodologies. In other words, by framing the central questions of International Relations in a certain way, the tools they used to address those questions were to some extent self-selecting.

The second theme addressed by the Committee in this period was their project for a collaborative publication on comparative states systems. Here we see the Committee following Wight's dictum that international society 'can be properly described only in historical and sociological depth.'[6] Interest in comparative states systems persisted after Butterfield relinquished the chair of the group in 1966, passing on to Martin Wight (1967–1971) and Adam Watson (1972–1978, following Wight's death). During this period, the Committee worked towards publishing a second volume of papers, with historical states systems as its theme although this never came to fruition. Hedley Bull's return to the Committee in 1977, to take up the Montague Burton chair in International Relations at Oxford, injected a greater degree of focus for the final 'round' of their proceedings. As Bull noted in his introductory paper on the expansion of international society, 'the goal of the study that I am proposing is to reach a deeper understanding of the nature of historical change, in which we are still involved.'[7] These words are important because they highlight the way in which, for the first time in their history, the Committee were embarking upon on a journey with a clear idea of the destination – the publication of a volume of essays written by contributors (many of whom were not 'members') chosen on the basis of their expertise rather than their congeniality.

Methodology

Given that Hedley Bull is portrayed in the 'new great debate'[8] as the arch-traditionalist, it is paradoxical that he was perceived by other members of the Committee as their leading expert on the behavioural revolution. In 1965, he gave two papers on 'Recent American Contributions to the Theory of International Relations',[9] motivated in good measure by the Committee's concern that they had to prepare for Schelling's visit later that year.[10]

Bull's research for these papers laid the groundwork for his notorious article 'International Theory: The Case for a Classical Approach'. In the first of the two papers, Bull begins by noting the peculiar insularity of the Committee from the new ideas, texts and approaches of mainstream American International Relations:

> It is very remarkable that the deliberations of our committee on the theory of international politics have been almost entirely unaffected by the vast literature that has grown up in the last ten years, bearing the stamp of the social sciences, emanating chiefly, although not exclusively, from the United States, and calling itself by the same name.[11]

Echoing C.P. Snow's famous polemic about the mutually exclusive mind-sets of arts intellectuals and scientists, Bull suggests that the Committee's ignorance can be put down to 'feelings of aesthetic revulsion against the American school's language and methods' rather than reasoned criticism. Bull then commends the 'new literature' for its high quality, which is why it 'should be taken seriously.' However, just in case his audience were beginning to think his year in America had persuaded him of the virtues of behaviouralism, Bull informed them that he should himself find it more congenial to dwell upon the weaknesses rather than the strengths of the new theory, but it is to the latter to which in the present essay I wish to draw attention.'[12] As an example, Bull cites Morton Kaplan's *System and Process in International Politics* which he regards as 'a necessary point of reference in any discussion of international systems and their transformation.'[13]

Hedley Bull did not dwell for long on the strengths of the new scientific theories. In September 1966, he presented to the Committee his polemical essay 'International Theory: the Case for a Classical Approach.'[14] By 'scientific approach', Bull was referring to the formulation of propositions 'based either upon logical or mathematical proof, or upon strict, empirical procedures of verification.'[15] evident to varying degrees in the work of Kaplan, Schelling, Deutsch and Boulding.[16] Bull dismisses these ideas with the following words:

> the scientific approach is likely to contribute very little to the theory of international relations, and in so far as it is intended to encroach upon and ultimately displace the classical approach, it is positively harmful.[17]

Bull justifies this sweeping critique of scientism by way of seven counterarguments.[18] First, their focus on methodology prevents scientific theorists from coming to grips with the central questions of international relations. Second, the status of science cannot provide shelter from the need for judgement. Third, the mistaken belief that theory can somehow evolve from a pre-theoretical stage to a final general theory. Fourth, the fashion for constructing 'models' is inappropriate for international politics and can even be harmful because it disengages the theorist from the real world. Fifth, the scientific school's 'fetish for measurement' leads to absurd conclusions about the degree of community between peoples varying according to the cross-references of countries in newspapers: 'Are the figures of "communication flow"', asks Bull, 'an index of political community at the international level, or a cause of it?'[19] Bull's sixth counter-argument is that the so-called scientific properties of 'rigour and precision' are qualities already present in the classical tradition, from antiquity (Grotius and Vattel) to modernity (Aron, Hoffmann, Wight and Waltz). The seventh and final proposition concerns the danger that the practitioners of the scientific approach 'by cutting themselves off from history and philosophy, have deprived themselves of the means of self-criticism.'[20]

The main thrust of Bull's argument rests upon an unqualified rejection of scientific standards as either a realisable or even worthy goal for the humanities. Here Bull is entering a long-standing debate within the philosophy of science between the social scientific positivists (from August Comte onwards) who see no essential difference between natural science and social science, and interpretivists who believe that the natural world and the social world demand different methodologies. By the early 1950s, proponents of the 'unity of the sciences' had triumphed intellectually and institutionally as political science displaced political theory and the behavioural sciences displaced philosophy. Interestingly, as we saw in Chapter 2, one of the first works in International Relations to reject categorically the 'unity of the sciences' argument was E.H. Carr's *The Twenty Years' Crisis*. Carr recognised that in the process of analysing the facts, social scientists transformed them.[21] His recognition that there can be no value-free enquiry in the social sciences received universal assent in the British Committee.

Hedley Bull's critique of scientism is more complete than his defence of traditionalism. He defined the classical approach as 'the approach to theorising that is derived from philosophy, history and law,'[22] but does not provide guidance on how each of these three master-subjects contribute to the classical approach. As we have already noted in Bull's argument, the traditionalists were contemptuous of the aspirations of the scientists for predictive capability. But if we look more closely at the traditionalists' use of history, it is apparent that they implicitly believed that the contemporary world can best be understood by applying the lessons of history. A good example of this appears in the editors' preface to *Diplomatic Investigations*: 'it is a useful enterprise to explore the corpus of diplomatic and military experience in order to reformulate its lessons in relation to contemporary needs.'[23] The point here is that although the language used is more understated, the assumption that there are recognisable patterns in history and that it is possible to apply the lessons of history, demonstrates that the traditionalists can impute to the historical process a degree of predictability. Indeed, as Hoffmann has pointed out, many philosophers of history caught on to the idea of rhythms and patterns long before positivists decided the social world was reducible to law-governed explanations.[24]

A related criticism of the traditionalists concerns the lack of empirical content of their historical papers.[25] The following criticism by Morton Kaplan is pertinent here,

> Those traditionalists who have done a significant amount of historical research – and they are the exceptions – confine themselves largely to problems of diplomatic history that are unrelated to their generalizations about international politics.[26]

As we noted in an earlier chapter, Herbert Butterfield's historical ruminations fell short of his own strictures on the need for the kind of technical history that would meet with the empirical criteria advocated by the scientists. This same criticism can be levelled at the other historians in the Committee. With the notable exception of Martin Wight's essays,[27] few of the Committee papers show any sign of being researched, and historical documents are seldom referred to.[28] In short, the criticism of the historical content of the classical approach is that traditionalists *use* history but they don't *do* history.

The second ingredient of the classical approach is philosophy. But apart from the rather often repeated priority of 'philosophical rigour', what did Bull and the traditionalists mean by philosophy? It is clear that they did not mean to address the epistemological foundations of knowledge, which is the starting point for metaphysics; or even undertake the depth of ethical investigations into international society of the type Michael Walzer provided in *Just and Unjust Wars*.[29] Instead, the philosophical content of traditionalism is restricted to the construction of a 'canon' of philosophical texts, and more significantly, the formulation of fundamental questions. In a famous passage from his 'International Theory: The Case for a Classical Approach', Bull asks the following questions:

For example, does the collectivity of sovereign states constitute a political society or system, or does it not? If we can speak of a society of sovereign states, does it presuppose a common culture or civilization? And if it does, does such a common culture underlie the worldwide diplomatic framework ... What is the place of war in international society? Does a member of international society enjoy a right of intervention in the internal affairs of another, and if so in what circumstances? Are sovereign states the sole members of international society, or does it ultimately consist of individual human beings, whose rights and duties override those of the entities who act in their name? To what extent is the course of diplomatic events at any one time determined or circumscribed by the general shape or structure of the international system; by the number, relative weight, and conservative or radical disposition of its constituent states, and by the instruments for getting their way that military technology or the distribution of wealth has put into their hands; by the particular set of rules of the game underlying diplomatic practice at the time?[30]

These questions are philosophical to the extent that they are general, contested, abstract and resistant to empirical verification. This point is turned into a powerful criticism by David Vital who argues that the strength of the questions posed by Bull 'lies in their power to stimulate interest in the field as a whole, rather than in such answers as might be furnished in direct response to them.'[31] In defence of Bull, and as a prelude to the following chapter, he did more than ask interesting questions. His approach to theory was rigorous and displayed a remarkable coherence, from his 1961 British Committee paper through to his lectures on justice. This does not mean that the content of Bull's understanding of philosophy is not open to criticism; two examples spring immediately to mind, the uncertain status of the 'primary rules of social life' and his rather idiosyncratic treatment of justice in *The Anarchical Society*.

Of the traditionalists' trilogy, international law remains the least studied. This is worthy of note given the centrality of law to society. To borrow R.J. Vincent's metaphor, international law locates international society 'like a miner's lamp locating gas'.[32] From the point of view of methodology, international law is more easily accommodated by the classical approach given its resistance to the hypothetic-deductive canon of social scientific investigation.[33] For example, the lawyer's stress on a sense of legal obligation requires an interpretative approach which rests on fundamentally different methodological assumptions than behaviouralism. In view of the affinity between international law, the method of the British Committee, and their belief in the existence of an international society, it is surprising that the Committee did not take international law more seriously. Recall how one of the striking features of Hedley Bull's paper 'The Grotian Conception of International Society' and the discussion which followed, was the hostility on the part of key members of the Committee towards an approach to law which addressed normative questions about the control or the elimination of the use of force without subordinating these considerations to the balance of power. Given the debate that Bull's paper provoked, it is surprising that the Committee did not pursue further the relationship between international law and international order. Perhaps they thought that, in the absence of Bull, they did not have the intellectual resources within their ranks to pursue such an inquiry.

A second set of questions provoked by the 'new great debate' concerns the degree to which Bull's arguments were representative of the Committee as a whole. Bull concluded his polemical essay, 'International Theory: The Case for a Classical Approach', by issuing the following warning to his colleagues: 'the distinctive methods and aspirations these theorists have brought to the subject are leading them down a false path, and to all appeals to follow them down it we should remain resolutely deaf'.[34] Did the members of the British Committee remain 'resolutely deaf' to the new 'scientific' theories of International Relations or was the project of comparative states-systems a concession to behaviouralism? In his memorial lecture to Martin Wight, Bull recalls their difference of opinion over the appropriate strategy to pursue against the 'scientists'. In rather colourful prose, Bull reflected on what he described as the 'correct strategy', which was 'to study their position until one could state their own arguments better than they could and then – when they were least expecting it – to turn on them and slaughter them in an academic Massacre of Glencoe. Wight entertained none of these bloody thoughts.'[35] Contrary to Bull's recollection, there is considerable textual evidence from the British Committee papers to suggest that Wight and the rest of the Committee were vocal in their disdain for behaviouralism. Although Wight never published an article relating directly to the 'new great debate', there are a number of criticisms in his work of the new thinking in International Relations theory. In the previous chapter we noted how Wight re-wrote the preface to *Diplomatic Investigations* for the very purpose of distinguishing the British Committee from American scientism. Here Wight states categorically that 'the political, diplomatic, legal and military writers who might loosely be termed "classical" have not been superseded as a result of recent developments in sociology and psychology.'[36]

Various references by Herbert Butterfield support the argument that the British Committee were very aware of the growing cleavage between themselves and mainstream American International Relations. In the first Martin Wight memorial lecture, Herbert Butterfield recalls Wight's response to the latest methodological developments: 'When Hedley Bull raised the large-scale question of the English way of dealing with international relations – the method of our committee – against the extravagant scientism of some of the Americans – Martin was in his element again.[37] Indeed, the members of the Committee were so confident of their 'way of dealing with international relations' that they considered publishing a collected volume on the subject.[38]

Butterfield's own position on the 'new great debate' is an interesting one. As Chapter 4 noted, Butterfield was obsessed with the eighteenth century balance of power system, and frequently drew parallels between the accumulation of 'scientific' knowledge in the natural world and the emerging science of politics and diplomacy. In correspondence with one of his Peterhouse *alumni*, Peter Savigear, Butterfield reveals his ambiguity regarding the application of 'science' to international politics.

> I always pleaded for a 'scientific' rather than a 'moralistic' attitude to international affairs; but the modern American developments give me a certain amount of dismay. I want to see the reassertion of the traditional Old World handling of these matters (the development of a quasi-scientific treatment inaugurated in the eighteenth century) and I should like to see an English movement which knew the American work without being enslaved by it.[39]

This passage is interesting because it expresses Butterfield's desire to understand the developments in American International Relations. More importantly, it demonstrates his view that science *was* traditional. The best example of this is Butterfield's argument that the balance of power 'occupies in this "science" the kind of place that gravitation had in the Newtonian system.'[40]

One of the most frequent explanations for the polarised methodological debate is the different academic cultures in Britain and in the United States.[41] The American International Relations academy in the post-war era is frequently characterised as being an integral part of a 'behaviourial revolution' which sought to adopt the scientific canon of the natural sciences.[42] This is in sharp contrast to the liberal-arts tradition in Britain of which the British Committee stands as a paradigmatic example. However, it would be a mistake to classify the 'new great debate' purely in national terms.[43] This point is amplified by the fact that the American traditionalist Stanley Hoffmann wrote a stinging critique of the pretensions of scientism a decade before Bull.[44] Similarly, a number of British scholars have dismissed traditionalism with opprobrium.[45]

What this analysis of the classical approach demonstrates is that the 'new great debate' was not solely a dispute about methodology. As is often the case, an argument over methodology usually signifies a deeper cleavage concerning the nature of the subject itself. This is crystal clear from Bull's list of central questions on the nature and limits of international society in contrast to the view of international relations maintained by behaviouralists which was normatively neutral, concentrating upon action/ reaction models of states and decision-making processes.

The one genuinely significant methodological difference between the 'classicists' and the 'scientists' turns on the nature of theory. Clearly, the members of the British Committee were using the notion of theory in an inductive sense, meaning theory generated by practice, and crucially, in a constructivist sense, meaning theoris*ing* can shape the conduct of individual and collective action. In describing the liberties of states, Vattel was in an important sense constituting them. Strict positivists (of which behaviouralism is a sub-species) would refute this argument, substituting a method which relies on a separation between subject-object, and fact-value. The aim of theory, for positivists, is to formulate laws of behaviour which can be tested for their predictive capability. Looking back on the last three decades of International Relations debates about the nature of theory – indulging in historical anachronism for a moment – Kenneth Waltz appears as the *real* proponent of a scientific mode of inquiry, and looks today like 'the most obvious target for Bull's strictures'.[46]

Comparing International Societies

In January 1964 Herbert Butterfield presented a general discussion paper reflecting on the progress of the British Committee.[47] The significance of Butterfield's paper is that it encouraged the Committee to apply their conception of 'theory' to the history of states-systems. His preference was for an analysis of the origins of the European states-system, with particular reference to the way in which the maxims associated with the post-Westphalian order 'have retained their validity.'[48] Butterfield concludes by suggesting the British Committee undergo a project of comparing the *internal* properties of historic states-systems.[49] Although the Committee papers did indeed manage to illuminate aspects of the internal relations of communities in historic states systems, some of their most interesting later work focuses upon the *external* dynamics civilisations and their 'others'.

From the beginning of their discussions on historic states systems, members of the British Committee were divided on the question of whether a common culture was a necessary condition for the existence of a states system. Martin Wight's first paper opened with the assumption that 'the histories of Greece and Rome were continuous and interdependent in a way which makes them a historic, and very largely a cultural, whole.'[50] At the following meeting, in January 1965, Desmond Williams drew the contours of the discussion around a lyrical definition of a state-system as 'an order possessing a kind of *unity*' which 'involves a degree of contract and commitment between the units'.[51] This prompted a combative response from Hedley Bull:

> we are not sufficiently flexible in our idea of what a 'system' is. Morton Kaplan regards an international system as a 'system of action'. You can take any area and look for the pattern of the relations between the states in that area. It will form some sort of 'system'. *There is no need to posit* even any *consciousness* of system amongst the states involved.[52]

Despite Bull's attempt to remove intentionality from the British Committee's conception of a states-system, Wight persisted in bringing a pre-existing common culture into the debate. As he put it forcefully in his paper 'De Systematibus Civitatum': 'We must assume that a states-system will not come into being without a degree of cultural unity among its members.'[53]

In his main contribution to the work on states systems Butterfield emphasised the role of agency in constructing the system.[54] He argues that the 'conscious effort' of statecraft is required to organise a states-system (re-invoking familiar themes in Butterfield's earlier writing particularly on the balance of power which he characterised as 'an elaborate artifice' rather than 'something bestowed by nature'.)

> The salient fact about the 'international systems' so far studied is that basically they do not seem to have been produced by the process of bringing together units which have been hitherto quite separate. The effective forces making for some sort of combination may be the elements of an antecedent common culture. Granted that a states-system is already in existence, it may not be difficult to add to it new units which were once outside it – even units that are of quite alien culture – as one might conceive of adding Turkey to the European system in the nineteenth century. But this itself does not seem to be very easy, and what emerges from our historical survey is an impression of the tremendous difficulty of actually creating an international order where no firm basis for it previously existed. It looks as though (in the conditions of the past at least) a states-system can only be achieved by a tremendous

conscious effort of reassembly after a political hegemony has broken down.[55]

Here Butterfield is arguing against Wight's contention that a common culture is not a necessary condition for a well-ordered states system. In its place, Butterfield asserts the role of enlightened state leaders following the maxims of classical European statecraft. Interestingly, the above passage also suggests that the system itself is doing some 'work' in socialising 'aliens' into the system,[56] emphasising again Butterfield's heightened sensitivity to the impact of international structures on the decisions of agents.

Hedley Bull's only contribution to the British Committee's investigation into historical states-systems was a paper distributed to the Committee in July 1967.[57] Herein Bull attempts to disentangle the blurring of interests and identity in the Committee's discussions of states systems; in so doing, we see the origins of the system-society dualism which is regarded by many to be a distinguishing feature of the English School. According to Bull, an international system is:

> A pattern of behaviour in which states are related to one another as a set of interacting parts ... It is obvious that two or more political units may constitute a system in this sense without their having a sense of common purpose or identity such as might find expression in observance of a system of law, operation of a common diplomatic procedure or awareness of the requirements of a balance of power. The political collectivities in question might have no other relations but war, but they would form a system if they interacted as parts of a whole.[58]

This notion of an international system constituted by purposeless interaction among states contrasts with Bull's interpretation of international society as a '*union* or association' for 'regulating the relations of states in the absence of a common superior'.[59] The distinguishing feature of a society of states was the element of consciousness on the part of agents to maintain order. In this sense, a society 'presupposed a system' of interacting parts:

> But it involved also *a sense of common identity* and an awareness of the need to operate common institutions in the pursuit of common purposes.[60]

Hedley Bull's substitution of the term international society for what Wight took to be the characteristics of a states-system, enables Bull to distinguish between systems of interaction and *societal* systems (or international society).[61] This distinction is one of the most significant conceptual innovations to occur during the second phase of the British Committee's proceedings. It reappears in Bull and Watson's edited collection of the final British Committee papers on *The Expansion of International Society* and in a number of other related works on the history of international society.[62] Although gaining widespread approval,[63] the separation of states system from international society is not without its critics. Geoffrey Berridge referred to Bull's revision as 'a gratuitous confusion'.[64] His most weighty criticism is that history does not conform to either of these ideal-types. More recently, Barry Buzan has argued that the English School in general has not delineated a clear boundary between 'system' and 'society'. When, for example, does 'society' emerge out of the 'system'? And *how* do international societies evolve? These issues are explored further in the British Committee's final proceedings, considered below.

In the conclusion to his preliminary paper on the modern international system, Bull considered the limitations of a systems approach. He berated systems thinking in general for presupposing that the survival of the system is the goal of the units, and for blurring descriptions of the system and justifications for the system. The lesson of applying 'systems theory', Bull argues, 'is not that the attempt to see international systems in relation to other systems is misguided, but that it should be pursued more critically.'[65] In subsequent correspondence, Adam Watson reluctantly agreed that the systems approach 'needs to be pursued more critically, with a greater awareness of its limitations, and with much greater clarity and less jargon in stating the results.'[66]

After a lull in the Committee's proceedings between the end of 1967 and 1970, Martin Wight (who had taken over the responsibility of the Chair from Butterfield) sent out a circular to the members informing them of the 'resumption of the meetings'. On 25 March 1970, Geoffrey Hudson, Adam Watson, Desmond Williams and Wight himself met in Brighton to discuss the next 'round' of their deliberations. They agreed to resume the pattern which Butterfield had established of three meetings a year, rotating between Oxford, Cambridge and Brighton. Their intellectual objective was to resurrect the collaborative project on states systems, as the minutes of the meeting make clear:

> We recognised that the renewal of the grant by the Rockefeller Foundation does not oblige us to work towards publication, though we all agreed that the aim of publication would give an edge to our work.

We hoped that we could maintain the tradition of spontaneous papers, each member of the Committee writing on what was interesting him at the moment. We hoped at the same time not to lose sight of our unifying theme of States-Systems, which we shall reconsider in about a year from now, to see whether a book would be feasible.[67]

A year later, in a letter dated 13 May 1971, the Committee decided 'to bury the noble but grandiose scheme of a collective volume on States-Systems .... It now seems common sense to lay it aside.'[68] The principal reason for abandoning the project was the fact that the papers lacked coherence, varying greatly 'in detail, length, and treatment of the subject matter.' They therefore decided, 'to encourage members of the Committee each, as the spirit moved him, to write his own book on the theme of States-Systems (or indeed any other theme), drawing upon the papers which the Committee had already produced.'[69]

In addition to Wight's papers from this period being published as a volume in their own right,[70] the origins of two other individual projects can be traced back to the early British Committee discussions on states systems. Hedley Bull's *The Anarchical Society* addresses, albeit cautiously, the question raised by Wight in 'De Systematibus Civitatum', namely, whether the present society of states is a 'more desirable' way of administering world politics 'than the alternatives'.[71] Adam Watson's ambitious work *Evolution of International Society* provides a survey of all identifiable states systems, noting the family resemblances between systems, their points of differentiation, and the mechanisms which facilitate their functioning.[72] But perhaps the best example of the avenues opened up by the Committee's discussions on states-systems can be seen in the ideas and arguments presented in Bull and Watson's edited collection of papers on *The Expansion of International Society*, a volume which should properly be seen as the swan song of the British Committee period.[73]

In the years after Wight's death in 1972, the profile of the Committee changed considerably. All Souls' College had become the principal venue, and funding from the Rockefeller Foundation had ceased. More significantly, of the original members, only Butterfield, Watson, Howard and Bull remained (although his participation was restricted to meetings which coincided with visits to the UK). In addition to these four, the Committee included: Christopher Andrew (Corpus Christi, Cambridge), Coral Bell (University of Sussex), Geoffrey Best (University of Sussex), Michael Donelan (LSE), Noel Dorr (Department of Foreign Affairs, Dublin), Robert L. Wade-Gery (FCO), Daniel O'Connell (All Souls', Oxford), Michael Palliser (FCO), Maurice Keens-Soper (University of

Leicester), William Wallace (Royal Institute of International Affairs), David Watt (Financial Times), Patrick Wormald (University of Glasgow). Among these later members, only Michael Donelan and Maurice Keens-Soper were 'specialists' in academic International Relations, suggesting that Wight never succeeded in his aim to build the Committee around a core of theorists who identified themselves with the discipline.

Michael Howard remembers the meetings in the final phase of the Committee as being far more 'businesslike'. This he put down to the 'firm grip' which Bull exerted, following his return from Australia in 1978.[74] At the first meeting, Bull presented a paper on 'Justice in World Politics'. He characterised it as an agenda setting paper, noting how the focus of the Committee's work to date had been 'concerned almost entirely with order in international relations rather than with the realisation of justice or just change.' The just claims he had in mind were those of Third World states, which he had been sensitised to in his years at the ANU. Bull felt that the Committee should not try to study the contemporary details of the demands of post-colonial states, rather, their 'distinctive contribution' would be to place the North-South debate 'in a broad historical and philosophical context'.[75] At the next meeting, Adam Watson gave a paper entitled 'From a European to a Global International Order', which both endorsed Bull's proposal and set in motion the body of work which became *The Expansion of International Society*.[76]

Conclusion

Examining the so-called 'new great debate' in the context of the British Committee papers provides a number of important insights. For instance, although it was only Bull who went 'public' in his condemnation of behaviouralism, it is evident that both Butterfield and Wight were increasingly aware of the differences between their classical approach and the social scientific methodology of theorists like Deutsch and Singer. With hindsight, these differences between the 'scientists' and the 'traditionalists' do not appear to be as great as the sound and fury of Bull's rhetoric suggested. The scientists of the 1960s were not as methodologically rigorous as the next generation of rational choice theorists of the 1980s and 1990s, and the English School were not as historical as the 'classical approach' implied. Indeed, the best English School work is a blend of history and social science, as Hoffmann and Buzan have noted.[77]

An explicit link was made in the chapter between the 'great debate' and the Committee's work on states systems. Bull wanted to restrict the notion of a system to a functional/mechanistic model favoured by those like

Kaplan who Bull identified as the 'American School'. What marked the interpretations of post-Westphalian Europe off from previous states systems was the sense of common identity on the part of monarchs, state leaders and the diplomatic community. Bull believed that the evolution of the shared rules and common language could only be understood using the 'classical approach' to international relations. Although other members of the Committee resisted Bull's terminological distinction, believing that their comparative study of states systems thinking need not imply a commitment to a scientific mode of enquiry. Their inductive approach to states systems treated them as ideas 'embodied and at work in practice'[78] rather than abstract representations or models.

In evaluating the Committee's papers from 1964–1984, there is evidence of a cumulative research programme, albeit one which ebbed and flowed. The early work on states systems, led by Wight, produced useful classifications, raised a number of crucial questions even though his answers are difficult to disentangle from the depth of historical (and rhetorical) detail. Wight prompted later English School 'system-thinkers' to be reflective about the relationship between a system of reciprocal interests (such as trade or communication) and a society marked by common identity (or shared culture). What interested Bull and Watson, during the final stage of the British Committee's proceedings, was whether the tension between order and justice could be managed in a world where the 'we feeling' of the European society of states had been displaced by global political and economic forces. Without a common identity, how could the interests of sovereign states be made to converge? In the final two chapters, we will look at the ways in which Bull and Vincent responded to this dilemma.

NOTES

1. Letter from Herbert Butterfield to K.W. Thompson (5 October 1962).
2. He gave two papers in this period, 'Arms and Institutions' (January 1965), 'Watchfulness between States' (October 1967) and one talk on 'The Press and Foreign Affairs' (January 1965).
3. The coexistence of these two themes is recorded in correspondence between Butterfield and Thompson. Letter from Herbert Butterfield to K.W. Thompson (2 March 1966).
4. Hedley Bull, 'International Theory: The Case for a Classical Approach', in Klaus Knorr and J.N. Rosenau (eds), *Contending Approaches to*

International Politics (Princeton: Princeton University Press, 1968), 21–38.

5. James Richardson suggests that Bull 'received little reinforcement from the traditionalists.' J.L. Richardson, 'The Academic Study of International Relations', in J.D.B. Miller and R.J. Vincent, *Order and Violence: Hedley Bull and International Relations* (Oxford: Clarendon Press, 1990), 155.

6. Wight, 'Western Values', in Herbert Butterfield and Martin Wight (eds), *Diplomatic Investigations* (London: Allen and Unwin, 1966), 96.

7. Bull, 'From a European to a Global International Order' (1978).

8. See Morton Kaplan, 'The New Great Debate: Traditionalism vs Science in International Relations', in Knorr and Rosenau (eds), *Contending Approaches*.

9. Hedley Bull, 'Recent American Contributions to the Theory of International Politics: Part I', (January 1965). Hedley Bull, 'Recent American Contributions to the Theory of International Politics: Part II', (July 1965).

10. In the minutes of the 'Business Meeting' (4 October 1964) Butterfield writes: 'It was agreed that the next meeting should be held on 8–11 January 1965 and that Mr. Schelling should be invited to attend. Hedley Bull undertook to produce for that occasion a paper on "American Developments in the Theory of International Politics".'

11. Bull, 'Recent American Contributions, part I', 1.

12 Bull, 'Recent American Contributions, part I', 1.

13. Bull, 'Recent American Contributions, part I', 10.

14. The paper was first presented to the 10th Bailey Conference on the teaching of International Relations, London School of Economics, January 1966. Four months later, it was published in *World Politics*. Mary Bull adds an interesting biographical postscript: 'I remember clearly Hedley saying that he would send it to *World Politics*; he wanted to keep up his connection with the journal, and he wanted to bring the article to the notice of the Americans – in England he was too much preaching to the converted. And they did notice it!' Letter from Mary Bull to the author, (17 January 1993).

15. Bull, 'International Theory', 21.

16. Bull provides a long list of works as examples of the 'scientific approach'. Bull, 'International Theory', footnote, 22.

17. Bull, 'International Theory', 26.

18. Bull, 'International Theory', 28–37.

19. This argument was first made in his paper 'Recent American Contributions: Part 2' (January 1966) in which he described and then subjected to critique, the ideas associated with Karl W. Deutsch. Although he objected to Deutsch's method, Bull applauded his attempt to replace national interest based explanations with the language of 'communication' and 'mutual identification'. The following comment by Bull shows that he was keenly aware of the way in which 'identity' shapes 'interests': 'The fact in British political life of a "we-feeling" that is experienced when judging the United States or Australia or New Zealand ... provides an element of our foreign policy which cannot be reduced to a function of the national interest. It may influence our conception of what the national interest is, and be influenced by it, but it is itself another thing and exerts an influence of its own on our policy.'

20. Bull, 'International Theory', 35, 37.

21. E.H. Carr, *The Twenty Years' Crisis 1919–1939* (London: Macmillan, 1939), 7.

22. Bull, 'International Theory', 20.

23. Butterfield and Wight eds., *Diplomatic Investigations*, preface, 12–13.

24. Stanley Hoffmann, *Janus and Minerva: Esays in the Theory and Practice of International Politics* (Boulder, Col.: Westview Press, 1986), 443.

25. Butterfield and Wight claim that their approach is 'empirical and inductive'. Butterfield and Wight (eds), *Diplomatic Investigations*, preface, 12.

26. Kaplan, 'The New Great Debate', 56.

27. As Murray Forsyth noted wryly, 'we trust him as a historian'. Forsyth, 'The Classical Theory of International Relations', *Political Studies* 26 (1978), 411.

28. The one exception to this is Herbert Butterfield's 'Eyre Crowe's Memorandum of 1st January 1907', (July 1960).

29. Michael Walzer, *Just and Unjust Wars* (New York: Basic Books, 1977).

30. Bull, 'International Theory', 27.

31. David Vital, 'Back to Machiavelli', in Knorr and Rosenau (eds), *Contending Approaches*, 147.

32. R.J. Vincent, 'Order in International Politics' in Miller and Vincent (eds), *Order and Violence*, 55.

33. This argument is made by Hoffmann, 'The Study of International Law and the Theory of International Relations', in Stanley Hoffmann, *The State of War* (New York: Praeger, 1965).

34. Bull, 'International Theory', 38.

35. Hedley Bull, 'Martin Wight and the Theory of International Relations', in Martin Wight, *International Theory: The Three Traditions* (Leicester: Leicester University Press, 1991), xi. In his introduction to Martin Wight, *Systems of States* (Leicester: Leicester University Press, 1977), Bull suggests Wight had 'simply no point of contact at all' with the social scientific school. Bull, 'Martin Wight and the Study of International Relations', 14.

36. Butterfield and Wight (eds), *Diplomatic Investigations*, preface, 12. In addition, as early as 1960 Wight argued in 'Why is there no International Theory?', that international politics is communicated better through historical writings, which do 'the same job' as the 'new methodologies' but with 'more judiciousness and modesty, and with closer attention to the record of international experience'. Martin Wight, 'Why is there no International Theory?' in Butterfield and Wight (eds), *Diplomatic Investigations*, 32.

37. Herbert Butterfield, 'Raison D'Etat: The Relations between Morality and Government', First Martin Wight Memorial Lecture (Brighton: University of Sussex, April 1975), 3.

38. Letter from Herbert Butterfield to K.W. Thompson, (2 March 1966). In this correspondence Butterfield adds: 'At the same time [as the study of states systems] we have been engaged in a study and critique of the recent American work on the Theory of International Politics, and I have long been pressing that we should find a way of introducing this into whatever book we publish next, as the issue is a big one, and we feel that the case for our own approach is a thing worth putting.' Also Butterfield wrote in a letter to Martin Wight (29 June, 1966): 'I hold the very strong view that if we could

produce a critique of the various American groups in which Hedley has been interested, this would be a real contribution and a most original piece of work, likely to command great interest and achieve higher importance than any miscellaneous collection.'

39.   Letter from Herbert Butterfield to Peter Savigear (16 February 1970).

40.   Herbert Butterfield, 'Notes for a Discussion on the Theory of International Politics', (January 1964), 6. As he noted earlier in the discussion: 'Perhaps also it could just be said that we are bound to be greatly concerned with what might be called the 'Political Science' of international relations, or with the attempt to treat these relations in a more scientific manner.'(4)

41.   See, for example, Steve Smith 'Introduction', in Smith (ed.), *International Relations: British and American Perspectives* (Oxford: Blackwell, 1985), ix–xiv.

42.   See K.J. Holsti, *The Dividing Discipline: Hegemony and Diversity in International Theory* (Boston: Unwin Hyman, 1985), esp. 31–40.

43.   This situation was recognised by Butterfield and Wight. As they wrote in the preface to *Diplomatic Investigations*, the discussions of the American committee were themselves in some respects traditional compared with the flourishing contemporary school of American and Australian international theory and systems analysis.' Butterfield and Wight (eds), *Diplomatic Investigations*, 12.

44.   Stanley Hoffmann, 'International Relations: The Long Road to Theory', *World Politics*, 11 (1959), 346–77.

45.   Roderick C.Ogley, 'International Relations: Poetry, Prescription or Science?', *Millennium*, 10 (1981), 170–86. R.E. Jones, 'The English School of International Relations: a case for closure', *Review of International Studies*, 7 (1981), 1–13. For an attack on a particular exponent of traditionalism see Michael Nicholson, 'The Enigma of Martin Wight', *Review of International Studies*, 7 (1981), 15–22.

46.   Brown, 'Sorry Comfort?' 91. Note also that Waltz's *Theory of International Politics* was published at a time when positivism was beginning to be discredited within the broader social scientific community, see for example, Richard Bernstein, *The Restructuring of Social and Political Theory* (London: Methuen, 1976).

47.   Herbert Butterfield, 'Notes for a Discussion on the Theory of International Politics', (January 1964).

48.   Butterfield, 'Notes for a Discussion', 6.

49.   Butterfield, 'Notes for a Discussion', 8. Committee papers on (or pertaining to) states systems included the following: Hedley Bull, 'Notes on the Modern International System' (January 1965); Herbert Butterfield, 'The Historic States-System' (January 1965); Geoffrey Hudson, 'The Extension of the Western International System to Asia and Africa' (July 1965); Maurice Keens-Soper, 'The Awareness of Diplomacy: François de Callières' (April 1972); E.I.J. Rosenthal (guest) 'The Medieval Islamic States-System'; Adam Watson, 'The Indian States System' (April 1967), 'The Nature of State Systems', (October 1967), 'The Macedonian States System (October 1972), 'The State System of the Dark Ages (October 1972); Martin Wight, 'The States System of Greece and Rome: Part 1', 'The States System of Greece and Rome: Part 2', 'De Systematibus Civitatem'

(April 1967), 'International Legitimacy' (April 1971), 'Triangles and Duels (Janary 1971); Desmond Williams, 'International Systems in the Middle Ages', (October 1960).

50. Martin Wight, 'The States-System of Greece and Rome: Part I', (October 1964). Reprinted as 'The States-System of Hellas' in Wight, *Systems of States*, 46–72. The meeting was the first session on states systems. It was opened by a guest speaker, Dr Rosenthal, who gave an unminuted talk on 'The Medieval States-System'. Other papers included Geoffrey Hudson's 'The Traditional Chinese Conception of International Relations' and Desmond Williams's paper 'The International State-System in the Middle Ages'. Adam Watson, on leave from the Embassy, also gave a talk on 'Cuba'. Watson's paper appears, with hindsight, to be a masterly analysis of Cuba's predicament. He carefully distances Castro from Communism: 'Cuba must be seen in the light of the polycentrism now current in the Communist world, and not as the pivot of a global conspiracy. She depends on Russia which cannot always give her what she wants and there are strains in the present system of collaboration. ... Castro would like, therefore, to move into a position in which he would be much less dependent on Russia; and the only way in which he can do this is by establishing better relations with the West.' Adam Watson, 'Cuba', (October 1964), 1–3.

51. Desmond Williams in the discussion, 'States-Systems', (January 1965), 1–2.

52. Hedley Bull in the discussion, 'States-Systems', (January 1965), 2. Emphasis added.

53. Wight continues, 'The three states-systems that we have taken as paradigms, the Greek, the Western, and the early Chinese, each arose within a single culture'. Martin Wight, 'De Systematibus Civitatum', (April 1967), reprinted in Wight, *Systems of States*, 21–45. As many scholars sympathetic to the English School have noted, Wight is primarily responsible for the terminological confusion that pervades this project, principally because he used the term 'systems of states' to mean what others denote by 'international society'. See Barry Buzan, 'From International System to International Society: Structural Realism and Regime Theory meet the English School', *International Organization* 47 (1993), 331.

54. Herbert Butterfield, 'The Historic States-Systems', (January 1965). Adam Watson believed that Butterfield's paper 'summed up and deepened its [the Committee's] discussions on the nature of such systems and why they have functioned as they have.' Watson, *The Evolution,* 5.

55. Butterfield, 'The Historic States-System', 2. Emphasis added.

56. Barry Buzan is on similar terrain when he brings Waltzian ideas of the system generating 'like units' to bear on the system-society debate in the English School. Buzan, 'From International System to International Society', 344.

57. Hedley Bull, 'Notes on the Modern International System', (July, 1967). Bull was not there to present it himself.

58. Bull, 'Notes on the Modern International System', 1–2.

59. Bull, 'Notes on the Modern International System', 2. Emphasis added. Buzan takes the issue of whether a common identity exists between states to be the key point of demarcation between an international society and an international system. See Buzan, 'From International System to International Society', p. 331.

60. Bull, 'Notes on the Modern International System', 1–2. Emphasis added.
61. Although in his Committee papers on *Systems of States* Wight uses international system and international society interchangeably, his draft chapter for the revised edition of *Power Politics*, written in 1967 (the same year Bull wrote his Committee paper 'Notes on the Modern International System') goes some way towards separating the terms. 'It can scarcely be denied', argued Wight, 'that there is a system of states, and to admit there is a system comes halfway to admitting there is a society'. Wight, *Power Politics* (Leicester: Leicester University Press, 1978), 105.
62. See Gerrit W. Gong, *The Standard of 'Civilization' in International Relations* (Oxford: Clarendon, 1984); and Iver B. Neumann and Jennifer M. Welsh, 'The Other in European Self-Definition: An Addendum to the Literature on International Society', *Review of International Studies* 17 (1991), 327–348. For a review of the system/society debate, see Alan James, 'System or Society?', *Review of International Studies* 19 (1993), 269–288.
63. Evan Luard, *Types of International Society* (Macmillan, 1976), esp. vii-viii. See also Maurice Keens-Soper, 'Political Philosophy and International Relations: The Case for the Night-watchman', *International Relations* 3 (1967), 259–272.
64. Geoffrey Berridge, 'The Political Theory and Institutional History of States-Systems', *British Journal of International Studies* 6 (1980), 86.
65. Bull, 'Notes on the Modern International System', 6.
66. Letter from Adam Watson to Hedley Bull, (6–9 October 1967), 4.
67. Martin Wight, minutes, (25 March, 1970), 1. Although publication was not a formal condition of the next stage of Rockefeller funding, the proposed volume on states-systems was one of the principal reasons for the award of $12 500, agreed in December 1971 for the year beginning January 1972. Letter from J. Kellum Smith, Jr. Secretary of the Rockefeller Foundation to Asa Briggs, Chancellor of The University of Sussex, 1971
68. Letter from Martin Wight to the Committee, 13 May 1971.
69. Letter from Martin Wight to the Committee, 13 May 1971.
70. Wight, *Systems of States*.
71. Wight, 'De Systematibus Civitatum', 44.
72. Adam Watson, *The Evolution of International Society: A Comparative Historical Context* (London: Routledge, 1992).
73. Hedley Bull and Adam Watson (eds) *The Expansion of International Society* (Oxford: Clarendon, 1984).
74. Michael Howard, letter to the author, 7 January 1993.
75. Bull, 'Justice in World Politics' (September 1978).
76. Adam Watson, 'From a European to a Global International Order', (January 1979).
77. Buzan, 'From International System to International Society', 329. Hoffmann, 'International Society', in Miller and Vincent (eds), *Order and Violence*.
78. Maurice Keens-Soper, 'The Practice of a States-System', in Michael Donelan (ed), *The Reason of States* (London: Allen and Unwin, 1978), 40.

7 Hedley Bull

In his memorial lecture to Martin Wight, Bull noted how he had been a 'constant borrower' from the mind of his mentor, 'always hoping to transcend it but never able to escape it.' There is no doubt that Bull thought about International Relations in quintessentially Wightean terms: the habit of thinking in threes; the search for patterns in the history of ideas about international relations; the belief that academics should keep a critical distance from the short-termism of policy-making; and finally, the recognition that an enquiry into the normative basis of international society must proceed on a comparative basis. These fundamental points of convergence have prompted a representation in the literature of the Wight-Bull lineage as the backbone of the international society tradition.

As we have seen from his British Committee papers, Bull favoured a pluralist conception of international society which provided a tolerable international order founded on a limited consensus to uphold the norms of sovereignty and non-intervention. In this sense, pluralism mediated the realist denial of the existence of international society, and the natural law assumption of its *a priori* existence. Although the body of his work argued for a pluralist conception of international society on the grounds that it preserved international order, his later work highlighted his increasing concern that the ideological polarisation of post-1945 international society threatened to undermine the very order that pluralism promised. In view of his growing disenchantment with pluralism, Bull was pulled back to consider whether justice could be placed on the agenda of international society without undermining international order.[1]

In the course of unravelling Hedley Bull's pluralist theory of international society and his subsequent explorations on the edge of solidarism, this chapter will address the following themes and questions in successive sections. The first section reflects on Bull's view of International Relations as a discipline, in particular, his understanding of the relationship between theory and history, scholarly enquiry and policy-relevancy. Part two considers how Bull arrived at pluralism through a critique of realist deniers of international morality and natural law thinkers who assumed an in-built and universal morality. With pluralism, Bull believed it was possible to balance the tension between order and justice. However, his later thinking reveals a deep ambiguity about whether it was possible to rethink the order-justice conundrum without privileging power and interests *or* falling foul of the criticisms he made of solidarism in his early British Committee paper. Finally, the chapter will consider how Bull would have interpreted the tectonic changes which have taken place in international society since the late 1980s. Would he have viewed the end of the Cold War, and reconciliation in South Africa, as evidence of growing ideological convergence? Or would he point to the new polarisation between the West and the rest as evidence of the deep divisions over values which continue to exist in global politics?

An Australian at the Gates of the 'English School'

In his address given at the memorial service to Hedley Bull in October 1985, his colleague Adam Watson recalled Herbert Butterfield saying to him, after Bull had attended the British Committee for only a few meetings: 'It looks as though Hedley Bull will be the ablest of us all.'[2] What is noteworthy about this passage is not the high praise so much as the idea that Bull had become one of 'us'. This touches upon the cultural question of how identities were formed in the encounter between Britain and its former colonies. In many respects, Bull's biography is a paradigmatic example of the socialisation of élites from former British colonies. For a graduate from the University of Sydney's Faculty of Arts in 1952, the transition to Oxford to undertake a B.Phil in Politics was no doubt considerably easier than for a British graduate with a first degree from outside the London-Oxford-Cambridge 'golden triangle'.

Bull's arrival in the UK in the 1950s coincided with a heightened sense of exceptionalism in Australian political culture.[3] The invention of a distinctive Australian identity inculcated a scepticism about accepted religious and ethical mores, an appreciation of iconoclasm, and a belief in egalitarianism (as long as this only extended as far as 'Australians' from 'British stock').[4] Adam Watson described Bull as 'a very dinkum Aussie', and Michael Howard's eulogy testifies to his iconoclasm which was in full flow at the time Bull was writing *The Control of the Arms Race*.[5] The decade he spent as Professor of International Relations in the Research School of Pacific Studies at the Australian National University in Canberra (from 1966 to 1975) no doubt put even more clear blue water between his worldview and the value system which underpinned the British Committee. In short, Bull was a hybrid of two political cultures which, whilst sharing certain affinities to a liberal constitutional tradition, nevertheless exhibited quite different positions on key postwar issues, from the personal to the international political.[6]

Hedley Bull's move up the academic ladder continued in 1955 with his appointment to an assistant lectureship in International Relations at the LSE (the choice of C.A.W. Manning). In a rather muted but amusing tone, J.D.B. Miller described how, although Bull's relations with Manning were 'complex', Bull nevertheless 'enjoyed the stimulation of trying to understand his themes.'[7] Although Manning may have been a source of intellectual amusement to Bull, nevertheless the two most important intellectual influences on Bull in the late 1950s were his senior colleague Martin Wight, and Philip Noel-Baker, an eminent writer on disarmament. Hedley Bull was recommended to Noel-Baker as a research assistant for his project on the arms race, but their working relationship could not withstand their widely differing views on the conditions for a stable international order. Noel-Baker published the book *The Arms Race: A Programme for World Disarmament* in 1958, and a year later Bull published a severe critique of it. Bull's central claim was that the disarmers had failed to understand the structural features of the international system which mitigate against comprehensive disarmament. The key difference between Bull and Noel-Baker was that Bull believed that security policies must work within existing institutions of international society (especially the balance of power) and not against them. In this respect, there is a unity of purpose in the two principle sub-fields of the discipline in which Bull worked, strategic studies and international theory.[8]

Revisiting the Three Traditions

As a junior academic, Bull attended Wight's lectures on the 'three Rs' (probably in 1955/6), noting later in life how they had made 'a profound impression on me.'[9] Bull was, however, ultimately more cautious than his mentor about the value of the three traditions *per se*. He was less interested in the hermeneutic act of reconstructing the conversation between philosophers and practitioners about the origins and development of norms and values in the society of states. The question which motivated Bull's theoretical investigations was not whether a certain state leader or diplomat conformed to a discernible Grotian or Marchiavellian tradition, but to what extent these practices can be identified within contemporary international society. This was the agenda that *The Anarchical Society* addressed, as did *The Expansion of International Society*. In these works, the 'three Rs' are used only in so far as they encapsulate co-existing patterns in international relations.[10] Bull's unstinting belief that inter-state relations constituted an international society, despite persistent challenges from the realist 'right' and the revolutionist 'left', led him to reflect more deeply than Wight about the relationship between Grotian ideas and the daily practices of states. It is this sustained examination of the *via media* which is Bull's most significant contribution to Martin Wight's three traditions.

Bull's treatment of Grotian ideas in *The Anarchical Society* is arguably more restrictive than in 'The Grotian Conception of International Society'. Following Wight, he defines the Grotian tradition descriptively in terms of 'economic and social intercourse' between states, and prescriptively as the subjective sense of being 'bound by the rules and institutions of the society they form.'[11] The idea of transnational solidarity in this schema is something which is accorded to 'revolutionists' like Kant.[12] Here we see the deep ambiguity in the international society literature as to whether 'solidarism' refers to horizontal movements which cut across states (transnational solidarity), or whether states themselves can act in solidarist ways (international solidarity).[12] In his consideration of alternative paths to world order at the end of *The Anarchical Society*, Bull reverts to considering Grotian solidarism in terms of the capacity of states to recognise common objectives and devise institutions and practices to promote them. In this discussion, solidarism is associated with the abolition of the resort to war for political ends, and the attempt to subordinate the use of force to the collective will of the society of states.

One of Bull's last projects was to bring together Grotian scholars for a lecture series in 1983 which eventually formed the backbone to the volume *Hugo Grotius and International Relations*, published after his death. In his essay on 'The Importance of Grotius', Bull clearly argues for the restrictive definition of solidarism as law enforcement. There is no mention of the broader idea of solidarism in respect to the obligation on states to act as 'guardians of human rights everywhere', as there had been twenty five years earlier. Although he recognises the Grotian 'turn' in the post-1945 international legal regime, where individuals can be held responsible for crimes carried out in accordance with a government's instruction, Bull did not make the case for the relevance of Grotius' treatment of individuals as subjects of international law in terms of solidarity between individuals and groups being oppressed in one state, and the practical and moral consequences this holds for individuals and their governments in other states.

In addition to the revisions Bull makes to the content of solidarism, what is striking about Bull's essay on 'The Importance of Grotius' is his more cautious approach to the history of ideas. Aware of the problems of anachronism, Bull argued that it was 'absurd to read Grotius as if he were speaking to us directly about the problems of our own times.'[14] That said, what interested him about Grotius was the fact that he was a man of his time; he stared into the abyss of the Wars of Religion and from that point on channelled his intellectual and political energy into dealing with complex normative questions about the changing conception of sovereignty evolving in the seventeenth century: what rights and duties did states have? what were legitimate reasons for the use of force? what rules were European states subject to in their relations with non-European peoples and states? Bull was not claiming that Grotius was responsible for the new European order, only that he was constitutive of it in both a theoretical and a practical sense. This combination of theoretical insight and practical foresight is one which Bull held in high regard. Grotius was not only a visionary, able to stand back from the prevailing assumptions of his day in order to articulate a different kind of international society, he was also a practitioner rooted in his own time and space. 'The seminal works of policy', argued Bull in the conclusion to his chapter, 'are those whose authors are not mere visionaries but are able to take account of the prevailing forces and reshape or redirect them.'[15]

Hedley Bull and the 'Two Worlds' of Theory and Practice

The vexed question of the relationship between the world of ideas, and their relevance to policy-making, was an issue which Bull gave considerable attention. Despite his admiration for what he regarded as Grotius' successful synthesis of the theory and practice and his own desire to engage with a world beyond theory, he remained of the opinion that the spheres of academia and policy-making should remain distinct. This reification of the quality of detachment is one which contains within it the kernel of two important liberal principles. The first is that the role of an intellectual is to be unrelentingly critical of *all* political principles, including his or her own. The second concerns his recognition of the need for distance from the short-termism of foreign policy-making. In the case of the former, he had in his sights Richard Falk; and in the latter, Henry Kissinger.

Bull never tired of turning the weapon of the relativity of thought against proponents of radical change, or what he pejoratively referred to as 'the Philip Noel-Baker Syndrome'.[16] The Peace Research movement 'suffered' from this affliction in the late 1960s and early 1970s, as did the Princeton group of WOMPers centred on Richard Falk's 'global salvationism'. For Falk, the role of the academic was to advocate universal moral values such as peace, economic and social justice, ecological sustainability and human rights. The belief that alternative theory can transform political practices leading to the development of a global community of humankind is what distinguishes Falk's conception of the role of an academic from that maintained by Bull.

Why was Bull so concerned to debunk those who espoused an overtly political doctrine? In an *adhominem* critique of Falk's work, Bull argued that Falk had fallen down the slippery slope 'from analysis to advocacy'. This is his stinging conclusion:

> The task of the academic inquirer is not to jump on bandwagons but to stand back and assess, in a disinterested way, the direction they are going. Any writer can join a political movement and devote his intellectual talents to supplying the rhetoric, the exaggeration, the denunciation and the slurring of issues which will help to speed it on its way. It does not seem the best use for the talents of the Albert G. Milbank Professor of International Law.[17]

Bull's critique of Falk would seem to imply that Bull believed it was possible to make a positivistic distinction between facts, which could be analysed in a disinterested way, and values, which belonged to a subjective realm more suited to moral philosophy than political science. This was not, however, the case. As Bull put it in his article on 'International Relations as an Academic Pursuit', there is 'no such thing as a "value-free" inquiry into International Relations.'[18]

From the mid-1960s onwards, Bull had become increasingly critical of the tendency in American International Relations to deny the role of values in shaping academic investigations. Although recognising the positive contributions of scholars such as Schelling, Kaplan and Deutsch, Bull argued that the American hegemony over academic International Relations was leading to the double closure of 'intellectual and political conformism'. Steering a middle course between the tendency towards the scholasticism of some of his British Committee colleagues, and the scientism of the behaviouralists, Bull's methodology is best summed up as 'a blend of intelligent social science and humanism'.[19] As a social scientist, the International Relations scholar should seek to explain and uncover answers to the big questions about war, power, justice, intervention, rights, law, sovereignty. As a humanist, the academic should be aware not only of the consequences of their ideas/theories, but the existence of an ethical dimension in all realms of political action.

There is one further ingredient to the humanist approach and that concerns the emphasis upon human agency rather than systemic structures in determining outcomes.[20] This explains why Bull had little time for those who failed to empathise with the concerns of state leaders. As he put it in his lectures on *Justice and International Relations*, in steering a path between conflicting moral values, 'terrible choices have sometimes to be made.'[21] One state leader which Bull exhibited less empathy towards was Henry Kissinger. The former US Secretary of State was a paradigmatic example of the dangers inherent in the explosive combination of advocacy and power. Bull argued that Kissinger should not have been bitter about his treatment by other academics and intellectuals. It is precisely the calling of academics 'to ask irresponsible questions'[22] and attempt to expose the hypocrisy and deceit of those at the helm of the ship of state. As a general rule, 'Professors do not make good policy-makers', and as a particular case study, Kissinger provided 'a very unfortunate example to a profession whose business is, after all, with thinking, and not with doing.'[23]

It is perhaps possible to see an overlay of the 'three Rs' accompanying Bull's understanding of the relationship between theory and practice, thinking and doing. Revolutionists were not to be trusted as they had a tendency to confuse political doctrines with intellectual enquiry. Even if their position had some merit, how can they be so sure of their foundations? At the other end of the continuum, realists evince too much complacency, allowing constraints upon action to mask over a lack of moral ambition. The more plausible position, according to Bull, was a middle path which embodied to some extent a combination of commitment (without partisanship) and detachment (without being unworldly). To this end, he recommended the addition of the rare quality of unrelenting criticism of one's own position and that of others. As Bull put it, in a very postmodern intervention, 'the best foundation for this is political nihilism.'[24]

It is worth noting that Bull saw in the 'British model' an adequate distance between the 'two worlds' of academe and policy-making.[25] He was however, critical of the lack of engagement with his other British Committee colleagues in contemporary debates with International Relations and the social sciences more generally. Perhaps this adds further weight to the argument that Bull represented a different political culture from his predecessors. He was less inclined to treat academic inquiry in terms of a polite conversation between the converted, and more motivated to take on opponents in order to force them (and himself in the process) to critically examine their own positions.

A Disenchanted Pluralist?

Despite the methodological weaknesses noted earlier, Bull's British Committee papers shows how he innovatively sought to develop the pluralist and solidarist wings of the English School as a way of mapping the normative possibilities of the society of states. Like E.H. Carr's manipulation of the dualism 'utopia' and 'reality', Bull's thinking exhibited a perennial tension between the two planes of pluralism and solidarism.

Pluralism as a Critique of Realism

As we saw in Chapter 1, E.H. Carr advanced a devastating critique of ethical universalism in *The Twenty Years' Crisis*. Carr's master-stroke was to relativise the universalist claims of statesmen in order to reveal the partial interests which were driving their arguments. Carr's insistence upon wielding the weapon of the 'relativity of thought' reflected his belief that there were no disinterested standards for judging political conduct.

In '*The Twenty Years' Crisis* Thirty Years On', Bull challenged head-on 'the weapon of the relativity of thought'[26] which Carr believed to be the apotheosis of realist thought. Relativism, argued Bull, was inadequate because it denied 'all independent validity to moral argument' thereby preventing Carr from an 'elaboration of the notion of the good of international society as a whole.'[27] The essence of Bull's dismissal of Carr's moral relativism is the purported existence of some values (for example, order) which may be for 'the good of international society as a whole.'[28] This is the key point with which Bull concluded his critique of Carr's:

> The idea of an international society – of common interests and common values perceived in common by modern states – is scarcely recognised in *The Twenty Years' Crisis*. In the course of demonstrating how appeals to an overriding international society subserve the special interests of the ruling group of powers, Carr jettisons the idea of international society itself. This is the idea with which a new analysis of the problem of international relations should now begin.[29]

The above passage underlines the depths of Bull's dissatisfaction with the normative void he felt Carr had left.[30] In place of Carr's political realism, Bull sought to construct an international theory which more closely reflected the practices of sovereign states. Bull asks the question how far the idea of international society is reflected in the thought of statesmen, and he concludes that 'the element of a society has always been present, and remains present, in the modern international system.'[31] According to Bull's famous definition, international society exists because states believe themselves to be '*bound* by a common set of rules and institutions.'[32]

International law was central to his vindication of the existence of international morality.[33] In response to the realist argument that states obey international law only when it is in their self-interest, Bull suggests what is more surprising is that states 'so often judge it in their interests to conform to it.'[34] This narrow argument about the motives of states in conforming to international law is projected onto the broader canvas of international society as a whole. Given the recognition by states that they have rights

and duties in their relations with one another, the case for international
society against *realpolitik* is that states will adhere to the rules and norms
of the society of states even when these conflict with their non-vital interests.[35] The argument which Bull is making – although at times somewhat
implicitly – is that states should act (implying an element of agency) in a
way which strengthens the normative principles of international society.[36]
It is at this point that Bull clearly departs from the core principles of political realism. In short, by strengthening the institutions of international
society, the logic of anarchy can be mitigated.[37]

Despite challenging Carr's ethical relativism, a number of Carr's realist
sirens can be detected in Bull's work. Both were cognisant of the fact that
in international politics conflicts of interest were, in Carr's words, 'real
and inevitable'.[38] For this reason, Bull was keen to remind the liberal idealists that the dilemmas of statecraft require state leaders to settle for the
least worst outcome. In addition to recognising the ubiquity of conflict,
Carr and Bull both recognised that international politics was a site upon
which the ritualistic clashes of power and morality, war and law, were
played out. A third area of agreement between Carr and Bull concerned
the centrality of the traditional practices of statecraft, such as the balance
of power and war, to the management of international relations.

In the final analysis, Bull acknowledged Carr's skill in mobilising the
weapon of the 'relativity of thought' to critique the fictional world community of the 'utopians', and as his attack on Falk demonstrated, showed
himself to be not adverse to slaying contemporary universalists with the
same weapon. But never losing sight of the critical power of realism, he
was dissatisfied with its narrowly defined ethics of self-interest. Bull's
interest was in the survival of the society of states, understanding the
nature of the rules which underpinned international society and the bonds
which shaped their social relations. For these reasons, it is unsatisfactory
to place Bull in the realist tradition.[39] Even when Hedley Bull entered the
mansion of realism, he remained detached from the paradigmatic claim
that international politics is a struggle for power among atomistic states
driven by the desire for self-preservation.

Pluralism and the Critique of Natural Law
Whilst Bull believed, in contrast to Carr, that it was possible to make distinctions between actions taken to promote a world common good, and
acts of naked self-interest, he nevertheless agreed with Carr that natural
law provided spurious grounds upon which to guide moral actions. In
a number of review essays in the late 1970s Bull was highly critical
of writers sympathetic to the natural law tradition who assumed that a

primordial community of humankind was 'already in place'. In this instance, his target was the natural law thinking of E.B.F. Midgley and Michael Donelan.

In his critique of Midgley in 'Natural Law and International Relations', Bull counselled against the foundationalist premise of 'a fixed point of reference' from where 'all moral disagreements can in principle be settled.'[40] World politics, according to Bull, is an arena where individuals and groups 'are in conflict about the most basic moral ends, and when that occurs there is sometimes no rational way of choosing between them.'[41] Bull also challenged the more 'empirical equivalent of natural law' evident in Michael Donelan's work. In his review of Donelan's edited collection *The Reason of States*, he offered a trenchant critique of the natural law principles which framed Donelan's understanding of the society of states:

> Michael Donelan writes that political theorists have assumed a world of separate states... He proposes that instead we begin with the assumption of 'a primordial community of mankind', of which the world of separate states is but a particular arrangement. ... The trouble with this is that while individual human beings are primordial, and separate states a mere arrangement of them, the community of mankind is not primordial but is on the contrary a mere figment of the imagination.[42]

Michael Donelan's response, galvanised by his adversary's accusation that some of the essays in the volume were 'half-baked', accused Bull of being a 'positivist' for not regarding the global community as anything other than a means by which diverse cultures 'agree enough about expediency and power to run an orderly states-system.'[43] In the letters page of the following month's *Times Literary Supplement*, Bull clarified his position in relation to Donelan's: '[t]he issue, as it appears to me, is not whether "in *reason*" there exists a moral community of mankind, but whether one exists in *fact*.'[44] By the term 'in fact', Bull means whether the moral community exists as a shared practice among state leaders and the extent to which universal values permeate the wider consciousness of humankind.

What is interesting about his exchanges with these two proponents of natural law thinking is the way in which they both underestimate the extent of Bull's moral universalism. E.B.F. Midgley accused him of being the slave of a 'liberal arts' modernism which prevented him from discovering 'what are the fundamental truths.'[45] Similarly, Donelan arguably misrepresented Bull as someone who regarded states as 'moral islands'. By way of a response to these critics, consider Bull's defence of the society of states as an instrument for delivering the moral value of 'world order'.

In *The Anarchical Society*, Bull defines 'world order' as 'those patterns or dispositions of human activity that sustain the elementary or primary goals of social life among mankind as a whole'.[47] He contrasts this with order among states (which he calls international order) and argues:

> Order among mankind as a whole is something wider than order among states; something more fundamental and primordial than it; and also, I should argue, something morally prior to it … 'world order' is more fundamental and primordial than international order because the ultimate units of the great society of all mankind are not states (or nations, tribes, empires, classes or parties) but are individual human beings … it is necessary at this point to state that if any value attaches to order in world politics, it is order among all mankind which we must treat as being of primary value, not order within the society of states as such.[47]

Therefore, in contrast to the natural lawyers, the underlying moral universalism in Bull's thinking concerns his insistence that individuals are the ultimate moral referent. International order is only to be valued to the extent which it delivers 'world order', which Bull makes the litmus test for the ethical claims of the society of states.[48]

Out of this two-pronged offensive against realism and natural law universalism, Bull constructed a pluralist theory of international society. Taking from the realists, pluralism recognises that states with different conceptions of justice must provide for a minimum inter-state order, and from the ethical universalists, the recognition that the moral value of a pluralist society of states has to be judged in terms of its contribution to individual well-being (since Bull makes this the ultimate test of any ethical position).[49] Surprisingly, Bull did not explicitly state this defence of pluralism, but what is implicit in Bull has been made explicit by Robert Jackson, Terry Nardin, Chris Brown and others.[50] The morality of a pluralist conception of international society, argues Jackson, depends upon the assumption that states 'are valuable in themselves'. In this sense, international society 'presupposes the intrinsic value of all states and accommodates their inward diversity.[51]

The later Bull and the Limits of Pluralism
Hedley Bull's pluralist conception of international society rests on the explicit claim that it can deliver inter-state order in conditions of cultural heterogeneity. However, later in life Bull came to express increasing

disillusionment with pluralism on the grounds that it could not provide for order among states and hence order among the wider society of humankind. The reason for Bull's worries about order can be traced to his analysis of the role played by the great powers. Hedley Bull identifies two prescriptive roles for the great powers in providing for international and world order: first, they should manage their own relations in an orderly manner,[52] and second, they ought to use their dominant position in relation to the rest of international society in such a way as to strengthen rather than weaken the society of states.[53]

Bull invested in the great powers the responsibility for managing the society of states and became increasingly disillusioned by their failure to act as global guardians. He recognises that although the practice of great power responsibility is at variance with the principle of sovereign equality, such an affront to inter-state justice is a necessary requirement for inter-state order. Thus, the legitimacy of the institution of the great powers depends upon how far their special privileges are made acceptable to others. In making their dominant position acceptable to international society, Bull argued that the great powers must accept their duties which include the following: they should refrain from disorderly acts themselves; they should show that they can be responsive to demands for just change; and they should co-opt aspiring secondary powers into the great power club. Here Bull is appealing to the argument he deployed against Carr, namely, that the desire for some minimum order is so 'powerful and universal' that states are willing to accept the benefits of an order even if this reflects the value of the dominant states.

Bull reflects on the descriptive role of the superpowers in sustaining inter-state order in the conclusion to *The Anarchical Society*. Echoing his critique of Carr's view of morality as a cloak for great power interests, Bull contends that the critics of 'superpower hegemonism' are too inclined to treat the superpower detente of the 1970s as simply serving the interests of the United States and the Soviet Union. Instead, Bull made the case that these tentative moves towards co-operation were in the wider interest of the society of states since all states benefited from steps taken to reduce the risks of nuclear war. Indeed, Bull suggested that the superpowers might be seen as 'trustees for mankind as a whole'.[54]

Bull's judicious thoughts in *The Anarchical Society* on the superpowers' claim to the mantle of the 'great responsibles' coincided with the period of US/Soviet detente. However, when he returned to these questions during the second Cold War, Bull was much more pessimistic as to the role of the superpowers in providing order. He wrote, '[t]he United States and Soviet Union have little claim to be regarded as nuclear trustees for mankind ... it is difficult to find evidence in any part of the world that they are still viewed as the great responsibles.'[55] Whatever hopes Bull had entertained in the mid-1970s of superpower responsibility as a means of sustaining a pluralist society of states had foundered on the rocks of US/Soviet antagonism.

Looking back on the failed experiment of superpower management in the 1970s, Bull characteristically resisted the temptation to blame one superpower or the other. Instead, he identified the deeper problem as lying in the ideological antipathy between East and West which prevented the superpowers from acting out their prescribed role as custodians of inter-state order. This failure cast considerable doubt as to whether pluralism – which promises order in a divided world – could accommodate the ideological polarisation of the Cold War.

Bull's concerns about the ability of the superpowers to provide for order was only one element in what he perceived to be the general malaise in the society of states at the end of the twentieth century. His anxieties centred on the consequences for order of the cultural heterogeneity of post-colonial international society. Bull's thinking on this question oscillates between optimistic and pessimistic readings.[56] With regard to the former, he was encouraged by the extent to which Third World states had accepted the cardinal norms of the European society of states. Southern states have sought to reshape existing rules and institutions to eliminate discrimination and to break down barriers of exclusion, but they have also recognised a strong common interest in respecting the ethic of coexistence. This reflects not only their desire to protect their new found sovereignty and independence in their relations with the western powers, but also their need for these rules in regulating their relations with each other. This is the case in particular with the non-intervention principle which remains the constitutive norm of the society of states, and is guarded most jealously by post-colonial states.[57] To this extent the southern states' demands for independence and sovereign equality are compatible with the pluralist theory of international society.

Bull's pessimistic thinking on the globalisation of European international society centred on the question of how far it could endure with only a 'thin' sense of common interests and common values? His doubts about the resilience of European international society are clearly evident in a passage towards the end of *The Anarchical Society*: 'the international history of this century so far may be regarded as a prolonged attempt to cope with the drastic decline of the element of society in international relations brought about by the single, catastrophic "accident" of the First World War.'[58]

The pluralist conception of international society promises order among ideologically heterogeneous states. But the question raised by Bull's analysis of the Cold War and decolonisation is how far does coexistence depend upon some minimal ideological consensus? Pluralists privilege order over justice in the belief that there is not sufficient solidarity among humankind to provide for the latter, but why should we accept this moral minimalism if pluralism cannot deliver an ethic of coexistence? This is where Bull arrived at by the end of *The Anarchical Society* where he argued that both order and justice depended upon developing more solidarist sentiments in the society of states.

Bull set about investigating the possibilities for cosmopolitan solidarism in the Hagey Lectures given at the University of Waterloo in 1983. There is no doubt that these lectures present more starkly than in any of Bull's other works the acceptance of solidarism as a legitimate voice in the debate about what constitutes justice in international society. On the face of it, this signals a movement away from his critique of solidarism in his 1962 British Committee paper. Moreover, the solidarist shadows in the lectures underscore how far Bull's disillusionment with pluralism went beyond considerations of whether it was providing for inter-state order. Bull's engagement with the 'revolt against the West' in these lectures on *Justice in International Relations* called into question the moral legitimacy of a society of states based upon norms of sovereignty and non-intervention.

Making explicit what had been suggested in *The Anarchical Society*, Bull argued that 'the question of justice concerns what is due not only to states and nations, but to all individual persons in an imagined community of mankind.'[59] The moral value of the society of states had to be judged in terms of what it contributed to the achievement of individual justice because the value of inter-state order is only a 'derivative value', and what 'ultimately' is important 'has to be reckoned in terms of the rights and interests of the individual persons of whom humanity is made up, not the rights and interests of the states into which these persons are now divided.'[60] Given Bull's awareness that the majority of the members of the South denied their citizens basic civil and political rights, and that a significant number of these states tortured and murdered them, he must surely have begun to doubt the normative basis upon which pluralism rests.[61]

Bull identified a 'growing cosmopolitan moral awareness', at least among the 'advanced countries', which was leading the West to increasingly 'empathise with sections of humanity that are geographically or culturally distant from us.'[62] He recognised that this emerging 'awareness' that states have responsibilities to maintain basic global welfare values was only reflected to a limited degree in foreign policy, and that it was possible to regard the humanitarian activities of governments in a 'cynical' and 'hypocritical' way. That said, in the final analysis, Bull thought that 'the mere existence of this moral concern with welfare on a world scale represents a major change in our sensibilities.'[63] Bull's sympathy for common humanity can be seen in his call for 'particular states to act as... local agents of a world common good.'[64] Nowhere in the lectures does he specify which states should fulfil this role, but the logic of his theory points to the great powers, since they assume such a prominent role in Bull's conception of international society.[65] However, this argument is clearly at odds with the scepticism he expressed in *The Anarchical Society* about the capacity of the great powers to provide for both order and justice.

Hedley Bull's project outlined in *Justice and International Relations* is certainly an ambitious one. It amounted to nothing less than an attempt to think through how the advanced industrial states and the poorer states might be drawn into a conversation as to what constitutes the 'world common good' at the end of the twentieth century. The presumption here is that the North[66] should seek to accommodate the demands of the South for a re-distribution of wealth, while those 'quasi-states'[67] which had little 'respect for constitutions or acceptance of the rules of law' would come to recognise that 'some degree of commitment to the cause of individual human rights on a world scale must follow.'[68] Bull was clear that in this dialogue the West need not apologise for its commitment to liberal values and institutions.[69] At the same time, he implied that the South's views on human rights as economic and social rights were 'equally legitimate topics of conversation.'[70]

These solidarist sentiments in the lectures are checked by an abiding scepticism as to how far they could be realised in practice. Having told us that individual rights and duties are the ultimate moral referent, and that a commitment to basic human rights must underpin any cosmopolitan culture, Bull points to the continuing lack of agreement among states as to what is meant by human rights:

> The cosmopolitanist society which is implied and presupposed in our talk of human rights exists only as an ideal, and we court great dangers if we allow ourselves to proceed as if it were a political and social framework already in place.[71]

Here Bull worried that particular states – setting themselves up as judges of what constituted universal human rights – would threaten the ethic of co-existence. Whilst there is a need for states to act as 'agents of a world common good', Bull was all too aware that 'states are notoriously self-serving in their policies, and rightly suspected when they purport to act on behalf of the international community as a whole.'[72]

Despite Bull's doubts about the capacity of states to act as agents of solidarism, he was increasingly drawn to the idea that without justice, there could be no lasting order. He had not forgotten his earlier doubts about whether it was possible to reach a consensus on justice, but the liberal solidarist in him wanted to believe that 'the measures that are necessary to achieve justice for the peoples of the Third World are the same measures that will maximise the prospects of international order or stability, at least in the long run.'[73] His growing conviction that justice was the precondition for a lasting order can be seen in an address Bull gave in Canberra, 1983:

> For all this the Western countries today, and especially the United States, display an appalling lack of vision in their policies towards the South.... No international order can endure in the future unless these states and people believe themselves to have a stake in its continuance. The issue that this raises for the Western powers is not mainly or even chiefly a moral one.... We must take the Third World seriously primarily because of the vital interest we have in constructing an international order in which we ourselves will have a prospect of living in peace and security into the next century and beyond. This requires that we in the West should be ready to accommodate the demands of Third World countries for a redistribution of wealth and power in the international system.[74]

E.H. Carr had advocated appeasement principally on prudential grounds,[75] and Bull's prescriptions seem to ultimately rest on the same instrumentalist foundations.

In the Canberra lecture, Bull was arguing that whilst the western states had a moral obligation to strengthen justice in world politics, the West had a 'vital interest' in creating a more just international order. Bull's solidarist aspirations required the western states to redistribute wealth to a minority of powerful southern states on the grounds that these states need to be 'co-opted' into the management of the global order. The problem is that he gives us no good reason to assume that southern states such as India and Brazil, will place the victims of international inequality at the centre of their domestic and foreign policies. What is striking about Bull's instrumentalist defence of justice is that ultimately he permits the content of justice to be cajoled by the convenience of power. In other words, the logic of Bull's position is that we only have a security interest in accommodating those who have the power to cause immense transnational harm.

In framing the case for a redistribution of wealth on grounds of order, Bull is unable to cast off the shadow of Carr's critique that 'power always creates a morality which is convenient to itself.' As we have seen, Bull's explorations on the edge of solidarism looked to the possibility of an imagined community of humankind but 'he is constantly pulled back to a position of profound scepticism.' Is this scepticism a product of the theoretical inadequacy of this articulate voice of the English School to liberate solidarism from the schackles of realism-cum-pluralism? Or was Bull's normative theory so imprisoned by the necessity of managing power and order during the Cold War that solidarism remained still-born? These questions will be considered in the final part of the chapter.

Solidarism in the Post-Cold War Period

When contemplating the solidarist potential of the post-Cold War world, it is instructive to return to *The Anarchical Society*, thirty years on. In Part Three of the book, Bull considers several alternatives to the contemporary states system. The 'solidarity of states' model, he argues, 'would be radically different from what exists now, but would represent a new phase of the states system, not its replacement by something different.'[76] What is sketched before us bears a striking resemblance to the reformist ideas put forward in the early post-Cold War period and assembled under the banner 'new world order'. Even the initial use of the phrase by President Bush was represented in terms of 'solidarity against aggression',[77] or what Bull referred to as 'solidarity, or potential solidarity, of most states in the world in upholding the collective will of the society of states against challenges to it.'[78] In the Gulf War there was undoubtedly a rare sense of solidarity among the 'law-enforcers' to uphold the constitutive principles of non-aggression and the right of Kuwait to be protected by the norms of sovereignty and nonintervention. However, this solidarity did not extend beyond the rights of sovereigns to encompass the rights of individuals and groups who were subject to mass killings after the 'cease fire'. Even at the creation of the 'new world order' then, solidarism was at best only partial.

Reflecting on the humanitarian crises of the 1990s,[79] Nick Wheeler and Justin Morris have pointed to the continuing relevance of Bull's earlier judgement that the society of states was not solidarist enough to legitimise collective humanitarian intervention. His concern centred on the dangers to international order of implementing particular conceptions of justice in a world where there was no shared understanding of what justice entails, and no consensus on what level of human suffering would justify humanitarian intervention. Writing in the mid-1980s, Bull stated forcefully: 'The reluctance evident in the international community even to experiment with the conception of a right of humanitarian intervention reflects not only an unwillingness to jeopardise the rules of sovereignty and non-intervention by conceding such a right to individual states, but also the lack of any agreed doctrine as to what human rights are.'[80]

When Bull was writing about the lack of consensus among states on the 'doctrine' of human rights he had in mind in particular the need to take on board the Third World's conception of human rights as economic and social rights. Although the referent for the Third World may have changed, as modernisation brings former Third World states into the 'core', and the remainder become consigned to a new global underclass, the question of the content and scope of human rights remains as contested as when Bull was writing.[81] In this new revolt against western values, Bull would no doubt have offered a similar prognosis: the West should permit the dilution and hybridisation of its culture and beliefs, whilst realising that the lack of consensus about those values does not invalidate them.[82]

Although Bull's scepticism about the potential for state leaders to act as moral guardians would not have been challenged by the way in which the society of states has responded to humanitarian crises, he might, however, have been more sanguine about the prospects of solidarity taking root in the wider world society (of individuals, peoples, and NGOs). The common culture of modernity, which Bull saw as something of an élite phenomena, is now far more widely distributed, particularly across metropolitan districts of world society. This blurring of the boundaries of difference creates the possibility for deeper solidarities beyond borders. No doubt Bull would have checked this sentiment by voicing concern about the potential for NGOs and global corporations to act as the new irresponsibles, given their relative autonomy from the society of states and its institutions. Nevertheless, there are good reasons for thinking that he would have accepted the need to include other actors in the attempt to forge a new consensus on the construction of trans-cultural moral solidarity. A related dimension to this argument, and one which finds Bull's ideas inadvertently dovetailing with the prevailing currents in philosophy, concerns his recognition that a new consensus cannot be grounded in natural law. In particular, having argued that there are no in-built human rights, Bull explored how far a consensus could be reached on the content of 'basic human rights' through the kind of inter-cultural conversation advocated in the 1990s by thinkers such as Bhikhu Parekh.[83]

A second reason why Bull might have looked at the 1990s with more optimism than the last decades of the Cold War, concerns the end of apartheid in South Africa. The endurance of a political system founded on ethnic exclusion was an issue which he devoted considerable attention to, not just because it was one of the great moral questions of the day, but also because the wider reaction to the apartheid regime posed important questions for the relationship between order and justice. Despite important economic and strategic considerations interests in maintaining normal diplomatic and political relations with South Africa (order), there exists a 'world consensus' which exists 'against this surviving symbol of white supremacism that all other societies in the world, to different degrees and in different ways, have repudiated over the last three decades' (justice).[84] What is particularly interesting about this discussion is that Bull believed South Africa to be a 'microcosm of the world'. Just as the white minority have had to come to terms with black majority rule, he prophetically argued that privileged western publics will have to adapt to the withering away of their dominance.[85]

There is one more reason why the post-Cold War period would have seemed more solidarist in Bull's mind. In a number of articles about European security in the early 1980s, Bull had become increasingly sceptical about the dependence of Western Europe on the security 'guarantees' of the US. Given the increasing divergence in American and European security interests, Europe needed to become more 'self-reliant' and in the process, 'make progress towards realising the idea of their unity'.[86] Indeed, Bull's analysis of the possibilities for new forms of governance to emerge in Europe were remarkably prescient. Recognising that sovereignty was being devolved down to regions and up to international institutions, and that states could no longer expect exclusive loyalty from their citizens, Bull anticipated that these changes would constitute a form of regional order which had gone 'beyond the state'.[87]

Conclusion

Just as Carr turned to utopianism, Hedley Bull's later work highlighted a growing recognition of the normative weakness of a pluralist society of states. For this reason he looked to solidarism and its promise of a deeper consensus on substantive goals such as distributive justice, environmental protection and universal human rights. An example of the inadequacy of pluralism was revealed in the consideration on Bull's reflections on justice in the context of North/South relations. In the final analysis, Bull's doubts about whether it was possible to mount a philosophical defence of justice, led him to make the case for justice in terms of its contribution to order. The reason why he buttressed this appeal with the claim that all states have an interest in order was that this would be more persuasive to western states than simply appealing to moral solidarity. This reveals Bull's deep inner tension between the rational intellectual speaking to policy-oriented constituencies, and the sympathetic will driving Bull to lend his voice to what he saw as the just claims of the Third World.

The fleeting moment of liberal solidarism in Bull's thought rests uneasily with his contention that terrible choices might have to be made between order and justice. As discussed above, Bull was fearful that to pursue partial conceptions of justice might undermine the rules of coexistence upon which the society of states rested. This explains his cautious response to those who claimed that international society recognised a right of humanitarian intervention. The failure of the society of states in the post-Cold War era to extend its enforcement of the law beyond inter-state order to encompass the policing of human rights abuses, confirms Bull's reluctant judgement that there was no consensus for collective action among the members of the society of states. In this sense, the post-Cold War world has proven Bull to be right. But a lingering doubt remains as to whether Bull's work furnishes an adequate explanation for the failure of the 'new world order'/'solidarity of states' project. Did solidarity against aggression collapse because of disagreements about what constitutes human rights abuses, as Bull argued, or because the voice of cosmopolitan moral awareness was muted in the West?

Bull identified a growing moral solidarity in the late twentieth century, and this is evident in the widespread moral outrage triggered by human suffering in the aftermath of the Gulf, in Bosnia and in Rwanda. But the key question is how far this awareness translates into sustained moral and political action. Given his recognition of the limits of 'cosmopolitan moral awareness' his only mechanism for heightening solidarity was through states acting as guardians over global human rights. Although Bull repeatedly cautioned us to be sceptical of those 'missionaries' who claim to speak on behalf of the global good life, his writings in the last decade of his life highlight his search for a theory of international relations which places morality at the centre whilst recognising that progress has to be negotiated in the society of states. In this sense as in many others, Bull occupied a *via media* in International Relations, between the merchants of theory-as-emancipation and the sceptics who view theory-as-power. In this precarious space, lies a cautious, yet critical, attempt to widen the moral horizon.

156 *Inventing International Society*

NOTES

1. I am grateful to Caroline Blacker for giving me permission to re-print material which first appeared in Nicholas J. Wheeler and Tim Dunne, 'Hedley Bull's Pluralism of the Intellect and Solidarism of the will; *International Affairs* 72 (1996), 91–107.
2. Watson, quoted by J.D.B. Miller 'Hedley Bull, 1932–1985' in J.O.B. Miller and R.J. Vincent (eds), *Order and Violence: Hedley Bull and International Relations* (Oxford: Clarendon, 1990), 199.
3. The paradigmatic text here is Russell Ward, *The Australian Legend* (Melbourne: Oxford University Press, 1978).
4. Professor John Anderson, Bull's philosophical mentor and tutor at the University of Sydney between 1949 and 1952, embodied these values of the new Australia. 'Anderson, probably the most original philosopher ever to have worked in Australia, was a renowned sceptic and iconoclast who aroused the wrath of governments and exhorted his students to adopt a critical approach to everything, including censorship, patriotism, religion and social conventions'. W.M. O'Neil quoted in Robert O'Neill and David N. Schwartz (eds), *Hedley Bull on Arms Control* (London: Macmillan, 1987), 3.
5. This is how Michael Howard remembered Bull's iconoclasm: 'I can still vividly recall the sessions where veteran disarmers, bureaucrats and warriors shook their heads over the lucid draft chapters, clear, uncompromising, sensible, in which this tall, diffident yet abrasive young man cut through half a century's emotional waffle and forced them to think again from first principles. It was this experience which first cast Hedley Bull in the role of the *enfant terrible* of International Relations. Michael Howard, 'Hedley Bull: A Eulogy for his Memorial Service', O'Neill and Schwartz, *Hedley Bull*, 275.
6. Bull recognised there was an English School. This is evident from his comment, no doubt delivered *ex cathedra*, to the effect that 'someone at BISA said there was no British school. Nonsense.' Bull, 'The Appalling State of IR Studies at the LSE and Elsewhere', talk given to the Grimshaw Club, 17.1.80.
7. Miller, 'Hedley Bull 1932–1985', 4.
8. The focus in this chapter will principally be on his contribution to international theory. For a useful compendium of Bull's writings on strategic studies, see O'Neill and Schwartz (eds), *Hedley Bull on Arms Control*.
9. Bull, 'Martin Wight and the theory of international relations', in Martin Wight, *International Theory: The Three Traditions* (Leicester: Leicester University Press, 1991). Although there is a remarkable degree of scholarly continuity between Wight and Bull, both Carsten Holbraad and J.L. Richardson note how Bull was more philosophical and less historical in his approach to ideas. See Holbraad, 'Conclusion' and Richardson, 'The Academic Study of International Relations', in Miller and Vincent (eds), *Order*.
10. As Bull noted after a brief overview of the three traditions: 'This is not the place to explore further the connections and distinctions within each

tradition'. Hedley Bull, *The Anarchical Society: A Study of Order in World Politics* (London: Macmillan, (1 ed., 1977), 27 .

11.   Bull, *The Anarchical Society*, 27.
12.   For critiques of this reading of Kant, see Stanley Hoffmann 'International Society' in Miller and Vincent (eds), *Order and Violence*, 23; and more extensively, Andrew Hurrell 'Kant and the Kantian Paradigm in International Relations', *Review of International Studies* 16 (1990), 183–205. For a critical treatment of Bull's general interpretation of political theory/history of ideas, see Ian Harris, 'Order and Justice in *The Anarchical Society*', *International Affairs* 69 (1993), 734–39.
13.   Solidarist international law includes not only using force collectively against a recalcitrant state who represents a threat to international society, but also the extension of the authority of international law over a wider range of subjects other than states.
14.   Hedley Bull, 'The Importance of Grotius', in Hedley Bull, Benedict Kingsbury and Adam Roberts (eds), *Hugo Grotius and International Relations* (Oxford: Clarendon), 91. Compare this view of the history of ideas with the more cavalier disregard for anachronism in Bull's 1962 British Committee Paper, 'The Grotian Conception of International Society'.
15.   Bull, 'The Importance of Grotius', 93.
16.   Talk on 'The Appalling State of IR Studies at the LSE and Elsewhere', Grimshaw Club, 17.1.1980.
17.   Bull, 'International Law and International Order', review essay, *International Organization* 26 (1972), 588.
18.   Bull, 'International Relations as an Academic Pursuit', *The Australian Outlook* 26 (1972), 262.
19.   Hoffmann, 'International Society', 18.
20.   For a structural account of world politics, see for example, Kenneth Waltz *Theory of International Politics* (New York: McGraw-Hill, 1979).
21.   Hedley Bull, *Justice in International Relations* (Hagey Lectures: University of Waterloo, Ontario, 1984), 18.
22.   Bull, 'Kissinger: The Primacy of Geopolitics', *International Affairs* 56 (1980), 487. The following argument, about the need to speak truth to power, Bull quoted approvingly from Chomsky in 'International Relations as an Academic Pursuit', 264.
23.   Bull, 'Kissinger', 487.
24.   Bull, 'International Relations', 265.
25.   He discussed the 'British model' and the 'American model' in a talk to diplomats on 'The Intellectual and the Bureaucrat in Foreign Affairs', Tuesday Group, 6.5.69.
26.   Carr, *The Twenty Years' Crisis* (London: Macmillan, 1 ed., 1939), 96.
27.   Hedley Bull, '*The Twenty Years' Crisis*, Thirty Years On', International Journal 24 (1969), 629.
28.   Bull, '*The Twenty Years' Crisis*, Thirty Years' On' 629.
29.   Bull, '*The Twenty Years' Crisis*, Thirty Years' On', 638.
30.   However, without engaging in an extended discussion of the interpretation of Carr's work, it could be argued that Bull's reading is unbalanced for two reasons. First, he underestimates the importance of morality in *The Twenty*

Years' Crisis, and Carr's prescription that political theory required both realism and utopianism, morality and power. Second, by focusing on only *The Twenty Years' Crisis*, Bull is not sufficiently sympathetic to the strong utopian undercurrent of Carr's other works in international relations (discussed more fully in Chapter Two).

31.   Bull, *The Anarchical Society*, 41.

32.   Bull, *The Anarchical Society*, 13. Emphasis added. Andrew Hurrell has argued that 'the subjective sense of being bound by a community was the cornerstone of his definition of international society'. Hurrell, 'International Society and the Study of Regimes: A Reflective Approach' in Volker Rittberger (ed.), *Regime Theory and International Relations* (Oxford: Clarendon, 1993), 63.

33.   This point is captured well by R.J. Vincent's epigram, '*ubi societas ibi jus est*'. Vincent, 'Order in International Politics'. 55.

34.   Bull, *The Anarchical Society,* 140.

35.   Andrew Linklater traces this argument back to Vattel, who argued that a responsible state is not 'legally obliged to act in ways that will jeopardise its survival or endanger its vital national interests, but it is beholden to other states to place the survival of order before the satisfaction of minimal national advantages'. Linklater, 'What is a Good International Citizen?', in Paul Keal (ed.), *Ethics and Foreign Policy* (Canberra: Allen and Unwin, 1992), 28–29

36.   Andrew Linklater, *Beyond Realism and Marxism: Critical Theory and International Relations* (London: Macmillan, 1990), 14.

37.   Stanley Hoffmann argued that although Bull showed that society could exist amidst anarchy, he left unanswered the question whether society could overcome the state of war. In Hoffmann's words, 'how much society, as it were, is likely to flourish in an anarchical structure?' See his essay on 'International Society', in Miller and Vincent (eds), *Order and Violence*, 26.

38.   Carr, *The Twenty Years' Crisis*, 70.

39.   Numbered among those who regard Bull as a realist include: Fred Halliday, 'International Society as Homogeneity', *Millennium*, 21 (1992), 438. Martin Griffiths, *Realism, Idealism and International Politics: A Reinterpretation* (London: Routledge, 1992), 155–167, Anthony McGrew and Paul G. Lewis *et al.*, *Global Politics* (Cambridge: Polity, 1992), 19.

40.   Bull, 'Natural Law', 180.

41.   Bull, 'Natural Law, 180.

42.   Hedley Bull, review of Michael Donelan (ed.), *The Reason of States. Times Literary Supplement* April 28 (1978), 474.

43.   Michael Donelan, *Times Literary Supplement* May 12 (1978), 528.

44.   Hedley Bull, *Times Literary Supplement* 26 May (1978), 585. Emphasis added.

45.   E.B.F.Midgley, 'Natural Law and the "Anglo-Saxons" – Some Reflections in Response to Hedley Bull', *British Journal of International Studies* 5 (1979).

46.   Bull, *The Anarchical Society*, 20.

47.   Bull, *The Anarchical Society*, 26.

48.   For Bull, it was possible to see these goals being achieved at the level of the state, at the level of international society, and at the level of world society.

His principal concern in *The Anarchical Society* was to show how these goals were provided for by the society of states.

49. Bull, *The Anarchical Society*, 21.
50. For deeper explorations of this argument, see Robert Jackson, 'Martin Wight, International Theory and the Good Life', *Millennium* 19 (1990), 261–272; Terry Nardin, *Law, Morality and the Relations of States* (Princeton NJ: Princeton University Press, 1983); Chris Brown, *International Relations Theory: New Normative Approaches* (Hemel Hempstead: Harvester Wheatsheaf, 1992).
51. Jackson, 'Martin Wight', 267. Ian Harris finds Bull's analysis of order and justice incomplete for the reasons that Bull does not adequately defend order on ethical grounds. Harris, 'Order and Justice in *The Anarchical Society*', International Affairs 69 (1993), 725–41.
52. Bull, *The Anarchical Society*, 200.
53. Bull, *The Anarchical Society*, 221–222.
54. Bull, *The Anarchical Society*, 288.
55. Hedley Bull, 'The Great Irresponsibles? The United States, The Soviet Union and World Order', *International Journal* 35 (1980), 447.
56. For an incisive discussion of this point, see Andrew Hurrell, 'Society and Anarchy in the 1990s', in B.A. Roberson (ed.), *The Structure of International Society* (London: Pinter, 1998 forthcoming).
57. An argument made by, among others, James Mayall, *Nationalism and International Society* (Cambridge: Cambridge University Press, 1990), and Robert Jackson, *Quasi-States: Sovereignty, International Relations, and the Third World* (Cambridge: Cambridge University Press, 1990).
58. Bull, *The Anarchical Society*, 249.
59. Hedley Bull, *Justice in International Relations*, (Hagey Lectures: University of Waterloo, Ontario, 1984), 18.
60. Bull, *Justice*, 13.
61. Chris Brown puts this point lucidly: 'If diversity entails that states have the right to mistreat their populations, then it is difficult to see why such diversity is to be valued'. Brown, *International Relations Theory*, 125.
62. Bull, *Justice*, 12.
63. Bull, *Justice*, 13, emphasis added.
64. Bull, *Justice*, 14.
65. It is possible that Bull may have envisaged a role for 'middle powers' as agents of a world common good, since they are powerful enough to be responsible but not so powerful as to be purely self-interested. See Paul Keal, 'Introduction' in Keal (ed.), *'Ethics and Foreign Policy'*, 9–11.
66. Not without reservations, I have decided to follow Bull's use of the terms 'North and 'South'.
67. Bull and Watson use the term 'quasi-states' in Hedley Bull and Adam Watson (eds), *The Expansion of International Society* (Clarendon Press: Oxford, 1994), 430.
68. Bull, *Justice*, 13.
69. Bull, *Justice*, 33.
70. Richard Shapcott, 'Conversation and Coexistence: Gadamer and the Interpretation of International Society', *Millennium* 32 (1994), 81–2.
71. Bull, *Justice*, 13.

72. Bull, *Justice*, 14.

73. Bull, *Justice*, 18.

74. Hedley Bull, 'The International Anarchy in the 1980's', *Australian Outlook*, 37 (December 1983), 128–9, emphasis added.

75. Although in the *Twenty Years' Crisis*, Carr makes the 'morality' argument in terms of self-determination. See Carr, *The Twenty Years' Crisis*, 282–83.

76. Bull, *The Anarchical Society*, 230.

78. Quoted in L.D. Freedman, 'The Gulf War and the New World Order', *Survival*, 33 (1991), 195–196.

78. Bull, *The Anarchical Society,* 230.

79. Nicholas J. Wheeler, and J. Morris 'Humanitarian Intervention and State Practice at the End of the Cold War', Jeremy Larkins and Rick Fawn (eds), *International Society after the Cold War: Anarchy and Order Reconsidered* (London: Macmillan, 1996).

80. Hedley Bull (ed.), *Intervention in World Politics* (Oxford: Clarendon Press, 1984), 193.

81. For a reassertion of the primacy of economic rights, see the literature on 'Asian Values'. For example, the collection in James T.H. Tang (ed.), *Human Rights and International Relations in the Asia Pacific* (London: Pinter, 1995). Clearly, disagreement about the nature and importance of different items on the shopping list of human rights is bound to constrain the scope of collective action to prevent human rights 'abuses', unless 'police action' is taken unilaterally by one ideological/civilizational block, with potentially disastrous consequences for international order.

82. Bull, Chatham House lecture on 'Western Values in a Hostile World', 23.9.1980.

83. Bhikhu Parekh, 'Non-Ethnocentric Universalism' in Tim Dunne and Nicholas J. Wheeler (eds), *Human Rights in Global Politics* (Cambridge: Cambridge University Press, forthcoming, 1998).

84. Hedley Bull, 'The West and South Africa', *Daedalus* 111, (1992), 266

85. Bull, 'The West', 265.

86. Hedley Bull, 'European Self-Reliance and the Reform of NATO', *Foreign Affairs* (Spring 1983).

87. For an insightful reading of Bull's schematic thoughts on 'neo-medievalism' and their relevance to critical thinking on new forms of community in Europe, see Andrew Linklater, 'Citizenship and Sovereignty in the Post-Westphalian State', *European Journal of International Relations* 2 (1996), 77–103.

8 R.J. Vincent

There is a remarkable similarity between R.J. Vincent's intellectual trajectory and that of his mentor, Hedley Bull. Both had an interest in strategic studies (although Bull's contribution was more pronounced in this area[1]), both deployed Wight's three traditions as a means to engage with classical theorists, and most significantly of all, they shared a theoretical investigation into the nature of order and justice in international society. Yet their common institutional affiliations and theoretical interests does not begin to convey the extent of their meeting of the minds. This is best illustrated by Vincent's admission that, even after Bull's death, his influence could 'be found on every page' of his work.[2]

The institutional route which Vincent took was the well-trodden path 'of English speaking trilateralism'[3] that united British, Australian and the west-coast North American centres of International Relations. He completed his first degree at the University of Wales, Aberystwyth, before undertaking an MA in Leicester and a PhD at the Australian National University from 1968–1971. His doctoral dissertation on *Nonintervention and International Order* was prepared for publication at Princeton University and has already attained the status of the classical treatment of the subject. Thereafter Vincent took up a research fellowship at the International Institute for Strategic Studies before moving to Keele University in 1976 where he remained for a decade. The last four years of his life were in some respects the most productive. His second book *Human Rights and International Relations* was published in 1986, and remains an essential point of departure for theorists working in this area. Following a three-year stint as a fellow and lecturer in International Relations at Nuffield College, Oxford, Vincent took up the Montague Burton Professorship at the London School of Economics. During his short residence in both these historic centres, Vincent had an enormous influence upon the first post-Cold War generation of International Relations scholars.[4]

By all accounts John Vincent was a combative intellectual who, so the apocryphal story goes, enjoyed bringing over-confident seminarians to book by suggesting they were 'half-way towards a good idea'. Articulated by a dusty don in a tweed suit, such faint praise might seriously damage the mental health of even the most resilient of postgraduate students, but coming from Vincent, it was invariably received in the spirit intended.

Like Bull, he brought to his academic work an appreciation of intellectual diversity. He was drawn to radical ideas which sought to cut a swathe through received views about the world; this was no doubt one of the reasons why he was favourably disposed towards graduates from Australia who invariably valued innovation over tradition, and irony over certainty.

Although it is tempting to dwell on his personal qualities and his ability as a teacher, the focus of this chapter will be an examination of Vincent's attempt to build a bridge between pluralist and solidarist theories of international society. The guiding question will be whether he is able to cross the bridge, and carry the tradition up the steep assent (whilst avoiding the pluralist crags and the realist chasms) to the summit of solidarism. In part one, I will consider Vincent's thinking on the relationship between academic theorising and political practice. The body of the chapter will then consider the elements in his solidarist or 'modified' conception of international society. Is it able to reconcile the two planes of order and justice? How does solidarism put to rest Bull's fear that new principles of international legitimacy might undermine international order? What are the prospects for solidarism intruding into the stubborn statism of the foreign offices around the world. Finally, it is important to address the question how Vincent grounds the cosmopolitan values of solidarism: what are the ethical foundations on which it rests?

Ideas and Practice in the Work of Vincent

R.J. Vincent's approach to the relationship between ideas and practice is classically Wightean in the way in which he excavated the writings of diplomats, state leaders, philosophers and jurists, in order to breathe life into international theory.[5] Before examining this approach in more depth, it is instructive to reflect on the theorists and practitioners who were the objects of his 'classical theories'. In particular, the section will examine whose classical theory Vincent was interested in, what his justification was, and why he believed classical theory to be relevant to the contemporary study of International Relations.

Vincent's essay on Edmund Burke filled an important gap in the English School's interpretation of the evolution of European international society. Martin Wight's essay on 'Western Values in International Relations', written over twenty years earlier, bore the imprint of Burke but did not make him the object of serious theoretical enquiry. Vincent was drawn to Burke's solidarist theory of European international society for two reasons. In the first instance, it overturns the pluralist norm of non-intervention. It was precisely because of the danger the French Revolution posed to the great 'Commonwealth of Europe' that Burke articulated a right of intervention. The Jacobins were thieves; the identity of France had been stolen; '[t]o be at peace with robbery was to be an accomplice with it'.[6] In a sense, Burke's solidarism can be likened to an international 'neighbourhood watch', where the members of the society of states must remain eternally vigilant, and prepared to act decisively, if the common European home was to be protected.

The second reason why Vincent believed Burke to be a worthwhile object for theoretical reflection concerns his understanding of the ties that bind peoples together. Rather than turning to natural law to furnish a reason for the unity of humankind, or to the legalistic idea of rights and obligations derived from formal agreements, Burke focused on an association of resemblances. Vincent often used to quote the following passage of Burke's which illustrates this romantic notion of solidarism:

> Nothing is so strong a tie of amity between nation and nation as correspondence in laws, customs, manners and habits of life. They have more than the force of treaties in themselves. They are obligations written in the heart.[7]

Crucially, these common bonds are not derived from reason or from conscious deliberation. These habits of co-operation, 'approximate men to men without their knowledge, and sometimes against their intentions.'[8]

The second 'classical theorist' who interested Vincent was Thomas Hobbes. His writings on Hobbes are perhaps more valuable for their insights into his general approach to the history of ideas than for his particular interpretation of Hobbes.[9] Vincent provides a reading of Hobbes for each of Martin Wight's categories: Hobbes's international anarchy constituting his realism; his rationalist recognition that the state mitigates the lawless savagery of the state of nature; and the revolutionary implications of extending the logic of his theory to embrace a world government following a social contract between states. The fact that a particular thinker can be 'read' in terms of all three traditions prompted Vincent to caution against 'treating great thinkers like parcels at the post office.'[10] But why did Vincent choose these particular 'parcels'? Once again we see an example of the English School's emphasis upon conservative political theorists to the detriment of a sustained examination of the revolutionist tradition. Indeed, in the essay on Burke, Vincent makes the important linkage between the 'three Rs' and the three hegemonic political positions of right (conservatism), centre (liberalism) and left (socialism).[11] Given Vincent's own politics, which could fairly be described as lying in the

'marchlands' between rationalism and revolutionism, it is surprising that
he did not reflect more deeply on an authentic figure in the revolutionary
tradition.[12]

In contradistinction to his Wightean treatment of Hobbes and Burke,
Vincent's two books do not focus explicitly on particular 'thinkers'. In
Nonintervention and International Order he presents a genealogy of the
idea of intervention and the way in which the theory and practice of
non-intervention has, in part, constituted the evolution of international
society.[13] *Human Rights in International Relations* considers the way in
which the discourse of universal human rights has been enunciated by
states and incorporated into international relations whilst at the same time
constituting a challenge to the ideology of *statism*. In both these works,
which will be considered in more detail in part two of the chapter, Vincent
presents us with the paradigmatic synthesis of theory and practice
promised by the international society tradition.[14]

Vincent's journey into the history of ideas about international relations
illustrates elements of continuity with the methodology outlined by Martin
Wight, but also a number of innovations. In terms of the former, Vincent
used theorists to illustrate particular positions on war, institutions, the balance
of power, law and ethics. Moreover, like the early British Committee work,
Vincent believed that the discipline had a longer history than had been
realised hitherto; a past which could be recaptured by analysing the classical
texts and speeches which contributed to the invention of international
society.[15] As he wrote in his essay on Burke, 'it is a legitimate enterprise to
seek to collect and order what was scattered and disordered'.[16] Where
Vincent was innovative in his use of traditions as an approach to international theory centres around his attempt to project the ideas of classical
thinkers into our world in the hope that they will provide us with a moral
compass which might guide us out of our present predicaments.[17]

Vincent also stepped outside of Wight's framework in one other important respect. More than any other member of the English School, Vincent
maintained a consistent interest in the theory and practice of foreign
policy.[18] His motive for these excursions was not to explore a particular
body of International Relations theory, but to consider 'theory as a guide
to policy'.[19] In this respect, Vincent viewed the two worlds of academic
International Relations and foreign policy as interconnected. Whilst he
endorsed Bull's general injunction that academics should remain resolutely independent from political advocacy,[20] he was also clear that this
independence should not be taken to mean separateness. The task for
'theory' was to act as something akin to what philosophers used to
describe as 'under-labourers', on whose shoulders policy-makers could

stand in order to see events more clearly, even distant events in global politics. Theorists have a 'duty to clarify and confront'[22] fundamental questions which practitioners may take for granted, an argument which will be returned to in the third section of the chapter.

Vincent's 'Modified' Theory of International Society

The pluralist theory of international society,[22] which Vincent defends in *Nonintervention and International Order*, must be read in the context of the practice of intervention and counter intervention by the superpowers in Eastern Europe and the Third World during the Cold War. 'It was against imperialism, and between legitimisms', Vincent later reflected, 'that I previously directed the principle of non-intervention.'[23] Vincent's defence of the norm of non-intervention follows a form of argument found in Bull's earlier work. Recognising that the norm places 'order between states before justice for individuals within them.'[24] Vincent justifies this position with the argument that international society is not ready to sanction intervention to promote justice or certain forms of government. In a world where there are only islands of order, rather than a continent of community, state sovereignty and non-intervention remain the guiding principles of statecraft. What is striking about Vincent's defence of nonintervention is that, like his predecessors, he does not provide a convincing account of why we should value the division of humankind into independent, sovereign communities. The nearest the author comes to justifying an order of sovereign states, is that the principle of nation-states 'continues to win the allegiance of men'.[25]

From this statist starting point, Vincent constructs an exemplary account of the theory and practice of a pluralist society of states. Following H.L.A. Hart and Hedley Bull, Vincent argues that the duty of states is to provide for the primary goals of security, trust and the sanctity of private property. From this assumption of the existence of 'islands of order' in an anarchical system, we see the function non-intervention serves:

It is a first principle, an elementary rule of orderly international relations because its observation would demonstrate the recognition by states of the existence of others and the legitimacy of their separateness in a society bound together only by mutual acknowledgement of the autonomy of its parts. It is fundamental to order in a society without government because it stands guard over the established enclaves of order. So long as international society is primarily composed of sovereign states, observance of a general rule of nonintervention can be regarded as a minimum condition for their orderly coexistence.[26]

More graphically, Vincent illustrates the norm of non-intervention by referring to it as analogous to a 'no trespassing' sign in customary domestic law.

There is no more effective critic of the view of order presented in *Nonintervention* than Vincent himself. In an essay on 'Order in International Relations' written almost two decades later, he offers weighty criticisms of Bull's use of the concept which he had taken for granted in his early work. Two in particular are pertinent here. The first is the recognition that an argument for order will generally be regarded 'in practice [as] a defender of particular orders'.[27] As we will see below, in his later works Vincent showed greater sensitivity to the question 'order for whom'? The second parallel criticism concerns the value of order as a sociological concept. Vincent was swept along, like many others in the 1970s, by the prevailing current of functionalist theory.[28] The reason why functionalism is now largely discredited is because of the circularity of its explanation. In short, both Bull and Vincent are ambiguous as to whether order presupposes or produces society. Functionalism is not only circular, it also stands accused of smuggling 'purposes' into society without articulating what they are or where they come from. What exactly is prior to (international) society, and how do we know?

The version of international society presented in *Nonintervention* is, ethically pluralist. All that binds states together is mutual recognition of their 'separateness', embodied in the norms of sovereignty and non-intervention. By the late 1970s, Vincent's theoretical interests broadened, as he grafted on to the order / nonintervention structure an interest in the cultural and civilizational bases of international relations. This coincided with his British Committee work on racial equality and stands as an intermediary stage in the evolution of his thinking from the statism of *Nonintervention* to the 'qualified statism' of his work on *Human Rights and International Relations* and after. What is interesting to note about this phase in his thinking is the tension between an expanding agenda pulling his theory of international society in a solidarist direction, but an equal and opposite reluctance to embrace more than an ethics of coexistence.

Vincent's preliminary sketch on an alternative framework to the morality of states is outlined in his 'Western Conceptions of a Universal Moral Order'.[29] The article is an attempt to explore within western thinking about international relations an alternative ontology to the morality of states. In Vincent's words, 'when the argument for equality is pressed on behalf of individuals ... it is one that must abandon altogether the "society of states" and come to grips with the hierarchical account of world society.'[30] His definition of world society is something of a 'menu' of all those entities whose moral concerns traditionally lay outside international society: the claim of individuals to human rights; the claim of indigenous peoples to autonomy; the needs of transnational corporations to penetrate the shell of the sovereign state; and the claim to retrospective justice by those who speak on behalf of the former colonial powers.[31] What Vincent had in mind when he uses the term 'world society' was an ontology which is opposed to statism, one which sees individuals or classes as the analytical referent object.

'Western conceptions of a universal moral order' turns out to be something of a false promise. Despite setting out on a course to find a moral order 'beyond international society to world society', Vincent concludes with a pluralist 'defence of the conventions of diplomacy'.[32] World society has an *empirical* content, but it lacks a *normative* community capable of judging and implementing moral claims. With this argument, Vincent takes on the neo-idealist assumption that transnational forces are withering away international society. In Vincent's words, 'this society remains "normatively relevant" so long as the justice constituency which exists in virtue of a sense of community is more visible within state frontiers than across them.'[33] The absence of a global 'justice constituency' remains an important reason for not abandoning the principle of non-intervention even in the case of human rights abuses which offend the conscience of the western world. Intervention, as he argued in *Nonintervention and International Order* is imprudent because of the problem of impartiality, the likelihood of military resistance, and the danger of military escalation into full-scale war.

This conclusion concerning the response of the society of states to the rights of individuals denied in other states, is not completely pessimistic. Consistent with the implicit constructivism in Vincent's approach to international theory, he argues that even if the moral claims made by agents in world society fall on deaf ears, there is a possibility that the articulation of these claims may, in themselves, 'assist in the building of a transnational justice constituency' which might civilise state behaviour.[34] Perhaps the most graphic example of the articulation of a moral claim in the contemporary history of world society was made by the anti-apartheid movement. Vincent's treatment of this issue in the late 1970s and early 1980s is surprisingly conservative. Although recognising that it was the injustice of the apartheid system in South Africa which brought the nineteenth century vocabulary of 'race' and 'civilisation' back into international society, Vincent allowed non-intervention to act as a cloak behind which international society could hide from its moral outrage. The problem with the doctrine of humanitarian intervention, Vincent argued, is that it invested too much trust in the motives of the interveners, and more importantly, the rule-consequentialist argument that countenancing intervention in a particular case may subvert international order itself.[35]

This pattern is repeated in his consideration of the issue of racial inequality as a factor in world politics. Despite recognising the power of metaphors such as the 'idea of a global caste system'[36], he concluded that 'some of the claims for the importance of race [ethnicity] in international politics are exaggerated.'[37] For instance, the argument made by neo-marxist inspired structuralists that there exists a global apartheid, with rich and poor falling on either side of the white/non-white colour divide, 'does not make of race', according to Vincent, 'any more than it does of poverty, the stuff of international politics.' In pulling back from making bold claims about the centrality of ethnicity to contemporary international politics, Vincent endorsed J.D.B. Miller's argument that racial solidarity will not displace the nation-state as the principle group referent, neither will racial discrimination become elevated above the national interest in thinking about reasons for resorting to the use of force.

By shifting the ontology of International Relations from the society of states to the wider world society, Vincent was at least forced to consider an alternative agenda to the one found in realist textbooks. In a dialectical manner, peering into the social forces of world society prompted him to rethink his earlier vindication of the morality of states. His article on culture, published in 1980, is illustrative of this process. The argument is set up in paradigmatic international society fashion. First he rejects the neorealist doctrine of the primacy of the system over the role of culture, then he dismisses the idea of cultural separateness, leaving a liberal middle way which holds that there is an international political culture which is not reducible to any particular constituent culture that participates in it.[38] In a typically Bullian manoeuvre, Vincent lays bare a three part outline for a study of global culture:

> Three themes for the study of culture in world politics have been suggested: the question of the relationship between culture and stability or order; the question of the quality of civilisation – culture as connected to justice or high achievement rather than to order; and the question of cultural engineering – of how the world order is to accommodate cultures as well as States, or regions, or individuals, or classes.[39]

This passage is pivotal to understanding Vincent's intellectual journey. Rather than focus on the relationship between culture and international order, Vincent sought to examine the solidarist question about the relationship between 'culture as connected to justice.' Through an examination of the human rights culture of late modernity, Vincent was able to bring justice to the fore by using the theory and practice of human rights as an indicator of the changing normative structure of international society.

In his commentary on Bull's contribution to International Relations, Vincent draws the reader's attention to his mentor's 'tanalizingly brief' passage in *The Anarchical Society* where Bull argues that world order was 'morally prior to order among states' for the reason that 'it is the purpose of those individuals which should inform the activities of states and the theoreticians and practitioners of order among them.'[40] Whilst Bull can legitimately be criticised for not thinking through the implications of this argument, given that states were obviously not providing for the conditions of world order, Vincent was considerably less complacent about the relationship between inter-state order and the primordial community of humankind. The guiding thought here – and one which the term 'solidarism' captures – is that the ties which bind individuals to the great society of humankind are deeper than the institutions and traditions which separate them. This does not mean that solidarism opposes the organisation of the human species into states, after all, this too develops out of the application of the universal principle of self-determination. Against 'realism', and its more civilised surrogate 'pluralism', solidarism is critically aware of the historical specificity of the present configuration of the states-system: moreover, solidarism evaluates the society of states according to its ability to deliver the conditions of moral progress for humankind. Respect for universal human rights therefore becomes, for Vincent, the key test for a civilised post-colonial international society.

The clearest indication of the solidarist 'turn' in Vincent's thinking can be found in his second and last major work *Human Rights and International Relations*, which was the source for a series of his contributions to books on theory, ethics and foreign policy.[41] Here he offers the reader a 'modified conception of international society'. The remainder of this chapter will interrogate how far Vincent wanted to modify the constitutive principles of the society of states. What was the ethical basis of solidarism? Did it rest, for Vincent, upon minimal moral universalism (a foundationalist epistemology), or one which is arrived at through an inclusive dialogue between competing conceptions of the content of universal human rights (a pragmatist epistemology)? How were diplomats and state leaders to act as local agents of a solidarist society of states?

Vincent begins the book *Human Rights and International Relations* by identifying three background models for thinking about the ethical basis of international politics. In the ensuing discussion, Vincent engages seriously with the work of leading political theorists like Beitz, Walzer and Shue,[42] something which Chris Brown noted as a failing in Bull's work.[43] Vincent provides a sympathetic reading of the realist view of the nature of 'community' in world politics, or more precisely, 'the part of that tradition that takes morality seriously.'[44] For realists, there may be a language of universal ethics, but there are no corresponding practices. It is in particularist communities (states) where morality is concretised. For this reason, we need to guard against states who speak in the name of universal human rights. But whilst we should remain sceptical of moral language disguising political interests, we should not, like the realists, seek to 'stop political conversation altogether.'[45] The antithesis of the realist model of community is expressed by the cosmopolitan idea of a universal moral law which applies to all individuals by virtue of their humanity. On the side of the cosmopolitans, Vincent draws on Kant's argument that a violation of an individual's rights in one state is felt by individuals in all other states.[46] But Vincent responds to this with the weighty objection that the cosmopolitan model too often assumes that 'we already inhabit a cosmopolitan world.'[47] The 'morality of states' model of community lies between the realist idea of rights as interests, and the cosmopolitan idea of universal rights and duties. It is a pluralist theory of international society in that it places sovereign states at the centre 'united by a principle of non-intervention which bears witness to their minimal solidarity'. Pluralism is not, therefore, the absence of morality 'but the recognition of its limits.'[48] The presumption here is that the state is a container for the common traditions and values of its citizens, and the primary function of the state is to protect this community from outsiders. 'The moral standing of any state', argues Vincent, 'depends on how well it does this.'[49]

Vincent realised that there are good empirical reasons for doubting the liberal statist claim that states stand guard over their citizens, leading him to revise the pluralist 'morality of states model'. Governments should no longer be assumed to be legitimate, rather, he argued, legitimacy is something which has to be earned. But how should the society of states respond to governments who commit acts of violence against their own citizens? To return to the 'egg-box' metaphor, how does the society of states avoid protecting and cushioning bad eggs? Vincent's solution to this dilemma is to elaborate a 'modified' solidarist conception of the morality of states. Two principles separate the solidarist from the pluralist morality of states; both develop out of the immanent critique of pluralism for its blindness to the daily round of human wrongs. In the first instance, individuals are entitled to the 'basic right' to life, meaning 'a right to security against violence and a right of subsistence'.[50] Second, there may fall on the society of states 'a duty of humanitarian intervention' in response to an occasion of 'extra-ordinary oppression'. Both of these solidarist sentiments will be examined further below.

The attraction of the idea of 'basic rights', was, for Vincent, primarily because it offered a resolution to the problem of relativism. In all his writings on human rights, Vincent displayed considerable sensitivity to the different ways in which the human rights discourse has been framed, both in terms of the history of ideas[51] and in terms of international political practice, particularly during the Cold War.[52] Indeed, it was the radically incompatible views about the nature and content of human rights which led him to take seriously the argument that 'human rights as an aspect of global politics indicate division rather than solidarity.'[53] Not content to end up with Bull's scepticism about the possibility of *universal* human rights, Vincent argued that 'basic rights' to security and subsistence allow for both unity and diversity. Unity in the sense that basic rights hold on to the core claim that *all* individuals have the right to life by virtue of their common humanity; diversity for the reason that basic rights only 'seek to put a floor under the societies of the world and not a ceiling over them.'[54] Above the floor, it is the business of the individual society to decide the content of their moral values.

Two related questions follow from the incorporation of basic rights into the morality of states. First, what correlative duties are implied and on whom do they fall? At the level of the individual, there is a duty to avoid depriving others of basic rights. At the level of the state, the failure of a government to provide for basic rights 'might now be taken as a reason for considering it illegitimate.'[55] And at the level of the international system, basic rights issue a warrant for a radical re-shaping of global economic resources. Each of these duties suggests that bringing basic rights into the society of states constitutes rather more than the 'minimal modification' suggested by Vincent.

The second question prompted by the solidarist society of states model concerns what type of international action is warranted by systematic abuses of basic human rights? Is humanitarian intervention, either unilateral or collective, a legitimate instrument for the enforcement of basic rights? A right of humanitarian intervention is, in many respects, a practice which bears witness to the existence of a modified morality of states, since humanitarian intervention 'presupposes a solidarist international society.'[56] To what extent, then, did Vincent believe that the principles of international legitimacy should be modified to incorporate a right of intervention in response to cases of extraordinary repression?

Whilst there is undoubtedly a shift in the way in which Vincent discusses humanitarian intervention in his two major works, as Nick Wheeler has argued,[57] there is also evidence of recurring doubts about the negative consequences of intervention for international order.[58] Even in his last article on the subject, when he was at his most sceptical about the dangers of allowing order between states to trump considerations of justice within them, he still falls short of endorsing humanitarian intervention as a legitimate practice.[59] Although recognising that non-intervention should only apply to protect 'good states from outside interference', this does not mean that rights violations would 'automatically' justify intervention.

In the final analysis, the 'solidarist' moment in his thinking on intervention resides not in the question of the appropriate response of the society of states to human rights abuses, but in the fact of the interdependence between domestic and international legitimacy. As Vincent argued,

the absence of a well-established doctrine of humanitarian intervention does not evaporate international concern, and now each state is quite legitimately exposed to the scrutiny and criticism of the international community on the relationship between government and governed within it.[60]

Here we see how pluralism and solidarism present two different conceptions of legitimacy in international society. It is no longer viable to iterate the pluralists line on legitimacy, namely, that 'we have to act *as if* other states are legitimate, not because they *are* legitimate but because to do otherwise would lead to chaos.'[61] Solidarism dismisses this as surrendering to prudential considerations. If the 'morality of states' is to be based on a moral defence of the state, then 'the principle of non-intervention would protect good states from outside interference, but not others'.[62]

The intrusion of solidarism into standard setting was only one side of the coin. The other was the record of states in what he called 'standard keeping', or what international lawyers more regularly refer to as the question of compliance. He cites a number of reasons why a state might not comply with the letter of human rights law. The first is the traditional concern that human rights issues get in the way of the business of diplomacy. It is obviously more difficult for a government to maintain good relations with another state, if, at the same time, it is accusing it of committing human rights abuses. This problem is obviously amplified in multilateral forums, when the 'freemasonry of diplomacy'[63] is forced out of its 'Grand Lodge' and comes under the spotlight of NGOs and their transnational constituencies. In addition, human rights are regularly shunted off the foreign policy agenda by two 'higher' goals, those of economic prosperity and national security. Governments rarely break diplomatic ties with states identified as denying basic rights to their citizens, this is motivated in good measure by economic imperatives like 'market access' or the need for 'foreign investment'. In support of this position, some exponents of universal human rights argue that trade can be a civilising device, providing liberal states with leverage to nurture the habits of good governance. But above all else, states fear that holding recalcitrant governments accountable for their misdemeanours might jeopardise the basis of international order. This argument was effectively mobilised by conservatives in the US during the Cold War against Carter's attempt to bring human rights to bear on superpower relations; it is being re-articulated in the 1990s, only this time it is China who is being labelled as the humanitarian pariah. There is one further reason, suggested by Vincent, why diplomats and state leaders make reluctant solidarists. Politicians live in fear of their prospects for re-election being dented by being seen to promote the good of a community beyond the state before the interests of their own people. At this point democracy and *raison d'état* become mutually reinforcing ideologies.

For all these reasons, Vincent noted wryly, 'foreign policy professionals are not excited about human rights.'[64] He believed that the current priority accorded to human rights by governments in general was too low, criticising the British Foreign and Commonwealth Office in particular. Ten years after Vincent presented this argument in a seminar at the London School of Economics,[65] a government has come to power committed to placing 'human rights at the heart of our foreign policy.'[66] Nowhere in Robin Cook's despatches does one read about the 'inescapable tension' between human rights and foreign policy, a tension which Vincent believed to be characteristic of the world of policy-making.[67] Does this long over-due arrival of an 'ethical dimension' onto the main menu of the foreign policy of a permanent member of the UN Security Council represent the advance of cosmopolitan values in the diplomatic community?

Vincent's answer to this question would have been mixed. Like many others, he would have noted how the end of the Cold War has reduced the risks to international order of pursuing human rights friendly foreign policies. Given the more favourable strategic climate, Vincent would probably have been disappointed with the human rights dimension in New Labour's ethical foreign policy.[68] In his first major speech to address issues concerning the content of the human rights favoured by the Government, Cook endorsed the key 'civil and political' rights (the truth of which he regarded as 'self-evident') but was silent about 'economic and social' rights which many developing countries hold dear. Of the two basic rights which Vincent put at the heart of his solidarist model of international society, only the right to security from violence was included in Cook's address.[69] The right to subsistence was conspicuously absent. Given that basic rights must be satisfied before all other rights can be enjoyed, Vincent would no doubt have been moved to ask the Foreign Secretary how someone who is starving is supposed 'to take part in the government of his or her country through democratic procedures'? The project for eradicating the scourge of the global poor, was, Vincent argued, more important than 'the global extension of a western conception of liberty' which lurks beneath the 'civil' list of rights.[70]

Before concluding the chapter, it is important to consider the question concerning the epistemological status of Vincent's universalism. As we have seen from the preceding discussion, importing basic rights into the society of states was an attempt to hold on to a universalist notion of humanity despite the competing conceptions of culture in international relations. The guiding thought here is that we share a moral nature, which is captured by the widespread belief that human rights are inalienable.[71] In *Human Rights and International Relations*, Vincent draws on this secular reading of natural law as the basis for his solidarist theory of international society. But in his 1992 chapter on 'Modernity and Universal Human Rights', Vincent questions the validity of relying on the naturalist tradition in establishing the universality of human rights. Instead, human rights must be anchored in a 'global cosmopolitan culture', where their content is arrived at by 'a social process by which global values are being worked out in an exchange between the cultures.'[72] There is a striking similarity between these thoughts and Richard Rorty's postmodern articulation of a 'global human rights culture'.[73] Both endorse a movement away from a foundationalist natural rights grounding for human rights in favour of a pragmatist epistemology which does not seek to establish *a priori* the universality of human rights. The question pragmatists ask about human rights, is not how do we *know* the inalienability of human rights, but how can we establish a framework for dialogue which might provide an anchor for universal human rights rather than a firm foundation. Consistent with this position, Vincent implied that we do not endorse human rights because of a legal convention or a meta-ethical truth claim, but ultimately for the reason that political life would lose its meaning without such a commitment.

Conclusion

An overwhelming concern for the victims of international politics marks an important personal and political difference between Vincent and other members of the English School. He had, as Christopher Hill noted, a 'personal feeling' for those 'who bore the brunt of high political decisions.'[74] This sensitivity to suffering humanity was extended to 'the voiceless masses' of Third World states 'without a part in the international conversation about justice.'[75] The depths of his humanism can, at times, serve to mask over the objections to full-blown idealism which recur in his thinking. Here the parallel with Bull once again comes into focus. In both cases, it is important to guard against the seductiveness of their solidarist sentiments, and to reveal the existence of the pluralist antithesis with its emphasis upon prudence and practice. We have already seen how, particularly in his early works, Vincent countered the anti-statism of thinkers like Richard Falk with arguments about the persistence of particularist allegiances of humankind to nation-states. Indeed, there is a striking parallel between his treatment of the state in *Nonintervention* and his chapter on 'Grotius, Human Rights, and Intervention' published sixteen years later. It is only in one of his last, and posthumously published articles, that he critically reflects on the reasons why we have decided 'to play [the game of] sovereign states in the first place'[76]

In Vincent's defence, solidarism – unlike cosmopolitanism – does not claim to transcend organised particularity. It is a theory of international society which accepts states and concedes their role as the principal containers of collective identity in global politics; at the same time as affirming difference, solidarism sets limits to the practices sanctioned by sovereignty. If a state fails to uphold the basic human rights of its citizens, it forfeits its right to immunity from intervention (whether this takes a coercive form or an act of collective censure). Although it is conceivable that international society might be able to establish a consensus on what constitutes internal legitimacy – civil rights, distributive justice, good governance – there are still important prudential considerations regarding the political and human costs of policing this moral code. Here we see how the British Committee's guiding thought, that the society of states is constituted by both the principle of 'moral obligation' *and* 'prudence', finds an echo in Vincent's argument in *Human Rights and International Relations* that 'prudence does not determine the moral agenda but it does condition its treatment.'[77]

As we saw towards the end of the chapter, solidarism is about more than deciding on a particular criterion for suspending the norm of nonintervention in response to gross human rights violations. For a solidarist model to be realised in practice, states need to act as guardians of basic rights everywhere. The implications this holds for contemporary international society are vast. It means addressing the plight of the global poor, which Vincent regarded as the twentieth century's equivalent of the slave trade. Liberating the world from this Holocaust of neglect requires promoting welfare internationalism, and this must be seen by the members of international society as an obligation and not a policy choice.

NOTES

1.   Vincent's main work in strategic studies was in his Adelphi paper: R.J. Vincent, *Military Power and Political Influence: The Soviet Union and Western Europe* (London: IISS, Adelphi paper 119, 1975).
2.   R.J. Vincent, *Human Rights and International Relations* (Cambridge: Cambridge University Press, 1986), viii.
3.   Christopher Hill 'Obituary: R.J. Vincent 1943–90', *Political Studies*, XXXIX (1991) 158–160.
4.   At Oxford, Vincent taught a number of postgraduates who have published widely in the discipline: Erica Benner, Iver B. Neumann, Geoffrey Wiseman, Jennifer M. Welsh and Ngaire Woods. At the LSE, Vincent helped to shape the work of younger scholars such as Peter Wilson and Mark Hoffman.
5.   Benedict Kingsbury puts the point well: the three traditions, or 'classical theories of international relations' constitute 'an approach that was both the inheritance and the legacy of the mush-missed R.J. Vincent.' Benedict Kingsbury, 'Grotius, Law, and Moral Scepticism: Theory and Practice in the Thought of Hedley Bull', Ian Clark and Iver B. Neumann (eds) *Classical Theories of International Relations* (London: Macmillan 1966), 42–70.
6.   R.J. Vincent, 'Edmund Burke and the Theory of International Relations', *Review of International Studies* 10 (1984), 211.
7.   Vincent, 'Edmund Burke', 212.
8.   Vincent, 'Edmund Burke', 212.
9.   R.J. Vincent, 'The Hobbesian Tradition', *Millennium* 10 (1981), 91–101.
10.   Vincent's other concern with traditions as a methodology for international theory was the problem of anachronism. His awareness of this is evident in his treatment of Hugo Grotius, written towards the end of his life: 'For while he [Grotius] gives one of the earliest statements of our modern idea of rights as moral possessions, and goes so far, it has been said, as to turn the law of nature into the injunction "to respect one another's rights" he does not explicitly distinguish a category of *human* rights from those of states or citizens or princes. And while it is possible to read into his work the basis of a fully fledged principle of non-intervention, and also a doctrine of humanitarian intervention as an exception to it, it is anachronistic to take Grotius's writings as indicating the arrival of these ideas in international society.' Vincent went on to argue that non-intervention did not become explicit in theory until the end of the eighteenth century and in practice in the nineteenth century, and

humanitarian intervention has still to be accepted as a legitimate practice today. R.J. Vincent, 'Grotius, Human Rights, and Intervention', in Hedley Bull, Benedict Kingsbury and Adam Roberts (eds), *Hugo Grotius and International Relations* (Oxford: Clarendon), 241–42.

11.   Vincent, 'Edmund Burke', 216.
12.   The fusion between rationalism and revolutionism in Vincent's thought is evident in his belief that 'a combination of Paine and Burke' was the best way to promote human rights. R.J. Vincent, 'The Place of Theory in the Practice of Human Rights', in Christopher Hill and Pamela Beshoff (eds), *Two Worlds of International Relations* (London: Routledge: 1995), 36.
13.   In Vincent's words: 'most states most of the time did in fact behave as if there were a rule of nonintervention prevailing between them.' R.J. Vincent, *Nonintervention and International Order* (Princeton: Princeton University Press, 1974), 385.
14.   Iver B. Neuman, 'R.J. Vincent', in Neuman and Waever (eds), *Masters in the Making* (London: Routledge, 1997), 4. In Neuman's words, 'more than any work in the international society tradition, *Nonintervention and International Order* is the exemplar of "theory-led empirical investigation" which the tradition espouses.'
15.   Note here Kingsbury's argument that '[t]he trialectic is itself a kind of Grotian solution by Wight, carried forward by Bull, to the theory/practice problem – a reproduction of the relations between a society and a practice of thinking about, and social criticism in, that society.' Kingsbury, 'Grotius, Law, and Moral Scepticism', 59.
16.   Vincent, 'Edmund Burke', 214.
17.   For example, he referred to Grotius' work as 'a text for our times'. Vincent, 'Grotius Human Rights, Intervention', 241.
18.   He was interested in US foreign policy in particular, especially when realism was at the helm during the Nixon and Reagan administrations. See R.J. Vincent, 'Kissinger's system of Foreign Policy', in *The Year Book of World Affairs*, 37 (1983); and R.J.Vincent, 'The Reagan Administration and America's Purpose in the World', *The Year Book of World Affairs*, 1.
19.   Vincent 'The Place of Theory', 33.
20.   In Vincent's words, '[m]embers of the Academy should be no-one's agents'. Vincent, 'The Place of Theory', 37.
21.   Vincent. 'The Place of Theory', 38.
22.   Pluralism is most graphically portrayed in his later book on human rights, where he likens the society of states to an 'egg-box': 'Sovereign states are the eggs, the goodness within contained by a (fragile) shell. The box is international society, providing a compartment for each egg, and a (less fragile) wall between one and the next. *The general function of international society is to separate and cushion.*' Vincent, *Human Rights and International Relations*, 123. Emphasis added.
23.   Vincent, *Human Rights and International Relations*, 118. Vincent defined intervention in militaristic terms: '[T]hat activity undertaken by a state, a group within a state, a group of states or an international organization which interferes coercively in the domestic affairs of another state. It is a discrete event having a beginning and an end, and it is aimed at the authority structure of the target state. It is not necessarily lawful or unlawful, but

it does break a conventional pattern of international relations'. Vincent, *Nonintervention*, 13.

24.   Vincent, *Nonintervention*, 344.

25.   Vincent, *Nonintervention*, 389.

26.   Vincent, *Nonintervention*, 331. Note the 'thin' nature of the society – 'bound' together by 'separateness'.

27.   Vincent, 'Order', 44.

28.   See, for example, his 'The Functions of Functionalism in International Relations', *Yearbook of World Affairs* 27 (1973), 332–344.

29.   Vincent, 'Western Conceptions of a Universal Moral Order', *British Journal of International Studies* 4 (1978), 20–46.

30.   Vincent, 'Western Conceptions', 44.

31.   Vincent, 'Western Conceptions', 29.

32.   Vincent, 'Western Conceptions', 45.

33.   Vincent, 'Western Conceptions', 45.

34.   Vincent, 'Western Conceptions', 44.

35.   Vincent, 'Western Conceptions', 41.

36.   R.J. Vincent, 'Race in International Relations', *International Affairs* 58 (1982), 670.

37.   Vincent, 'Race', 669. His later treatment of the question of race would seem to be more solidarist. In 1990, he cited the example of racial equality as a element in international human rights law 'which states undertake internationally to abide domestically.' Vincent, 'Grotius, Human Rights, Intervention', 254.

38.   R.J. Vincent 'The Factor of Culture in the Global International Order', *The Yearbook of World Affairs* 34 (1980), 260.

39.   Vincent, 'The Factor of Culture', 262.

40.   Vincent, 'Order', 43.

41.   In particular: 'The Idea of Rights in International Ethics' in Terry Nardin and David Mapel (eds), *Traditions of International Ethics* (Cambridge: CUP, 1992); 'Modernity and Universal Human Rights' in Anthony G. McGrew and Paul G. Lewis et al.; *Global Politics* (Cambridge: Polity, 1992); 'Beyond Non-Intervention' co-written with Peter Wilson, in Ian Forbes and Mark Hoffman (eds), *Political Theory, International Relations and the Ethics of Intervention* (London: Macmillan, 1993); and 'The Place of Theory'.

42.   Vincent and Wilson reflect on this relationship between 'political theory' and 'international theory' in 'Beyond Non-Intervention', 129.

43.   Chris Brown, 'Sorry Comfort? The Case Against "International Theory"', in F.R. Pfetsch ed., *International Relations and Pan-Europe* (Hamburg: Lit Verlag, 1993), 95–96.

44.   Vincent, 'The Idea of Rights', 259

45.   Vincent, *Human Rights*, 124.

46.   Cosmopolitans, from Kant to Beitz, argue that prudential considerations cannot undermine ideal theory. Note here also the thorough-going cosmopolitanism of Allott, and the argument that international theory took a wrong-turn at the end of the eighteenth century.

47.   Vincent, *Human Rights*, 124.

48.   Vincent, *Human Rights*, 114.

49.   Vincent, *Human Rights*, 115.

50. Vincent, *Human Rights*, 125.
51. In an early essay, he argued against a cosmopolitan reading of Rawls because it arose out of 'a particular philosophic tradition and has an appeal which is unlikely to be felt outside it'. Vincent, 'Western Conceptions', 31.
52. Vincent, 'The Idea of Rights', 262–64; 'Modernity and Universal Human Rights', 272–80; *Human Rights* Ch. 4 and 5.
53. Vincent, 'Modernity', 279.
54. Vincent, *Human Rights*, 126.
55. Vincent, *Human Rights*, 127.
56. Vincent, *Human Rights*, 104.
57. Nicholas J. Wheeler, 'Pluralist or Solidarist Conceptions of International Society: Bull and Vincent on Humanitarian Intervention', *Millennium* 21 (1992), 463–87.
58. Vincent, *Human Rights*, 114.
59. Here I depart somewhat from the position taken by Wheeler. In his otherwise judicious treatment of the question, there are good reasons for believing he overstates the extent to which Vincent and Wilson defend a right to humanitarian intervention. The argument that non-intervention should only apply to good states does not necessarily mean that the society of states has a duty to intervene in the affairs of bad states. This, as Vincent and Wilson argue, will depend 'on the nature and the extent of those violations and the definition we give to the concept of the "good state"'. cf. Vincent and Wilson, 'Beyond Non-Intervention', 125 and Wheeler, 'Pluralist or Solidarist', 480.
60. Vincent, 'Grotius, Human Rights and Intervention', 255.
61. Vincent and Wilson, 'Beyond Non-Intervention', 124.
62. Vincent and Wilson, 'Beyond Non-Intervention', 125.
63. Vincent, *Human Rights*, 132.
64. R.J. Vincent, 'Human Rights in Foreign Policy', in Dilys Hill (ed.), *Human Rights and Foreign Policy: Principles and Practice* (London: Macmillan, 1989), 58.
65. Vincent, 'The Place of Theory'. In the preface, Vincent's original seminar, which became his contribution to the book (revised for publication by the editors) was dated as November 1987. Hill and Beshoff (eds), *Two Worlds*, Preface, xiii.
66. Robin Cook, FCO Mission Statement, London 12 May, 1997 http://www.cto. gov.uk/texts/1997/may/12/mspc.txt
67. 'Taken in a foreign minister's baggage on a world tour' might 'spoil the whole trip'. Vincent, *Human Rights*, 137. compare this with Robin Cook's forthright statement on the aims of New Labour's foreign policy. 'The Labour Government does not accept that political values can be left behind when we check in our passports to travel on diplomatic business!' Opening Statement by the Foreign Secretary; London (May 12 1997).
68. On this occasion, I can be confident of gazing into the crystal ball since the answer is, so to speak, written in the book. Vincent criticised the last Labour Government's human rights policy (outlined in 1978) on similar grounds to that suggested below. Vincent, *Human Rights*, 144.
69. The human rights principles articulated by Cook were the following, first set out in the Universal Declaration of Human Rights: 'Everyone has the

right to life without fear of violence sponsored or tolerated by the state. Everyone has the right to liberty and freedom from arrest without due process of law. Everyone has the right to freedom from torture or cruel and inhumane treatment. Everyone has the right to freedom of thought and the right to express their thoughts. Everyone has the right to practice the religion of their choice. Everyone has the right to take part in the government of his or her country through democratic procedures.' Speech by the Foreign Secretary, Mr Robin Cook, To the Malaysian Institute of Diplomacy and Foreign Relations, Kuala Lumpur, 28 August, 1997. http://www.fto.gov.uk/texts/1997 aug/28/malaysia.txt.

70.   Vincent, *Human Rights*, 150.
71.   Vincent, *Human Rights*, 14.
72.   Vincent, 'Modernity', 286.
73.   Richard Rorty, 'Sentimentality and Human Rights', in S. Shute and S. Hurley (eds), *On Human Rights* (New York: Basic Books, 1993).
74.   Hill, 'Obituary: R.J. Vincent (1943–1990)', 59.
75.   Vincent, 'Order', 61. Interestingly, he believed that the book *Human Rights and International Relations* 'signed up with the Third World' to the extent that it interpreted the right to life as an argument about subsistence as well as security from violence. Vincent, *Human Rights*, 144.
76.   Vincent and Wilson, *'Beyond Non-intervention'*, 127.
77.   Vincent, *Human Rights*, 124.

Conclusion

> Perhaps the time is ripe for the enunciation of new concepts of universal
> political organisation which would show how Wales, the United
> Kingdom and the European Community could each have some world
> political status while none laid claim to exclusive sovereignty.
>
> Hedley Bull.[1]

All histories of ideas are open to contestation. Methodologically, the temptation is to re-write the text, re-interpret the idea, according to current
scholarly conventions or prevailing political ideologies. Whilst recognising the twin dangers of presentism and imposing undue coherence upon a
particular group of thinkers, the book has shown that there exists a family
resemblance linking the work of key thinkers, in British International
Relations from E.H. Carr to R.J. Vincent. In a loosely Wittgensteinian
sense, a family resemblance denotes the presence of networks of similarities 'overlapping and criss-crossing.'[2] The first part of the conclusion
retraces these similarities and in so doing serves as a précis of the 'story'
of the English School.

In contemporary academic International Relations, those who belong to
the tradition are participating in a much wider-ranging conversation than
many of their predecessors. As the paragraphs below suggest, certain elements of the British Committee agenda have fallen by the wayside: few
academics who identify with the English School today are interested in
the processes of diplomacy or the parallels between Newtonian science
and the eighteenth century balance of power. In their place, we find a
growing interest in normative questions relating to culture, community and
identity. The latter stages of the conclusion consider the relevance of
English School thinking to these themes. Although the assessment made
below is a broadly favourable one, this is not meant to imply a blanket
endorsement of the School. As I have tried to show at a number of points
in the text, there are plenty of skeletons in the cupboard; none more chilling than Carr's blindness to Stalin's reign of terror, or more obfuscating
than the intrusion of Augustinian dogma into Butterfield's thinking.

In the course of making an assessment of the contribution of the English
School, I am aware that the terms of reference of the book are shifting
from one where the author tries to be a critical observer, to one where the
author becomes an 'advocate' (or what Quentin Skinner once colourfully

described as the difference between a 'recording angel' and a 'hanging judge'). By way of a background justification for the advocacy below, I will be deploying what I take to be Andrew Linklater's approach to the history of ideas, which rejects the search for authenticity in favour of seeking out the normative potentiality of a theorist or text. The question, for Linklater, is not whether one interpretation is more faithful than another, but rather, what can we make of it?

I

The development of the English School begins with the work of Carr for the principal reason that he exerted an immense influence over writers like Wight, Butterfield, Bull and Vincent. Carr was the provocateur, whose critique of the degeneration of liberalism into complacent and self-interested statism was regarded as the point of departure for other writers. Apart from broadly agreeing with Carr's view of the breakdown of the inter-war period, Carr's critique of the assumption that there is a latent harmony of international interests enabled post-war theorists to study International Relations from the basis that international society was not a given but had to be created. The conscious attempt by Butterfield and Wight to bring together a group of scholars to engage in a collective enquiry into the morality of states is what marked the English School off from other traditional realist thought of the time.

The need to speak moderation to power was what motivated Butterfield to establish the British Committee as a vehicle for understanding and explaining international relations. The family resemblances shared by Wight and Butterfield, which could be dimly perceived in the 1940s, became institutionalised in the meetings of the Committee. As Michael Howard recalled, it was Martin Wight who provided the intellectual leadership in the first phase of the Committee's proceedings. He prompted his colleagues to ask fundamental questions about the practices of states and the values of civilisations. Wight's own thinking on International Relations had shifted considerably by the late 1950s. It is in his 'international theory' lectures that the evolution in Wight's thinking between the original *Power Politics* and his British Committee work can be discerned. In the lectures, Wight convincingly argued that neither realism nor idealism was able to capture the experience of state practice; instead, he invented a third position, rationalism, which he compiled from the writings and speeches of lawyers, politicians and the handful of philosophers who concerned themselves with inter-state relations. Apart from Hedley Bull, it is difficult to know how far other members of the Committee positively endorsed Wight's approach or whether they were powerless to resist, lacking Wight's range and depth in the history of ideas. Nevertheless, there was unanimity in the Committee as to the need to resist the current wave of scientism sweeping all before it in American International Relations.

Whilst it was Wight's approach to 'international theory' which informed the Committee's understanding of the task at hand, it was Hedley Bull who, more than anyone else, brought to the fore the ontological questions about the depth and breadth of international society. The most significant of the early British Committee meetings examining the nature of international society was in October 1961, when Martin Wight presented 'Western Values in International Relations' and Hedley Bull presented 'Society and Anarchy in International Relations'. Herbert Butterfield's painstaking minutes record the consensus which had emerged in the early meetings around the idea that sovereign states constituted a society: 'Wight and Bull in their respective papers were agreed in holding that there is an international society; and no one, in the course of the discussion, questioned this view.'[3] The discussion which followed the papers by Wight and Bull raised a number of fundamental questions about international society. Was a common culture a necessary condition for the element of society to flourish? Or could a rule-governed society be maintained despite the cultural diversity of its participants? Did a society of states require leadership by enlightened great powers acting in accordance with the balance of power? Is a society of states preferable to other kinds of world order, such as empire or hegemony? Recognising that there could not be purely theoretical answers to these questions, from 1964 onwards the British Committee's deliberations shifted from grand theory to a comparative history of earlier states-systems, how they were formed, and the means by which they are sustained or transformed. In these discussions Wight took the lead, excavating new avenues for investigation which others took up in the post-Wightean years of the Committee and after.

II

It would be easy to draw conservative conclusions from this particular episode in the discipline's past. Although a case was made in Chapter 1 for disengaging the English School from its cultural base, a sociological study of the British Committee would no doubt interpret it as an old boys club, imbued with élitist values in a quintessentially English institution, which was sheltered from the prevailing currents of cultural and technological change. This study has suggested we might want to draw a different kind of conclusion. The argument which will be outlined in the final pages of the book is that, during the British Committee era, the English School found themselves on the 'right' side of the key debates of their time. And crucially, even judged by today's standards, their approach to International Relations remains an important voice in the post-positivist dialogue which has, in the last decade, proven to be more resilient than other mainstream theoretical approaches.[4]

One of the reasons for its resilience is due to the distance the English School maintained from policy driven agendas. Even during the *Expansion* project, the most 'applied' phase in the series of meetings which spanned over two decades, the leaders of the group were keenly aware that their comparative advantage was in taking a broad brush to the canvass of colonialism and decolonisation. However, it would be wrong to believe that the principal members of the Committee turned their backs on global politics all together. Butterfield's writings on the Cold War, for example, reveal a deep unease about the crusading 'moralism' advocated by the likes of John Foster Dulles in the 1950s; similarly, Bull was highly critical of the 'belligerence' which accompanied the return of moralism in American foreign policy in the 1980s.[5] In the spirit of 'rationalism', Butterfield, Wight and Bull believed that the Soviet Union had the right to be treated with the same respect as any other great power; failure in the West to advocate co-existence with communism was the cause of insecurity rather than a policy of maintaining security.[6]

Related to the English School's unease about the ideological diplomacy pursued by the US were their misgivings about the replacement of the balance of power with a 'balance of terror'. For Butterfield and Wight in particular, nuclear weapons overturned centuries of accumulated wisdom about the just ends and means of the use of force. Wight detected that weapons of mass destruction had re-activated an interest in doctrines saturated with rationalism such as limited war, although the arms race posed a dialectical dilemma for rationalism; can one side hold on to these principles unless it is confident that its adversary shares them?[7] Alongside these Grotian influences on their thinking about the Cold War, there was an overlay of religious themes (evident in Butterfield's thinking in particular) about how good and evil was a matter for the contest between the city of man and the city of God, not East versus West.

Hedley Bull's approach to nuclear weapons was free from these otherworldly thoughts. In this sense, Bull was more rationalist than Butterfield and Wight on the question of the regulation of the use of force during the Cold War. His pioneering work on arms control in the late 1950s and early 1960s emphasised a middle way between the strategists gunning for superiority and the disarmers who, unwittingly, were jeopardising security. In place of these realist and revolutionist approaches, Bull advocated a policy of limited arms control agreements on the condition that these enhanced national and international security. Throughout Bull's writings on strategic studies, the term 'balance' recurs, as it had done in Butterfield's thinking on structures of governance within the state and in the society of states.

The wind of change sweeping through the international system in the post-war period, as the last phase of decolonisation gathered apace, was never central to the early work of the English School. During the 1960s for example, only Adam Watson wrote a number of papers about the experiences of 'new' states, but these were mostly restricted to discussions about the management of the transition to independence. We should not infer from this any sympathy on their part for the age of empire. From the scattered comments of various members of the English School, it was clear that they opposed colonial control over the non-European world. In a letter to the *New Statesman*, Martin Wight protested against Britain's acquiescence in the annexation of Sarawak by Indonesia, calling the episode the 'most repugnant form of imperialism'.[8] This anti-colonial sentiment received more consideration in his essay on 'Western Values' which suggested that intervention was legitimate in order to maintain 'civilised standards', a position which his head of Department at the LSE, Charles Manning, rejected for fear that this would bring white South African rule to an end. On the question of self-government for former colonial territories, as on so many others, Bull aligned himself with Wight. Towards the end of his life, Bull regarded South Africa as the only case where there was a consensus throughout the world on the injustice of a state founded on the principle of white supremacism.

III

The judgements of Wight, Butterfield, and Bull on some of the central questions of their day do not seem out of step when measured against a liberal or social democratic standard. In the closing paragraphs below, I will make the related but more important claim that the English School finds itself on the 'right' side of the main cleavages in the discipline today: first, it operates with a constructivist meta-theory; second, its understanding of theory is normative all the way down; and third, the agenda which has preoccupied the English School from the late 1950s onwards remains relevant to the theory and practice of international relations as the discipline approaches the start of its ninth decade.

In his famous address to the International Studies Association in 1988, Robert Keohane noted that the principal rupture in the field was between 'rationalists' and 'reflectivists'. What is striking about this distinction, and the equally influential distinction by Martin Hollis and Steve Smith between 'explaining' and 'understanding', is that the English School was excluded from both.[9] According to Keohane, the rationalist dimension – the mainstream of International Relations – represented a merger between neorealism and neoliberalism. What holds them together is principally their common interest in the need to 'explain behavioural regularities.'[10] Although Wight believed there were patterns in the history of ideas, these were of a historicist kind. It was this realisation which prompted Keohane to dismiss Wight's work for 'his neglect of the scientific or behavioural search for laws of action.'[11]

A good example of a specific debate in which the English School finds itself in opposition to the 'rationalists' is in terms of its critique of neoliberal understandings of co-operation. In terms of international institutions, there are differences not only in terms of what exactly the institutions are but also the part the institutions play in international society. For English School theorists, institutions are practices embedded in the fabric of international society. As we have seen with Wight and Bull, the institutions of international society have a longer history than the proliferating regimes of the late twentieth century; moreover, English School scholars equate institutions with practices such as sovereignty, balance of power, international law, the diplomatic dialogue, and war. In order to understand the institution of sovereignty, for example, an English School approach would advocate a historical sociology of the term and the meanings given to it by state leaders at particular historical junctures. Such an investigation is not amenable to the 'neo-neo' requirement of framing testable hypotheses across like cases.

The differences between the American and British approaches can also be discerned in terms of their understanding of how co-operation emerges. For neo-liberals and (some) neo-realists, the specific institutional arrangements (or regimes) emerge as a response to the co-ordination problem where unrestrained individualism leads to sub-optimal outcomes for the players in question. Therefore, the task for neo-liberals is to show how compliance with the rules is maintained by the requisite proportion of incentives and sanctions. In short, the crucial contention of the neo-liberal model is that co-operation can be understood *without* recourse to common beliefs or shared values.[12] But as Andrew Hurrell has noted, a core assumption of Hedley Bull's is the way in which international co-operation is rooted in the sense of being bound by inter-subjectively created rules.[13]

The discussions within the British Committee on methodology highlighted their opposition to key tenets of positivism. International relations were not amenable to the search for behavioural laws of action, and there was no such thing as value-free enquiry in the social world. In place of positivism, the English School argued for an interpretive understanding of international relations; one which revealed the contingency (and tragedy) of human decision-making, the often irreconcilable meanings that different actors give to the same event, and the way in which cultural values shape diplomatic and political practice. A sense of collective identity and legitimacy in European international society cruicially shaped the foreign policy of the great powers towards the Ottoman 'other'. In our own century, the end of the Cold War was brought about in part because the 'enemy' reinvented itself, and in so doing, shifted the boundaries of Europe eastwards and prompted western European states to re-calculate their interests.

Having suggested reasons why the English School is incompatible with the rationalists, the next move is to consider the location of the School on the 'reflectivist' (or 'constructivist') side of the divide. The number of post-positivist positions is far greater than Keohane alluded to in his category of 'reflectivist'. Most writers now take it to include feminism (in most of its variants), critical theory, post-structuralism, and constructivism. It in this last category that the English School should be situated, although with one crucial qualification. Before outlining the reasons why the English School is constructivist,[14] it is worth re-capping the key elements of constructivism as laid down by Alexander Wendt. He defines the project according to three claims: 'first, states are the principal units of analysis for international political theory; second, the key structures in the state system are inter-subjective rather than material; and third, state identities and interests are an important part of these social structures, rather than given exogenously to the system by human nature or domestic politics.'[15]

It should be apparent that there is an affinity between the theoretical core of the English School and these primary colours of constructivism. Writers like Wight, Bull and Vincent, clearly take the state as the central actor (even if the great society of humankind is ultimately the key normative referent). Moreover, the identity of states, given by the term sovereignty, has no meaning outside of the ideas and practices of the society of states where the rules of membership and succession are located. For the English School, sovereignty and nonintervention are constitutive of the society of states, in other words, it is sustained by the reproduction of these practices.

There is also common ground in conjunction with Wendt's second claim in that, for the English School, the notion of a society of states is founded precisely on a belief in the power of inter-subjective structures such as common rules, values and institutions. Here we see how the English School treats practices like war and the balance of power as *ideas*, unlike consistent realists who predominantly regard them as material structures. Moreover, for their effective operation, the 'positive' institutions of international society, such as diplomacy and law, require a highly developed form of what Wight called 'an international social consciousness'. This was in evidence during long periods of European international society, where the needs of the society 'became imprinted on the minds of practising diplomats'.[16] Bull's fear was that the cement which held European international society together might crack under the weight of decolonisation. What is interesting about Bull's thinking on relations between the west and the post-colonial world is the way in which, consistent with the third claim of constructivism, the newly independent states saw it in their interests to play the game of international society. In other words, the act of acquiring a sovereign identity generated common interests in maintaining the diplomatic dialogue and respecting the rights and duties of other states (despite the memory of what they regarded as their own rights as 'peoples' being trampled upon by the colonial powers).

In addition to the consensus on the institutions which sustain international society, there has been some progress in delivering justice in terms of humanitarian principles of universal rights and racial equality. Bull always doubted whether the current structure of sovereign states could deliver both order and justice; he felt the Third World was unlikely to endorse the *status quo* indefinitely, and any attempts to institutionalise just change would (in the absence of consensus) undermine the basis of international order. Bull's thinking on order and justice, which was taken up by Vincent in the late 1980s, makes a significant contribution to constructivist thinking. Not only do these two authors show how norms are generated, and what effect they have on the actors who interpret (and contest) them, the purpose of the English School's theoretical investigations is avowedly normative. Whilst the prevailing North American strand of constructivism has only described norms; the point for Vincent, was to change them.

A further question which has attracted the attention of North American constructivists, and which the English School has had a significant impact upon, relates to the impact of globalisation on regional, cultural and local identities. As one influential text put it, 'culture and identity' are making a 'return' to International Relations. But the work of the British Committee, from Wight's paper on 'Western Values' to Bull and Watson's collection, *The Expansion of International Society*, suggests that for the English School, questions of culture and identity never went away. What was driving their interest in culture was the question whether the framework of rules set by states to regulate their practices could cope with cultural diversity. This acceptance of cultural heterogeneity and the attempt to regulate diversity is an aspect of English School thinking which appeals to communitarians. Writers like Terry Nardin in the US endorse the 'egg box' view of international society, in which the purpose of the rules and institutions is to 'separate and cushion' a plurality of states. This is a useful metaphor because it draws our attention to the fragility of political communities, who join together to form a 'practical association' in order to facilitate co-operation whilst preserving their difference. This should not be confused, so the argument runs, with an association which engages in universalist practices such as setting (and policing) civilised standards of conduct.

As a number of theorists have pointed out, there is a point at which the neat distinction between 'practical' and 'purposive' associations breaks down.[17] The society of states since 1945 has engaged in an ever-widening normative agenda which has as its goal some notion of a 'good' which is shared by all states and peoples. In their more solidarist moments, English School theorists put this idea of a world common good at the centre of their enquiries. The idea that the international society tradition can offer critical openings into theorising a universal moral order, has provoked contradictory responses from the International Relations community. For critical theorists like Ken Booth,[18] the society of states cannot be an 'agent' of emancipation, since it is the normative structure of international society which is the permissive cause of human wrongs in the first place. On this reading, the society of states 'is never to be loved, and seldom to be trusted.'[19] Nick Wheeler has taken up this challenge, arguing convincingly that the English School is not complacent about the state. The fact that too many states were acting like 'gangsters', resorting to political violence and repression of their own people, rather than 'guardians' as pluralism implied, was the reason why Vincent sought to modify the 'morality of states' model. Pushing international society theory in a cosmopolitan direction, Vincent thought there should be clear limits to what practices of 'diversity' were permitted. In a solidarist world order, the idea of what it means to be a sovereign state would change; membership of international society, would become conditional upon satisfying minimum standards of civilised conduct.

Other critical theorists have found the English School more congenial. Andrew Linklater's project of deepening and widening the sense of community in global politics is one which he shares with solidarists. Like many other cosmopolitan thinkers, Linklater is agnostic about the particular institutional form that the community takes, privileging instead the historical and praxeological dynamic of moral inclusion and exclusion. In this critical constellation, individuals, bureaucracies, states, international institutions, NGOs and so on, all have the potential to act in inclusive ways. Not only do states have the potential to act as 'local agents of a world common good', they have considerably more agency than most other actors in world politics. Clearly the question of the contribution that states can make to the transformation of community is one which invites a critical international society approach, combining the insights of Bull's thoughts on alternative forms of community, Carr's understanding of the 'scourges' of economic and social exclusion, Wight's interest in constitutionalism, and Vincent's attempt to modify the principles of international legitimacy in accordance with cosmopolitan values.

The last decade has shown that the ideas and agenda of the English School remain pertinent; in some respects, their search for an understanding of how the institutions of international society can manage the tension between 'the ethic of difference' and the search for 'consensus' on normative issues[20] has never been more urgent. The next stage of the English School needs to build on this normative agenda without losing sight of the traditional pluralist contention that theory should build from the floor up rather than the ceiling down.

NOTES

1. Hedley Bull, *The Anarchical Society* (London: Macmillan, 1977), 267.
2. Ludwig Wittgenstein, *Philosophical Investigations*, G.E.M. Anscombe and R. Rhees (Oxford: Blackwell, 1953), 66–67
3. "The Meaning of "International Society"'', British Committee discussion (October 1961, 5–8).
4. Chris Brown, *Understanding International Relations* (London: Macmillan, 1997), 54.

5. See his 'The Classical Approach to Arms Control Twenty Three Years After', in Robert O'Neill and David N.Schwartz (eds), *Hedley Bull on Arms Control* (London: Macmillan, 1987), 126.

6. Carr had quite different reasons for being critical of the West's policy towards the Soviet Union; as far as he was concerned, communism offered the possibility of overcoming the scourges of war and unemployment which had been a feature of late capitalism. Hysteria in the West was not only ill-founded (resting on the assumption that 'our' form of governance was democratic and 'their' political system was tyrannical), it was likely to harm the prospects for the Soviet Union to build a new society.

7. Martin Wight, *International Theory: The Three Traditions* (Leicester: Leicester Universy Press, 1991), 231.

8. I am grateful to Roger Epp for drawing this to my attention. See Epp, 'Martin Wight: International Relations as Realm of Persuasion', in Francis A. Beer and Robert Hariman (eds), *Post-Realism: The Rhetorical Turn in International Relations* (East Lansing: Michigan State University, 1996), 129–131.

9. Hollis and Smith thought that the hegemony of 'explanatory' approaches in International Relations was such that they turned to philosophy to furnish examples for the category of 'understanding'. Martin Hollis and Steve Smith, *Explaining and Understanding International Relations* (Oxford: Clarendon, 1990), see especially Ch.4.

10. Robert Keohane, *International Institutions and State Power* (Boulder, Col.: Westview, 1989), 8. Note that Keohane's use of 'rationalism' is in sharp contrast to Wight's reading of a rationalist tradition in European thinking on international relations. Compare Keohane with Andrew Linklater, 'Rationalism' in Scott Burchill, Andrew Linklater et al., *Theories of International Relations* (London: Macmillan, 1996).

11. Robert Keohane, review of Wight, *International Theory* in *American Political Science Review* 86 (1992), 1112.

12. Keohane expresses this point clearly: 'International Cooperation does not necessarily depend on altruism, idealism, personal honour, common purposes, internalised norms, or a shared belief in a set of values embedded in a culture. At various times and places any of these features of human motivation may indeed play an important role in processes of international cooperation; but cooperation can be understood without reference to any of them.' Keohane, *International Institutions,* 159.

13. Note that this view of the English School and the 'neo-neo's' as opposed to each other has been challenged by Buzan 'From International System to International Society: Structural Realism and Regime Theory meet the English School', *International Organization* 47 (1993), 350. For an interesting meta-theoretical objection to the 'rationalist' / 'reflectivist' synthesis, see Hollis and Smith, *Explaining and Understanding*.

14. This argument is expounded upon in more depth in Timothy Dunne, 'The Social Construction of International Society', *European Journal of International Relations* 1 (1995).

15. Alexander Wendt, 'Collective Identity Formation and the International State', *American Political Science Review* 88 (1994), 385.

16. Herbert Bufferfield, 'Crowe's Memorandum of January 1, 1970' (July 1960).
17. See, for example, *Understanding International Relations*.
18. Ken Booth, 'Human Wrongs and International Relations', *International Affairs* 71 (1995), 103–26.
19. This, of course, is an adaptation of David Luban's remark about the state.
20. Andrew Hurrell 'Society and Anarchy in the 1990s' in B.A. Roberson (ed.), *The Structure of International Society* (London: Pinter, 1998 forthcoming).

Bibliography

This list is a compilation of the key works on the English School. The first section is a general list of articles, chapters and books on (or relating to) the English School. Subsequent sections relate to the key thinkers considered in the text; gathered up here are works on International Relations theory by the thinker in question, as well as commentaries on their work.

I The English School

Bartelson, J. 'Short Circuits: Society and Tradition in International Relations Theory', *Review of International Studies*, 22 (1996), 339–60.

Beer, A. and Hariman, R. (eds), *Post-Realism: The Rhetorical Turn in International Relations*. East Lansing, Michigan State University Press, 1996.

Berridge, G. 'The Political Theory and Institutional History of States-Systems', *British Journal of International Studies*, 6 (1980), 82–92.

Booth, K. 'Human Wrongs and International Relations', *International Affairs*, 71 (1995), 103–26.

Brown, C. 'International Theory and International Society: The Viability of the Middle Way', *Review of International Studies*, 21 (1995), 183–96.

Buzan, B. 'The Timeless Wisdom of Realism?', in S. Smith, K. Booth and M. Zalewski (eds), *International Theory: Positivism and Beyond*. Cambridge: Cambridge University Press, 1996.

Buzan, B. 'From International System to International Society: Structural Realism and Regime Theory Meet the English School', *International Organization*, 47 (1993), 327–52.

Clark, I. and Neumann, I.B. (eds), *Classical Theories of International Relations*. London: Macmillan, 1996.

Cutler, A.C. 'The "Grotian Tradition" in International Relations', *Review of International Studies* 17 (1991), 41–65.

Der Derian, J. 'Introducing Philosophical Traditions in International Relations', *Millennium: Journal of International Studies*, 17 (1988), 189–93.

Der Derian, J. (ed.) *International Theory: Critical Investigations*. Foreword by Adam Watson. London: Macmillan, 1995.

Der Derian, J. (ed.) *Critical Investigations*. London: Macmillan, 1994.

Donelan, M. (ed.), *The Reason of States*. London: Allan and Unwin, 1978.

Donelan, M. *Elements of International Political Theory*. Oxford: Clarendon Press, 1990.

Dunne, T. 'International Society: Theoretical Promises Fulfilled?', *Cooperation and Conflict*, 30 (1995), 125–54.

Forsyth, M. 'The Classical Theory of International Relations', *Political Studies*, 26 (1978), 411–416.

Fox, W.T.R. (ed.), *Theoretical Aspects of International Relations*. Notre Dame: University of Notre Dame Press, 1959.

Gallie, W.B. 'Wanted: A Philosophy of International Relations', *Political Studies*, 27 (1979), 484–92.

George, J. *Discourses of Global Politics: A Critical (Re)Introduction to International Relations*. Colorado: Lynne Reinner, 1994.

George, S. 'The Reconciliation of the 'Classical' and 'Scientific' Approaches to International Relations', *Millennium: Journal of International Studies*, 5 (1976), 28–40.

Gong, G.W. *The Standard of Civilization in International Relations*. Oxford, Clarendon Press, 1984.

Grader, S. 'The English School of International Relations: Evidence and Evaluation', *Review of International Studies*, 14 (1988), 29–44.

Griffiths, M. *Realism, Idealism and International Politics: A Reinterpretation*. London: Routledge, 1992.

Griffiths, M. 'Order and International Society: The Real Realism?', *Review of International Studies*, 18 (1992), 217–40.

Halliday, F. 'The Pertinence of International Relations', *Political Studies*, 38 (1990), 502–16.

Hill, C. 'The Study of International Relations in the United Kingdom', in H.C. Dyer and L. Mangasarian (eds), *The Study of International Relations: The State of the Art*. London: Macmillan, 1989.

Hill, C. '1939: The Origins of Liberal Realism', *Review of International Studies*, 15 (1989), 319–28.

Hoffmann, S. 'An American Social Science: International Relations' in *Janus and Minerva: Essays in the Theory and Practice of International Politics*. Boulder, Colorado: Westview Press, 1977.

Jackson, R. *Quasi-States, Sovereignty, International Relations and the Third World*. Cambridge: Cambridge University Press, 1990.

Jackson, R. 'Pluralism in International Political Theory', *Review of International Studies*, 18 (1992), 271–81.

Jackson, R. 'The Political Theory of International Society', in K. Booth and S. Smith (eds), *International Relations Theory Today*. Cambridge: Polity Press, 1995, 110–18.

Jackson, R. 'Is There a Classical International Theory?', in S. Smith, K. Booth and M. Zalewski, *International Theory: Positivism and Beyond*. Cambridge: Cambridge University Press, 1996.

Jones, R.E. 'The English School of International Relations: A Case for Closure', *Review of International Studies*, 7 (1981), 1–13.

Kaplan, M., 'The New Great Debate: Traditionalism vs Science in International Relations', in Knorr and Roseneau (eds), *Contending Approaches to International Relations*. Princeton: Princeton University Press, 1969.

Linklater, A. *Beyond Realism and Marxism: Critical Theory and International Relations*. London: Macmillan, 1990.

Linklater, A. 'What is a Good International Citizen?' in P. Keal (ed.), *Ethics and Foreign Policy*. Canberra, Allen and Unwin, 1992.

Linklater, A. 'Rationalism', in Scott Burchill, Andrew Linklater et al., *Theories of International Relations*. London: Macmillan, 1996.

Little, R. 'International Relations and the Methodological Turn', *Political Studies*, 39 (1991), 463–78.

Luard, E. *Types of International Society*. London, Macmillan, 1976.

Lyons, G.M. 'The Study of International Relations in Great Britain: Further Considerations', *World Politics*, 38 (1986), 626–45.

Manning, C.A.W. *The Nature of International Society*. London, Macmillan, 2 ed, 1975.

Mayall, J. (ed.), *The Community of States*. London: Allen and Unwin, 1982.

Mayall, J. *Nationalism and International Society*. Cambridge: Cambridge University Press, 1990.

Midgley, E.B.F. 'Natural Law and the 'Anglo-Saxons' – Some Reflections in Response to Hedley Bull', *British Journal of International Studies*, 5 (1979), 260–72.

Millennium: Journal of International Studies, Special Issue, 'Beyond International Society', 21 (1992).

Navari, C. (ed.), *The Condition of States*. Buckingham: Open University Press, 1991.

Navari, C. 'English Machiavellism', European International Studies Conference Paper. Heidelberg, September 1992.

Neumann, I.B. and Welsh, J.M. 'The Other in European Self-Definition: An Addendum to the Literature on International Society', *Review of International Studies*, 17 (1991), 327–48.

Ogley, R.C. 'International Relations: Poetry, Prescription or Science?' *Millennium: Journal of International Studies*, 10 (1981), 170–86.

Richardson, J.L. 'The Academic Study of International Relations', in J.D.B. Miller and R.J. Vincent (eds), *Order and Violence: Hedley Bull and International Relations*. Oxford: Clarendon Press, 1990.

Rosenberg, J. *The Empire of Civil Society: A Critique of the Realist Theory of International Relations*. London: Verso, 1994.

Smith, S. (ed.), *International Relations: British and American Perspectives*. Oxford, Blackwell, 1985.

Smith, S. 'Paradigm Dominance in International Relations: The Development of International Relations as a Social Science', in H.C. Dyer and L. Mangasarian (eds), *The Study of International Relations: The State of the Art*. London, Macmillan, 1989.

Smith, S. 'The Self-Images of a Discipline: A Genealogy of International Relations Theory', in K. Booth and S. Smith (eds), *International Relations Theory Today*. Cambridge, Polity Press, 1995.

Suganami, H. 'The Structure of Institutionalism: An Anatomy of British Mainstream International Relations', *International Relations*, 7 (1983), 2363–81.

Thompson, K.W. 'Idealism and Realism: Beyond the Great Debate', *British Journal of International Studies*, 3 (1977), 159–80.

Waever, O. 'International Society: Theoretical Promises Unfulfilled?', *Cooperation and Conflict*, 27 (1992), 97–128.

Wheeler, N.J. 'Pluralist and Solidarist Conceptions of International Society: Bull and Vincent on Humanitarian Intervention', *Millennium: Journal of International Studies* 21 (1992).

Wheeler, N.J. 'Guardian Angel or Global Gangster: A Review of the Ethical Claims of International Society', *Political Studies*, 44 (1996), 123–35.

Wilson, P. 'The English School of International Relations: A Reply to Sheila Grader', *Review of International Studies*, 15 (1989), 49–58.

II E.H. Carr

Booth, K. 'Security in Anarchy: Utopian Realism in Theory and Practice', *International Affairs*, 67 (1991), 527–46.

Bull, H. '*The Twenty Year's Crisis* Thirty Years On', *International Journal*, 24 (1969), 625–38.

Carr, E.H. *International Relations since the Peace Treaties*. London: Macmillan, 1937.

Carr, E.H. *The Twenty Year's Crisis 1919–1939: An Introduction to the Study of International Relations*. London: Macmillan, 1 ed., 1939.

Carr, E.H. *The Twenty Year's Crisis 1919–1939: An Introduction to the Study of International Relations*. London: Macmillan, 2 ed., 1946 (1981 printing).

Carr, E.H. *Britain: A Study of Foreign Policy From the Versailles Treaty to the Outbreak of War*. London: Longmans, 1939.

Carr, E.H. *Conditions of Peace*. London: Macmillan, 1942.

Carr, E.H. *Nationalism and After*. London: Macmillan, 1945.

Carr, E.H. 'The Moral Foundations for World Order', in E.L. Woodward et al., *Foundations for World Order*. Social Science Foundation: University of Denver, 1949.

Carr, E.H. *What is History?*, R.W. Davies (ed.), London: Penguin, 2 ed., 1987.

Davies, R.W. 'Edward Hallett Carr 1892–1982' *Proceedings of the British Academy*, LXIX (1983), 473–511.

Evans, G. 'E.H. Carr and International Relations', *British Journal of International Studies*, 1 (1975), 77–97.

Fox, W.T.R. 'E.H. Carr and Political Realism: Vision and Revision', *Review of International Studies*, 11 (1985), 1–16.

Forsyth, M. 'The Classical Theory of International Relations', *Political Studies*, 26 (1978), 411–16.

Grader, S. 'The English School of International Relations: Evidence and Evaluation', *Review of International Studies*, 14 (1988), 29–44.

Haslam, J. '"We Need a Faith": E.H. Carr, 1892–1982', *History Today*, August (1983), 36–9.

Howe, P. 'The Utopian Realism of E.H. Carr', *Review of International Studies*, 20 (1994), 277–97.

John, I., Wight, M., and Garnett, J. 'International Politics at Aberystwyth 1919–1969', in B. Porter (ed.), *The Aberystwyth Papers*. London, Oxford University Press, 1972.

Johnson, W. 'E.H. Carr's Theory of International Relations: A Critique', *Journal of Politics*, 39 (1967), 861–84.

Jones, C. *Carr and International Relations*. Cambridge: Cambridge University Press, forthcoming, 1998.

Linklater, A. 'The Transformation of Political Community: E.H. Carr, Critical Theory and International Relations', *Review of International Studies*, 23 (1997), 321–38.

Lynch, C. 'E.H. Carr, International Relations Theory, and the Societal Origins of International Legal Norms', *Millennium: Journal of International Studies*, 23 (1994), 589–619.

Morganthau, H. 'The Surrender to the Immanence of Power: E.H. Carr', *Dilemmas of Politics*. Chicago: Chicago University Press, 1962.

Smith, M.J. 'E.H. Carr: Realism as Relativism', in *Realist Thought from Weber to Kissinger*. Louisiana: Louisiana State University Press, 1986.

Stone, N. 'Grim Eminence', *London Review of Books*, 20 January–3 February (1983), 4.

Wilson, P. 'Carr and his Critics: Responses to *The Twenty Years' Crisis*', paper presented to the 'E.H. Carr: A Critical Reassessment' Symposium held at the University of Wales, Gregynog, 13–15 July 1997.

III Herbert Butterfield

Booth, K. and Wheeler, N. *The Security Dilemma*. London: Macmillan, forthcoming, 1998.

Butterfield, H. *The Peace Tactics of Napoleon, 1806–1808*. Cambridge: Cambridge University Press, 1929.

Butterfield, H. *The Whig Interpretation of History*. London: George Bell, 1949.

Butterfield, H. *Statecraft of Machiavelli*. London: Macmillan, 1940.

Butterfield, H. *The Englishman and His History*. Cambridge: Cambridge University Press, 1944.

Butterfield, H. *Christianity and History*. London: George Bell, 1949.

Butterfield, H. *History and Human Relations*. London: Collins, 1951.

Butterfield, H. 'The Scientific versus the Moralistic Approach in International Affairs', *International Affairs*: 27 (1951), 411–22.

Butterfield, H. *Christianity, Diplomacy and War*. London: Epworth, 1953.

Butterfield, H. 'The Balance of Power', British Committee paper, (April 1959) Later published in H. Butterfield and M. Wight (eds), *Diplomatic Investigations*. London: Allen and Unwin, 1966.

Butterfield, H. *International Conflict in the Twentieth Century: A Christian View*. New York: Harper and Brothers, 1960.

Butterfield, H. 'Eyre Crowe's Memorandum of 1st January 1907', British Committee paper, (July 1960).

Butterfield, H. 'Alternative Conceptions of International Law', British Committee paper, (July 1962).

Butterfield, H. 'Notes for a Discussion on the Theory of International Politics', British Committee paper, (January 1964).

Butterfield, H. 'The Historic "States-System"', British Committee paper, (January 1965).

Butterfield, H. 'The Balance of Power', British Committee paper, (April 1959) in H. Butterfield and M. Wight (eds), *Diplomatic Investigations*. London, Allen and Unwin, 1966.

Butterfield, H. 'The New Diplomacy and Historical Diplomacy', British Committee paper, (September 1960) in H. Butterfield and M. Wight (eds), *Diplomatic Investigations*. London, Allen and Unwin, 1966.

Butterfield, H. 'Morality and an International Order', in B. Porter (ed.), *The Aberystwyth Papers: International Politics, 1919–1969*. London, Oxford University Press, 1972.

Butterfield, H. 'Historiography', *The Dictionary of the History of Ideas*, Vol. 1. New York: Scribner's, 1973, 464–98.

Butterfield, H. 'Raison d'Etat: The Relations between Morality and Government', The First Martin Wight Memorial Lecture, University of Sussex, 23 April 1975.

Butterfield, H. 'Global Good and Evil', in K.W. Thompson and R.J. Myers (eds), *A Tribute to Hans Morgenthau*. Washington: The New Republic Book Company, 1977.

Cowling, M. 'Herbert Butterfield: 1900–1979', *Proceedings of the British Academy*, LXV (1979), 595–609.

Epp, R. 'The 'Augustinian Moment' in International Politics: Niebuhr, Butterfield, Wight and the Reclaiming of a Tradition', International Politics Research Occasional Paper No. 10, Aberystwyth, Department of International Politics, 1991.

Coll, A. *The Wisdom of Statecraft: Sir Herbert Butterfield and the Philosophy of International Politics*. Durham: Duke University Press, 1985.

Thompson, K.W. (ed.), *Masters of International Thought*. Baton Rouge, Louisiana State University Press, 1980.

Thompson, K.W. (ed.), *Herbert Butterfield: The Ethics of History and Politics*. Washington: University Press of America, 1980.

IV   Martin Wight

Bull, H. 'Introduction: Martin Wight and the Study of International Relations' in M. Wight, *Systems of States*. Leicester: Leicester University Press, 1977.

Bull, H. and Holbraad, C. 'Introduction', in M. Wight, *Power Politics*. London: Penguin, 2 ed., 1978.

Bull, H. 'Martin Wight and the Theory of International Relations' in M. Wight, *International Theory: The Three Traditions*. Leicester: Leicester University Press/Royal Institute of International Affairs, 1991.

Epp, R. 'Martin Wight: International Relations as Realm of Persuasion', in F.A. Beer and R. Hariman (eds), *Post-Realism: The Rhetorical Turn in International Relations*. East Lansing: Michigan State University Press, 1996.

Clark, I. 'Traditions of Thought and Classical Theories of International Relations', in I. Clark and I.B. Neumann (eds), *Classical Theories of International Relations*. London: Macmillan, 1996, 1–19.

Dunne, T. 'Mythology or Methodology? Traditions in International Theory', *Review of International Studies* 19, (1993), 305–18.

Dunne, T. 'Colonial Encounters in International Relations: Reading Wight, Writing Australia', *Australian Journal of International Affairs* 51 (1997), 309–23.

Howard, M. 'Ethics and Power in International Policy', Martin Wight Memorial Lecture, reprinted in *The Causes of War and Other Essays*. Cambridge, Mass: Harvard University Press, 1984.

Jackson, R. 'Martin Wight, International Theory and the Good Life', *Millenium: Journal of International Studies*, 19 (1990), 261–72.

James, A. 'Michael Nicholson on Martin Wight: A Mind Passing in the Night', *Review of International Studies*, 8 (1982), 117–23.

Nicholson, M. 'The Enigma of Martin Wight', *Review of International Studies*, 7 (1981), 18.

Nicholson, M. 'Martin Wight: Enigma or Error', *Review of International Studies*, 8 (1982), 125–8.

Porter, B. 'Patterns of Thought and Practice: Martin Wight's "International Theory"', in M. Donelan (ed.), *The Reasons of States*. London: Allen and Unwin, 1978.

Wight, M. 'Christian Pacifism', *Theology*, 33 (1936), 12–21.

Wight, M. *Power Politics*. London, Royal Institute of International Affairs, 'Looking Forward' Pamphlet No.8, 1946.

Wight, M. *The Development of the Legislative Council 1606–1945*. ed. M. Perham, London: Faber, 1946.

Wight, M. Review of *'The Twenty Years' Crisis'* by E.H. Carr, *The Observer*, (21 July 1946).

Wight, M. *The Gold Coast Legislative Council*. ed. M. Perham, London: Faber, 1947.

Wight, M. 'The March of History', *The Observer* (5 January 1947) Review of A.J. Toynbee, *A Study of History*. Abridgment of Volumes 1–6 by D.C. Somervell, London, Oxford University Press, 1947.

Wight, M. *British Colonial Constitutions 1947*. Oxford: Clarendon, 1952.

Wight, M. 'Eastern Europe', 'Germany', and 'Balance of Power' in A.J. Toynbee and F.T. Ashton-Gwatkin (eds), *The World in March 1939*. London: Oxford University Press.

Wight, M. 'The Tragedy of History', *The Observer* (2 September 1951) Review of H. Butterfield, *History and Human Relations*.

Wight, M. 'Morals and Warfare', *The Observer* (16 August 1953). Review of H. Butterfield, *Diplomacy and War*.

Wight, M. 'The Crux for a Historian Brought up in the Christian Tradition', in A.J. Toynbee, *A Study of History*. London: Oxford University Press/Royal Institute of International Affairs, 1954, 'Universal States Universal Churches', Vol. 7. Annex 3, 373–748.

Wight, M. 'War and International Politics', *Listener* (13 October 1955), 584–5.

Wight, M. 'Why is there no International Theory?', British Committee paper, (January 1959). Later published in *International Relations*, 2 (1960), 35–48/62, and reprinted in H. Butterfield and M. Wight (eds), *Diplomatic Investigations*. London: Allen and Unwin, 1966.

Wight, M. 'The Balance of Power', British Committee paper, (April 1961) Later published in H. Butterfield and M. Wight (eds), *Diplomatic Investigations*. London: Allen and Unwin, 1966.

Wight, M. 'Western Values in International Relations', British Committee paper, (October 1961). Later published in H. Butterfield and M. Wight (eds), *Diplomatic Investigations*. London, Allen and Unwin, 1966.

Wight, M. 'Comment on Hedley Bull's paper 'The Grotian Conception of International relations', British Committee paper, (August 1962).

Wight, M. 'European Studies', in D. Daiches (ed.), *The Idea of New University: An Experiment at Sussex*. London: Andre Deutsch, 1964.

Wight, M. 'The States-System of Hellas and Persia' and 'The States-System of Hellas', British Committee paper, (October 1964) Later published in M. Wight, *Systems of States*. Leicester: Leicester University Press, 1977, 46–72, 73–109.

Wight, M. 'International Legitimacy', British Committee paper, (April 1971). Later published in M. Wight, *Systems of States*. Leicester, Leicester University Press, 1977.

Wight, M. *Power Politics*. London: Penguin, 2 ed., 1978. Edited by Hedley Bull and Carsten Holbraad.

Wight, M. *Systems of States*. Leicester: Leicester University Press, 1977. Edited by Hedley Bull.

Wight, M. 'An Anatomy of International Thought', *Review of International Studies*, 13 (1987), 221–7.

Wight, M. *International Theory: The Three Traditions*. Leicester: Leicester University Press/Royal Institute of International Affairs, 1991. Edited by Brian Porter and Gabriele Wight.

V Hedley Bull

Bull, H. 'Society and Anarchy in International Relations', British Committee paper, (October 1961). Later published in H. Butterfield and M. Wight (eds), *Diplomatic Investigations*. London: Allen and Unwin, 1966.

Bull, H. 'The Grotian Conception of International Society', British Committee paper, (April 1962). Later published in H. Butterfield and M. Wight (eds), *Diplomatic Investigations*. London, Allen and Unwin, 1966.

Bull, H. 'Recent American Contributions to the Theory of International Politics: Part 1', British Committee paper, (January 1965).

Bull, H. 'Recent American Contributions to the Theory of International Politics: Part 2', British Committee paper (July 1965).

Bull, H. 'International Theory: The Case for the Classical Approach', British Committee paper, (September 1966). Published in *World Politics*, 3 (1966), 361–377; and reprinted in K. Knorr and J.N. Rosenau (eds), *Contending Approaches to International Relations*. Princeton: Princeton University Press, 1969.

Bull, H. '*The Twenty Year's Crisis* Thirty Years On', *International Journal*, 42 (1969), 626–38.

Bull, H. 'International Law and International Order', *International Organization*, 26 (1972), 583–8.

Bull, H. 'International Relations as an Academic Pursuit', *The Australian Outlook*, 26 (1972), 251–65.

Bull, H. *The Anarchical Society. A Study of Order in World Politics*. London: Macmillan, 1 ed., 1977.

Bull, H. Review of M. Donelan (ed.), *The Reason of States* in *The Times Literary Supplement*. (28 April 1978), 474.

Bull, H. 'The Appalling State of IR Studies at the LSE and Elsewhere', talk given to *The Grimshaw Club* (17 January 1980).

Bull, H. 'The Great Irresponsibles? The United States, The Soviet Union and World Order', *International Journal*, 35 (1980), 437–47.

Bull, H. 'Kissinger: The Primacy of Geopolitics', *International Affairs*, 56 (1980), 484–87.

Bull, H. 'Western Values in a Hostile World', Chatham House Lecture (23 September 1980).

Bull, H. and Watson, A. (eds), *The Expansion of International Society*. Oxford: Clarendon Press, 1984.

Bull, H. (ed.), *Intervention in World Politics*. Oxford: Clarendon Press, 1984.

Bull, H. *Justice in International Relations*. Hagey Lectures, University of Waterloo, Ontario, 1984.

Bull, H. 'The Importance of Grotius', in H. Bull, B. Kingsbury and A. Roberts (eds), *Hugo Grotius and International Relations*. Oxford: Clarendon Press, 1990.

Bull, H. 'The West and South Africa', *Daedalus*, 111 (1982), 255–70.

Dunne, T. and Wheeler, N.J. ' Hedley Bull and the Idea of a Universal Moral Community: Fictional, Primordial or Imagined?' in B.A. Roberson (ed.), *The Structure of International Society*. London: Pinter, forthcoming, 1998.

Harris, I. 'Order and Justice in *The Anarchical Society*', *International Affairs*, 69 (1993), 725–41.

Hoffmann, S. 'International Society', in J.D.B. Miller and R.J. Vincent (eds), *Order and Violence: Hedley Bull and International Relations*. Oxford, Clarendon Press, 1990.

Holbraad, C. 'Conclusion', in J.D.B. Miller and R.J. Vincent, *Order and Violence: Hedley Bull and International Relations*. Oxford: Clarendon Press, 1990.

Hurrell, A. 'Society and Anarchy in the 1990s', in B.A. Roberson (ed.), *The Structure of International Society*. London: Pinter, forthcoming, 1998.

Vigezzi, B. 'The British Committee on the Theory of International Politics', (1958–1985), Introduction to *L'Espansione Della Societa Internazionale: L'Europa e il Mondo della fine del Medioevo ai tempi nostri*. Milan: Jaca Books, 1994, trans. Roberta Guerrina.

Wheeler, N.J. 'Pluralist and Solidarist Conceptions of International Society: Bull and Vincent on Humanitarian Intervention', *Millennium: Journal of International Studies*, 21 (1992), 463–89.

Wheeler, N.J. and Dunne, T. 'Hedley Bull's Pluralism of the Intellect and Solidarism of the Will', *International Affairs*, 72 (1996), 91–108.

VII R.J. Vincent

Hill, C. 'Obituary: R.J. Vincent 1943–1990', *Political Studies*, XXXIX (1991), 158–60.

Miller, J.D.B. and Vincent, R.J. (eds), *Order and Violence: Hedley Bull and International Relations*. Oxford: Clarendon, 1990.

Neumann, Iver B., 'R.J. Vincent', in I.B. Neumann and O. Waever (eds), *Masters in the Making*. London: Routledge, 1997.

Vincent, R.J. *Nonintervention and International Order*. Princeton: Princeton University Press, 1974.

Vincent, R.J. 'Western Conceptions of a Universal Moral Order', *British Journal of International Studies*, 4 (1978), 20–46.

Vincent, R.J. 'Modernity and Universal Human Rights', in A.G. McGrew and P.G. Lewis et al., *Global Politics: Globalization and the Nation-State*. Cambridge: Cambridge University Press, 272–80.

Vincent, R.J. 'The Factor of Culture in the Global International Order', *The Yearbook of World Affairs* 34 (1980), 252–64.

Vincent, R.J. 'The Hobbesian Tradition in Twentieth Century International Thought', *Millennium: Journal of International Studies*, 10 (1981), 91–101.

Vincent, R.J. 'Edmund Burke and the Theory of International Relations', *Review of International Studies*, 10 (1984), 205–18.

Vincent, R.J. *Human Rights and International Relations*. Cambridge: Cambridge University Press, 1986.

Vincent, R.J. 'Grotius, Human Rights, and Intervention', in H. Bull, B. Kingsbury and A. Roberts, (eds), *Hugo Grotius and International Relations*. Oxford: Clarendon Press, 1990.

Vincent, R.J. 'Order in International Politics', in J.D.B. Miller and R.J. Vincent (eds), *Order and Violence: Hedley Bull and International Relations*. Oxford: Clarendon Press, 1990.

Vincent, R.J. 'The Idea of Rights in International Ethics', in T. Nardin and D. Mapel (eds), *Traditions of International Ethics*. Cambridge: Cambridge University Press, 1992.

Vincent, R.J. and Wilson, P. 'Beyond Non-Intervention', in I. Forbes and M. Hoffman (eds), *Political Theory, International Relations and the Ethics of Intervention*. London: Macmillan, 1993.

Vincent, R.J. 'The Place of Theory in the Practice of Human Rights', in C. Hill and P. Beshoff (eds), *Two Worlds of International Relations*. London: Routledge, 1994.

Index

Aberystwyth, xi
American Rockefeller Committee, 90, 106
apartheid, 154, 167, 168, 185
Armstrong, William, 91, 97

balance of power, 97, 100, 122, 186
  see also Butterfield, Wight
behaviouralism, 124
  Bull on, 116, 118, 120–4
  Butterfield on, 123, 129
  Hoffmann, 123
  Kaplan, 118, 120
  new great debate, 3, 9, 117, 129
  versus traditionalism, 117–118, 120, 122–4
  Wight on, 122–3, 129, 186
Berridge, Geoffrey, 127
Booth, Ken, xii, 23, 27, 77, 46, 189
British Committee
  aims, 96–7, 182
  Cambridge University, 82, 93
  classical approach, 122–4, 164
  Expansion phase, 128–9
  founding of, 90–4; Butterfield, xiii, 73, 82–3, 91, 182; Thompson, xii, 72–3, 89–90
  membership of, 12–13, 82, 91–4
  proceedings of, 93–4; balance of power, 98, 99; international theory, 94–5, 182–3; international society, 96–9, 101, 103–4, 117, 182–3; *see also* international society; - international law, 97, 121–2; state-systems, 124–9, 183; publications of, 104–5, 117; states-systems phase, 128–9
  see also individual authors
Brown, Chris, 95, 146, 170, 190
Burke, Edmund, 60–1, 98–100, 162–4
Bull, Hedley
  British Committee, 92, 117

European security, 154
influence of Carr, 102, 144
international society, 97–9, 143–4, 147–8, 183; balance of power, 138; international law, 100, 143; international order, 147–9, 151; international system, 125–7
new great debate: critique of behaviouralism, 116–117, 119; classical approach, 119–121; *see also* behaviouralism
pluralism, 100, 103–4, 136, 142, 145–6; and realism, 102, 143–4, 152; and relativism, 143–4; disillusionment with 146–9, 154; great powers, 147
solidarism, 100–1, 103–4, 142, 149–52; after the Cold War, 152–5; and apartheid, 154; ethical universalism 103, 149; justice, 136, 149–51, 188; theory and practice, 139–42
Third World, 35, 129, 148, 151, 153; and decolonisation, 188
three traditions, 56, 136, 138, 142; and Vincent, 161, 165; and Watson, 127, 130
Butterfield, Herbert
  British Committee, 73, 82–3, 91, 98, 103–4
  Christianity, 75
  history, 71; technical history, 74, 78, 120; diplomatic history, 74, 79, 97
  Hobbesian fear, 77–8, 83; security dilemma, 77, 80
  international system, 76, 79, 124–5, 126; balance of power, 77–8, 98, 123; diplomacy, 74, 79; international society, 80, 83, 96–7, 104
  League of Nations, 76